FISH
& SHELLFISH

Acknowledgments

We would like to thank Marine Mora and the Matfer Bourgeat Group as well as the Mora store for the utensils and equipment.

matferbourgeat.com
mora.fr

FERRANDI Paris

Project Coordinator: Audrey Janet
Chefs: Bastien Ancelet, Alexander Dreyer, and Baptiste Salomon
Students: Sulki Park and Valentin Pelier

Flammarion

French Edition
Editorial Director: Clélia Ozier-Lafontaine,
assisted by by Héloïse Moulard
Editorial Collaboration: Estérelle Payany
Design: Alice Leroy

English Edition
Editorial Director: Kate Mascaro
Editor: Helen Adedotun
Translation from the French: Ansley Evans
Copyediting: Wendy Sweetser and Nicole Foster
Typesetting: Alice Leroy
Proofreading: Nicole Foster
Indexing: Chris Bell
Cover design: Audrey Sednaoui
Production: Julie Hautecourt
Color Separation: IGS-CP, L'Isle d'Espagnac
Printed in China by Toppan Leefung

Originally published in French as
Poissons et Fruits de Mer: Recettes et Techniques d'une École d'Excellence

Éditions Flammarion
82 Rue Saint-Lazare
75009 Paris
editions.flammarion.com
@flammarioninternational

26 27 28 3 2 1
ISBN: 978-2-08-049811-3
Legal Deposit: 03/2026

Flammarion is actively committed to reducing the ecological footprint of its publications. The book you hold in your hands was printed on paper made from wood sourced from sustainably managed forests, using mineral oil-free inks, by a printer committed to environmental protection, and is compliant with European Union Deforestation Regulation (EUDR). Send regulation (EU) 2023/988 inquiries to latelier@flammarion.fr

FERRANDI
PARIS

FISH & SHELLFISH

RECIPES AND TECHNIQUES FROM THE FERRANDI SCHOOL OF CULINARY ARTS

Photography by Rina Nurra

Flammarion
PARIS • SINCE 1875

PREFACE

For more than one hundred years, **FERRANDI Paris** has taught all of the culinary disciplines to students from around the world. Following the success of our seven previous works published by Flammarion—a comprehensive guide to French pâtisserie, as well as volumes focused on chocolate, vegetables, fruit and nuts, charcuterie, French boulangerie, and meat—it is now time to explore the art of cooking with fish and shellfish, which offers a wealth of flavors.

Today, resources from the world's oceans and seas are precious and fragile. That is why we believe it is crucial to share our expertise on preparing fish and shellfish, while also raising awareness of threats to their sustainability.

Cooking with fish, shellfish, and cephalopods requires creativity and technical expertise. Beyond our mission to share this craft, we are also dedicated to the conservation of marine resources.

Both traditional skills and creative innovation—and an ongoing dialogue between the two—are central to **FERRANDI Paris**'s teaching philosophy. France boasts a rich variety of dishes made with fish, shellfish, and cephalopods. These time-honored recipes and techniques are part of the French culinary heritage that our teachers are dedicated to preserving. Moreover, the chefs at **FERRANDI Paris** are continually enriching this repertoire with regional recipes from around France (such as bouillabaisse, seafood pâté en croûte, and trout pithiviers) and the world.

Our school's close ties with industry specialists allow us to offer content that is both authentic and future-oriented. This book not only features delicious recipes but also demonstrates fundamental techniques and shares expert advice for anyone who wishes to explore the inspiring culinary world of fish and shellfish with confidence, whether at home or in a professional kitchen.

I extend my warmest thanks to the talented members of **FERRANDI Paris** who have brought this book to fruition, particularly Audrey Janet, who coordinated the project, and Bastien Ancelet, Alexander Dreyer, and Baptiste Salomon, chef instructors at the school. Drawing on their expertise, culinary sensibility, and dedication to responsible seafood cuisine, they have produced a book that honors the incredible richness and nuances of the ocean's bounty.

Thomas Allanic
Executive Director of FERRANDI Paris

CONTENTS

INTRODUCTION

A Portrait of
FERRANDI Paris

In over one hundred years of history, **FERRANDI Paris** has earned an international reputation as one of the premier culinary and hospitality schools in France. Since its inception, the school—a member of the prestigious Conférence des Grandes Écoles and hailed "the Harvard of gastronomy" by the press—has trained generations of groundbreaking chefs and entrepreneurs who have left their mark in the industry around the world. Whether at its historic campus in the Saint-Germain-des-Prés neighborhood in Paris, or its campus in Saint-Gratien, Bordeaux, Rennes, or Dijon, this institution is dedicated to world-class teaching with the aim of training future leaders in the culinary and pastry arts, hotel and restaurant management, and hospitality entrepreneurship.

Founded more than a century ago by the Paris Île-de-France Regional Chamber of Commerce and Industry, **FERRANDI Paris** is the only school in France to offer the full range of degree and certification programs in the culinary and hospitality arts, from vocational training to the master's degree level, in addition to international programs. The school takes pride in its 99 percent exam pass rate, which is the highest in France for degrees and certifications in the sector. No matter the level, a **FERRANDI Paris** education is rigorous and combines mastering the basics with an emphasis on innovation, management, and entrepreneurial skills, as well as hands-on practice in a professional environment. Committed to corporate social responsibility, **FERRANDI Paris** strives to limit its greenhouse gas emissions and foster social inclusion and diversity within its establishments, while integrating sustainable and ethical practices into the school's curriculum.

Strong Ties to the Professional World

A space for discovery, inspiration, and exchange—where the culinary arts mingle with science, technology, and innovation—**FERRANDI Paris** brings together the most prestigious and pioneering names in the hospitality sector and creative culinary world. The school trains 2,500 apprentices and students each year, in addition to three hundred international students of over forty nationalities and two thousand adults who come to the school to perfect their skills or change careers. The one hundred instructors at the school are all highly qualified: several have received prominent culinary awards and distinctions, such as the

Meilleur Ouvrier de France title (Best Craftsman in France), and all have at least ten years of work experience in the culinary field in prestigious establishments in France and abroad. To give students maximum opportunities and the chance to connect with other fields and the greater global community, the school has formed collaborative partnerships with several other institutions. In France, partner schools include the ESCP Europe Business School and AgroParisTech; abroad, the school collaborates with Johnson and Wales University in the United States, the ITHQ tourism and hotel management school in Canada, Hong Kong Polytechnic University, the Macao University of Tourism, and Başkent University in Turkey, among others. Since theory and practice go hand in hand, and because **FERRANDI Paris** strives for excellence in teaching, students also have the chance to participate in a number of official events through partnerships with several leading culinary associations in France, including Maîtres Cuisiniers de France, Société des Meilleurs Ouvriers de France, Euro-Toques, and more. In addition, the school offers numerous prestigious professional competitions and prizes, giving students many opportunities to demonstrate their skills and knowledge. A dedicated ambassador of French culture, **FERRANDI Paris** draws students from around the world every year and is a member of the French Interministerial Tourism Council; the Collège Culinaire de France (an association dedicated to upholding culinary craftsmanship); the Strategic Committee of Atout France (the French tourism development agency); and the Conférence des Formations d'Excellence au Tourisme (CFET), a group of institutions in France offering top-quality training in tourism-related fields.

Extensive Savoir Faire

FERRANDI Paris's expertise, combining practice and close collaboration with professionals in the field, has been shared in seven previous volumes, devoted to French pâtisserie (a Gourmand World Cookbook award winner), chocolate making, vegetables, fruits and nuts, charcuterie, bread and *viennoiseries*, and meat, intended for both professional chefs and amateur cooks alike. In this next book in the successful series, **FERRANDI Paris** now brings the art of cooking with fish and shellfish into the spotlight.

Fish, Shellfish, and Cephalopods

Deeply rooted in French culinary heritage, fish and shellfish are essential to many cuisines around the world. Mastering their preparation requires a thorough understanding of textures, cooking times, and appropriate techniques, whether you are working with round fish, flatfish, mollusks, crustaceans, or cephalopods. Knowledge of sustainable practices is also crucial. A founding member and signatory of the Ethic Ocean organization since 2018, **FERRANDI Paris** is committed to promoting the responsible use of marine resources among professionals and individuals. In this book, the chefs at **FERRANDI Paris** share essential techniques and recipes for preparing all types of seafood—from filleting to shucking, and from flavorful lobster sauce or fish soup to perfectly cooked turbot and tender octopus—giving readers the keys to bring out the best in the ocean's bounty.

FISH & SHELLFISH: THE ESSENTIALS

Definition and classification of seafood products

Oceans, seas, and freshwater bodies, including rivers and lakes, teem with incredible biodiversity. The wide range of fish, shellfish, crustaceans, and other types of seafood offers a world of flavors and textures, inspiring chefs everywhere. Rich in protein, minerals, and healthy fats, seafood is an essential part of our culinary heritage worldwide.

There are three main categories of products sourced from aquatic habitats:

Fish: Aquatic vertebrates that have fins and, usually, scales, and breathe through gills.

Cephalopods: Mollusks without an external shell, divided into octopods (with eight tentacles, like octopuses) and decapods (with ten tentacles, including cuttlefish and squid).

Shellfish: These are divided into two subcategories.

• **Crustaceans:** Arthropods with a shell. Those we eat are either decapods, which have five pairs of legs—including lobsters, crayfish, crabs, and shrimp—or cirripedes, such as barnacles, that attach themselves to various surfaces.

• **Mollusks** with a protective shell, divided into the following groups:

› **Bivalves**: Mollusks with two shells connected by a hinge (oysters, mussels, clams, cockles, razor clams, etc.).

› **Gastropods**: Mollusks with a single spiral shell (such as whelks, periwinkles, and abalones).

› **Echinoderms**: Mollusks with a calcareous exoskeleton and often spines (such as sea urchins).

Selecting seafood

As of 2021, over 35 percent of the world's fish stocks were overexploited, according to the 2024 edition of "The State of World Fisheries and Aquaculture," published by the Food and Agriculture Organization of the United Nations (FAO). Before considering criteria like freshness or taste, prioritize sustainability by learning about endangered species and choosing products that are responsibly caught or farmed. FERRANDI Paris is a founding member and signatory of Ethic Ocean, an organization that promotes the responsible use of marine resources among professionals and consumers. The association's app (ethic-ocean .org/index.php/application-mobile/) and species guide provide up-to-date information on each species (in French). In the US, Canada, the UK, and elsewhere, look for the blue Marine Stewardship Council (MSC) label, which certifies that products have been fished sustainably. Additionally, the Monterey Bay Aquarium Seafood Watch in the US and the Marine Conservation Society's Good Fish Guide in the UK are also helpful resources.

Sustainability criteria to consider when buying seafood

• Check the scientific (Latin) name, as common names can refer to different species with varying stocks.

• Look for the place of origin, also known as the FAO Major Fishing Area, where it was caught.

• Consider the status of the stocks.

• Find out the method used to catch or harvest it.

• If possible, learn the size at which the species reaches sexual maturity (which may differ from the legal size for sale).

• Consider the conditions in which farmed fish and other seafood are raised.

Fishing techniques

There are several categories of fisheries, including industrial (usually on large ships), artisanal (generally on small boats near the coast), coastal (close to shore), and deep-sea (in the open ocean, with expeditions lasting several days). Different fishing methods and gear types are used depending on the target species, their habitat (such as the seabed, open water, or the surface), and their behavior. Fishing methods and gear types fall into two categories: active and passive.

Active methods and gear types

• **Trawls**. Bottom trawls, pelagic trawls, and bottom seines, consisting of funnel-shaped nets with a closed end, used to catch fish such as cod, whiting, and haddock.

• **Surrounding nets**: Purse seines (sliding or non-sliding) that encircle schools of fish.

• **Dredges**: Metal-framed baskets or nets that are dragged along the seafloor, mainly for catching shellfish (scallops, cockles, clams, etc.).

Active gear is often more harmful to the environment because it can damage marine ecosystems and is not very selective, leading to bycatch.

Passive methods and gear types

- **Nets**: Passive nets such as flat gill nets or three-layered trammel nets that entangle fish and other seafood, including monkfish, rays, soles, lobsters, sea bass, and more.
- **Lines and longlines**: Lines fitted with baited hooks or lures.
- **Traps**: Pots, traps, and other devices used to lure and catch crustaceans and cephalopods, including lobsters, crabs, whelks, octopus, and cuttlefish.
- **Hand-digging, raking, or diving,** typically used for shellfish such as clams, scallops, razor clams, shrimp, and crabs.

In France, the fishing method must be listed on the label, unless the product has undergone processing. Whenever possible, opt for fish and other seafood caught using gentle (passive) methods to minimize the environmental impact.

***IKEJIME* IN BRIEF**

Ikejime, or *ike jime*, is not a fishing technique but a Japanese method for killing fish. It involves disabling the fish's central nervous system by inserting a spike into the brain. This process reduces stress and preserves the quality of the meat, which lasts longer and tastes better. Fish slaughtered this way can be aged to develop new flavors.

Seasonality

Seafood is not considered seasonal in the same way as fruits, vegetables, and other ingredients from the land. Their peak season does not necessarily coincide with the times when they are least expensive and most readily available. Marine species reproduce during specific times of the year, depending on their nature and habitat. They gather to spawn (i.e., reproduce), which makes them easier to catch in large numbers at that time. What is often referred to as a fishing "season," characterized by greater market availability, is not necessarily a reliable indicator of sustainability or quality. Each species and stock must be evaluated individually.

Mackerel, for instance, are fattier and more flavorful during their reproductive period. But the meat of some spawning flatfish, including sole and flounder, deteriorates more easily and is harder to work with, resulting in up to 30 percent losses. In the case of some shellfish, such as scallops, regulated fishing seasons that support the sustainability of the species have made it possible to manage stocks in France effectively.

Farmed fish, including trout, sea bass, salmon, and sea bream, are available year-round. Talking to your fishmonger is the best way to gain insight into the impact of the fish and other seafood you buy.

What about aquaculture?

Aquaculture is the practice of cultivating fish, shellfish, and other aquatic organisms in marine or freshwater environments for food. The main categories include fish farming, or pisciculture, for species like salmon, sea bass, and sea bream; shellfish farming, which encompasses mollusks such as oysters, clams, mussels, and scallops, as well as crustaceans like shrimp and crayfish; and algaculture, or seaweed farming. While aquaculture helps meet the growing food demand, it can also cause environmental damage itself. The quality of farmed seafood depends on factors like stocking density, feed, water quality, animal welfare, veterinary care, and farming and harvesting techniques. Well-managed farms can produce high-quality products while reducing pressure on wild populations. However, some intensive farms may cause significant environmental harm and yield lower-quality meat. When purchasing farmed seafood, it is essential to learn how they were produced.

In brief

Five tips for purchasing sustainable seafood

1. Talk to your fishmonger to obtain more detailed information.

2. Find the exact name of the species you are buying and check its stock status using the Monterey Bay Aquarium Seafood Watch, the Marine Conservation Society's Good Fish Guide, or an app such as Ethic Ocean or the WWF-SASSI FishID app.

3. Prioritize fish caught using less aggressive techniques and gear.

4. When buying fish, consider their size and choose ones that have had the opportunity to reproduce. Keep in mind that the legal size for sale does not always indicate sexual maturity.

5. Cook non-endangered species to discover new flavors and help reduce pressure on overfished populations.

Official quality labels

Several labels certify the origin or other specific features of seafood products.
Below are several of the most important ones:

Logo	Label	Description
PÊCHE DURABLE MSC www.msc.org/fr	**MSC (Marine Stewardship Council)**	Certifies fish from sustainably managed fisheries, with well-managed stocks and minimal impact on the marine ecosystem.
FARMED RESPONSIBLY asc CERTIFIED ASC-AQUA.ORG	**ASC (Aquaculture Stewardship Council)**	Certifies that farmed fish and other seafood have been raised in a sustainable, socially responsible way.
AB AGRICULTURE BIOLOGIQUE	**AB: Agriculture Biologique (Organic Agriculture) and the European Union organic logo**	Guarantees environmentally friendly production methods and animal welfare. The regulations are consistent across the EU, and imported products must meet the same standards. This label is only found on aquaculture products, not on wild-caught fish and seafood.
Naturland	**Naturland Aquaculture**	Certifies that farmed seafood has been raised according to EU organic standards, in a socially responsible way. Criteria include species-specific cultivation, protection of aquatic environments, and abstention from the use of genetic engineering and chemical additives.
FRIEND OF THE SEA	**FOTS (Friend of the Sea)**	Certifies both wild and farmed seafood. Criteria for wild fish include no overfishing or significant impact on the seabed, and bycatch must be limited to 8%.
INDICATION GÉOGRAPHIQUE PROTÉGÉE	**Protected Geographical Indication** (PGI, or IGP in French)	Identifies products with a quality, reputation, or other traits linked to their geographic origin. At least one stage of production must take place within a specific geographic region. This label safeguards the product's name across the EU. French seafood products with PGI status: • Huîtres Marennes Oléron (oysters) • Huîtres de Normandie (oysters) • Caviar d'Aquitaine (caviar) • Bulots de la Baie de Granville (whelks) • Coquilles Saint-Jacques des Côtes-d'Armor (scallops)
APPELLATION D'ORIGINE PROTÉGÉE	**Protected Designation of Origin** (PDO, or AOP in French)	Designates a product entirely produced using traditional methods within the same geographical area, conferring its unique qualities. The PDO protects the product's name throughout the EU. Moules de Bouchot de la Baie du Mont-Saint Michel (mussels) are the only seafood product with a PDO in France.
label Rouge DÉCRET DU 12.03.96	**Label Rouge**	A French label recognizing products that are superior in quality to other identical ones. Currently, thirty-two seafood products carry the label, including farmed shrimp and sea bream, smoked haddock, canned products, and processed items like fish soup.
PAVILLON FRANCE	**Pavillon France**	Identifies products caught by French vessels in compliance with European quotas.

Fish

The term "fish" encompasses a remarkably diverse range of species, with over 28,000 identified to date. From a culinary standpoint, it is helpful to organize these species into broad categories.

Fish classifications

Fish may be classified according to their shape, nutritional qualities, meat type, or the method of capture.

According to their morphology:

- **Round fish *(poissons ronds)***: These fish have cylindrical bodies and, when cut crosswise, produce round or oval-shaped steaks (*darnes*). They yield two fillets. Examples include sea bass, trout, cod, mackerel, hake, red mullet, and monkfish.
- **Flatfish *(poissons plats)***: True flatfish—including flounder, sole, plaice, and brill—are bottom-dwellers with flattened bodies and both eyes on the same side of their bodies. They yield four fillets. Other fish also have flattened bodies, but they swim upright and have one eye on each side. These include John Dory, sea bream, and porgy. The latter are considered round fish in English-speaking countries, but *poissons plats* in France, so they are found in the Flatfish chapter of this book. They yield two fillets.

According to their habitat:

- **Saltwater fish**: Species that live in marine environments, including whiting, sole, red mullet, sardines, tuna, and sea bream, to name but a few.
- **Freshwater fish**: Species that live in freshwater bodies like rivers, lakes, and ponds, including trout, pikeperch, pike, carp, and some eel species.
- **Migratory fish**: Fish that migrate between salt and fresh water during their life cycle, such as shad, salmon, eel, and sea trout.

According to their fat content:

- **Lean fish (less than 3% fat)**: Hake, pollock, cod, sole, flounder, perch, etc.
- **Medium fatty fish (3–10% fat)**: Sea bass, sea bream, trout, turbot, etc.
- **Fatty fish (more than 10% fat)**: Tuna, mackerel, herring, sardines, anchovies, etc.

According to their meat color:

- **White fish**: Their meat remains a pale color after cooking (cod, whiting, sole, etc.).
- **Blue fish**: Their meat has a deeper color and is generally fattier (tuna, sardines, mackerel, etc.).

Selecting fish

When purchasing whole fish, look for bulbous, glistening eyes, bright red gills, and shiny skin with the scales firmly attached. The flesh should be firm and spring back when pressed. For fresh fillets, look for a firm texture and glossy appearance with no visible gaps between the muscle layers and no browning around the edges. Fish should have a faint ocean smell but should never have a strong "fishy" or ammonia-like odor. Fresh flatfish, held by the head, should remain rigid without bending. The flesh, whether whole or filleted, should always be firm, and not soft, dull, or slimy.

Storing fish

It is best to consume fish as soon as possible after purchasing it. Whole fish should be scaled, gutted, and wrapped in a clean dish towel or placed in an airtight container. It can be stored for 24–48 hours in the coldest part of the refrigerator (32°F–35.6°F/0°C–2°C). Place fish fillets and steaks on a rack with the skin side facing up and store them in the coldest part of the refrigerator, for up to 24 hours.

If you plan to serve the fish raw—in sushi, sashimi, or carpaccio, for example—it must first be frozen for at least 24 hours at -4°F (-20°C) to eliminate any parasites such as anisakis. After thawing, the fish should be consumed within 24 hours.

Meticulously wrapped fish can be frozen for 3–6 months at a minimum temperature of 0.4°F (-18°C). Thaw it in the refrigerator before preparing it.

Smoked fish, such as smoked salmon, herring, and trout, have varying shelf lives depending on whether they are cold-smoked or hot-smoked. Dried and salted fish can be stored at room temperature and must be soaked in several changes of water to remove excess salt before consumption.

Preparing and cooking fish

Cooking fish requires careful attention because it is more delicate than meat and can dry out quickly. White fish—such as monkfish, pollock, and cod—have particularly fragile flesh that can break apart or lose significant water during cooking. Brining is an effective way to prevent this. Prepare a 10 percent saltwater solution—⅓ oz. (10 g) coarse gray sea salt per 4 cups (1 liter) water—and soak white fish fillets or steaks in the brine for 10–12 minutes before cooking, then pat them dry without rinsing. This traditional technique strengthens the flaky meat, preventing it from falling apart, and significantly decreases water loss during cooking. It is a simple yet effective treatment that produces firmer, more flavorful fillets suitable for all cooking methods.

Whether you are poaching, baking, grilling, or pan-frying, follow the recommended internal temperatures below for perfectly cooked fish:

- **Tuna and swordfish**: 100°F (38°C) in the center for a rare to medium-rare finish.
- **Salmon and trout**: 108°F–113°F (42°C–45°C) for tender meat.
- **White fish** (cod, hake, pollack, etc.): 118°F–126°F (48°C–52°C) for pearly white meat that flakes easily.
- **Monkfish**: 126°F–130°F (51°C–54°C) for optimal results.
- **Sole**: 131°F (55°C) for perfect doneness.

Unlike meat, which needs a long rest after cooking, fish does not retain heat as well. Typically, oven-cooked fish does not require resting before serving, unless you are preparing large cuts.

To reduce waste and save money, use the whole fish, from the head to the tail.

- Buy whole fish rather than fillets whenever possible.
- Use leftover heads and bones to make stocks and soups.

GOOD TO KNOW: Blue fish and fatty salmonids are not suitable for this type of preparation.

- Make use of fish roe, monkfish liver, cheeks, and collars from whole fish.
- Turn leftover cooked fish into terrines, fish meatballs, stuffed clam or scallop shells, and more.

Beyond reducing food waste, whole fish cookery offers the opportunity to explore new dishes and flavors while helping to preserve marine resources.

Cephalopods

Octopuses, cuttlefish, and squid have the reputation of being difficult to cook. Traditionally used in Mediterranean and Asian cuisines, they are becoming increasingly popular worldwide.

Species consumed

Among the edible cephalopods, there are two large families: octopods (which include octopuses) and decapods, which include cuttlefish and squid.

Octopuses, with their eight identical arms, are prized for their tentacles, mantle, and head.

Cuttlefish, which have an internal calcareous structure known as the cuttlebone, have more tender meat that can be eaten raw.

Squid, with their elongated, hydrodynamic bodies, are highly valued for their versatility. The common names for squid in France can be confusing. The term *encornet* refers to certain types of squid, particularly *Loligo vulgaris*, which is appreciated for its delicate, tender meat. It is sometimes called *chipiron* in southwestern France, or *supion* or *tautène* in the southeast. The meat becomes tender when cooked either very quickly or very slowly—there is no middle ground. In English, the term "calamari" refers to squid that is prepared as food.

Selecting cephalopods

Look for bright, vivid, and even iridescent skin, which indicates freshness. Both the body and tentacles should be firm yet elastic, returning to their original shape after being pressed. Look for squid with a white, pearly color that is nearly translucent and free of yellowish spots. It should have a slight, pleasant sea smell, never a strong one. Fresh cephalopods will not be slimy, and their texture will be supple yet firm.

Storing cephalopods

Cephalopods are especially fragile and should be eaten soon after purchase, within 24 to 48 hours maximum. Quickly remove them from their original packaging, whether paper or plastic, as these materials retain moisture and accelerate spoilage. Clean cephalopods thoroughly (see below), then store them in an airtight container in the coldest part of the refrigerator (32°F–35.6°F/0°C–2°C). To keep them as fresh as possible, wrap them in a clean, damp dish towel before placing them in the container. Never freeze fresh cephalopods that have not been cleaned. Once cleaned, however, squid, cuttlefish, and octopus can be frozen for up to 3 months at 0.4°F (-18°C). Freezing them for 24 hours can even tenderize their meat.

Preparation and cooking

All cephalopods consist of three parts: a head, a mantle that contains the organs and ink sac, and arms or tentacles with suction cups. If you want to save the ink for cooking (for risottos, sauces, etc.), be careful not to pierce the silvery sac that contains it.

To prepare octopus, separate the head from the tentacles by making a cut below the eyes. Once the head has been emptied and skinned, remove the beak: the hard central part that connects the tentacles. Wash everything thoroughly and dry before cooking.

To prepare squid and cuttlefish, pull on the tentacles to separate them from the body (mantle), pulling out the innards and ink sac as well (see techniques pp. 72 and 75). Remove the quill or beak (known as the cuttlebone in cuttlefish).

To clean squid and cuttlefish thoroughly, rub them with cornstarch, which helps impurities and residue clump together. This makes rinsing easier and helps ensure no grains of sand remain.

When cooking cephalopods, the time needed to make them tender rather than rubbery varies greatly, depending on the species. Octopus requires long simmering, while squid and cuttlefish cook more quickly, especially when they are small. In the latter case, brief, high-heat cooking—such as 2–3 minutes on the grill—is sufficient.

Shellfish

Encompassing everything from oysters and mussels to lobsters and shrimp, shellfish are remarkably diverse. They offer a broad spectrum of unique oceanic flavors and are appreciated by enthusiasts worldwide. Once limited to coastal regions, shellfish are now more widely available.

Crustaceans

The following are among the most consumed crustaceans:

• **Lobster (*homard*)**: There are two primary varieties of this noble crustacean with asymmetrical claws, which can weigh from 14 oz. (400 g) to over 2¼ lb. (1 kg):

› The **European or common lobster**, also known as the Breton lobster or blue lobster, is found in the northeast Atlantic Ocean.

› The **American lobster**, whose other names include the Canadian or Maine lobster, has a brown and red shell and larger claws. It is found in the northwest Atlantic Ocean.

• **Langouste**: Also known as spiny lobsters, langoustes have long antennae and no claws. There are several species, including the red ones caught in the Mediterranean Sea and the Atlantic Ocean, as well as the pink ones imported from the Caribbean. They typically weigh between 1¼ lb. (600 g) and 4½ lb. (2 kg), and their meat is quite firm.

• **Crayfish (écrevisses)**: The European crayfish (*Astacus astacus*), native to France, is becoming increasingly rare. This small freshwater crustacean measuring 2–6 in. (5–15 cm) in length is being replaced by the American crayfish (*Faxonius limosus*), introduced from North America and now an invasive species in Europe. Crayfish are traditionally used in quenelles, bisques, and sauces for their highly flavorful meat and shell.

• **Langoustine**: Also known as Norway lobsters or Dublin Bay prawns, these crustaceans have a pinkish-orange shell and their size is between a crayfish and a lobster. Their meat is especially tender and can be eaten raw when very fresh. They are sometimes also referred to as "scampi."

• **Crab**: The term "crab" covers a wide range of species, from the meaty brown or edible crabs (*tourteaux*) to delicate spider crabs and the massive king crabs. Other types include rock crabs, commonly used in soups, and soft-shell crabs, which are often served fried.

• **Shrimp**: From rock shrimp to king prawns, all shrimp are classified by size, expressed as numbers that indicate the count per pound or kilogram. Sizes range from under 10 for colossal shrimp to over 100 for mini shrimp. The flavor also varies, from the mild taste of small common shrimp to the stronger flavor of wild prawns. Shrimp may be farm-raised (the vast majority consumed today) or wild-caught.

• **Barnacles**: Mainly harvested on the coasts of Portugal and Galicia, in Spain, gooseneck barnacles have distinctive, plated heads, and they cling to rocks with meaty, edible stalks. The meat is firm and has an intense ocean flavor.

Bivalves and gastropods

Bivalves and gastropods are both groups of mollusks whose soft bodies are protected by a hard outer shell.

The following are among the widely consumed bivalves and gastropods:

• **Oysters**: Most edible oyster species belong to the Ostreidae family. The following two species are farmed on French coasts:

› Plump **Pacific oysters (*Magallana gigas*)**, also known as Japanese or Miyagi oysters, can have a mild, sweet, or intense flavor, depending on where they come from. In France, they are cultivated in the Marennes-Oléron basin, Cancale, and Arcachon. Native to Japan and southern China, Pacific oysters have been introduced to every continent except Antarctica.

› **European flat oysters (*Ostrea edulis*)** are native to Europe and have a more delicate, hazelnutty flavor. They were once far more abundant in the wild and are considered a priority species, with efforts underway to

reintroduce them in the UK and Ireland. They were introduced in the waters off Maine (US), where they now grow in the wild. In France, they are farmed in Brittany under the name Belon.

Pacific oysters are classified by size, ranging from 0 to 5, with the smallest numbers indicating the largest oysters. Wild (or diploid) oysters spawn between May and August in the northern hemisphere, which can give them a milky taste and texture that is not to everyone's liking. This is part of the reason for the traditional advice to eat them only in the months containing the letter "r"—from September to April. Warmer summer weather can also increase the risk of contamination, but with proper transportation and handling, this risk is minimal today, so always buy oysters from a trusted source. Sterile farmed oysters, also known as triploid oysters, are genetically manipulated and never become milky, so they can be eaten all year round.

• **Mussels**: Mussels have orange-colored flesh with a mild, briny flavor that varies in intensity depending on their origin and farming methods. Around 90 percent of the mussels consumed globally are farmed.

› Bouchot mussels are the most widely consumed type of mussel in France. They are farmed on wooden poles called *bouchots* located in intertidal zones along the Atlantic coast and the English Channel. Since 2013, the name "Moules de Bouchot" has been legally protected in the European Union as a Traditional Specialty Guaranteed (TSG). This ensures that mussels with this designation have been produced according to traditional methods, without specifying their geographical origin. They are available from July to February.

› Rope-grown mussels are cultivated on suspended ropes that are permanently underwater. They have a more intense flavor and are available from May to the end of August.

› Bottom-grown mussels, cultivated on the seabed in coastal areas, are available from May to February in France.

• **Scallops**: These bivalves have a characteristic fan-shaped shell that protects the firm yet tender meat inside. In some cases, orange or red coral—the female reproductive organ, or gonad—is also attached. Like shrimp, they are classified by size, based on the number of shelled scallops per pound or kilogram. Scallops are generally divided into two categories: the larger, meatier sea scallops and the smaller, sweeter bay scallops. A prominent example of the former is the great scallop (*Pecten maximus*), known as the *coquille Saint-Jacques* in French—a reference to the Camino de Santiago, or Way of Saint James pilgrimage route, whose emblem is this scallop shell. All the scallop recipes in this book were made with this species.

• **Cockles and clams**: With their firm flesh and delicate taste, these burrowing bivalves from the Veneridae family are often confused. The following are the three main types:

› Cockles (*coques*), the smallest, have a rounded shell with pronounced ridges. The meat is sweet, slightly briny, and relatively firm.

› *Palourdes,* also known as "*clovisses*" in the south of France, are generically referred to as "clams" in English. The term *palourde* is used for two different species in France—the *palourde européenne* (*Ruditapes decussatus*)—the grooved carpet shell or palourde clam, which has a pronounced oval shell and grayish stripes, and the *palourde japonaise* (*Ruditapes philippinarum*), or the Manila clam, which is rounder and has more colorful stripes. Both species are similar in taste.

› Warty Venus shell clams (*praires*) have a highly rounded shape and deep ridges. They are the heaviest and meatiest, but the least flavorful, of the three.

• **Periwinkles and whelks**: Members of the gastropod family, like land snails, periwinkles and whelks are gaining popularity for their firm meat and bold flavor.

› Periwinkles (*bigorneaux*), also known as "sea snails," are small, edible whelks, recognizable by their dark gray conical spiral shells. They are mainly found on rocky coasts.

› Common whelks (*bulots*), larger in size and very meaty, have yellow or brown conch-shaped shells. The western part of the Cotentin (or Cherbourg) Peninsula is the

leading French and European fishing area for this species (*Buccinum undatum*). Harvested in the area, Granville Bay Bulots, were awarded Protected Geographical Indication (PGI) status in 2019.

• **Sea urchins**: Beneath their spiny surface, sea urchins hide a delicacy: five lobes of uni arranged in a star shape around the inside of the shell. Often mistakenly referred to as "roe," uni are actually gonads, not eggs. They range in color from creamy yellow to orange, depending on whether the sea urchin is female or male. Their intense, slightly sweet flavor is particularly prized in Japan, the world's leading consumer of uni, and in France, the world's second-largest consumer.

Selecting shellfish

Fresh crustaceans have a pleasant ocean-like smell, firmly attached appendages, and a shiny, moist shell. When purchasing live crustaceans—whether crabs, lobsters, langoustines, or langoustes—touch them to gauge their responsiveness; they should react by moving. Fresh shrimp and prawns should have a firm texture and clean, vibrant colors. Their heads should be firmly attached. Avoid all crustaceans that smell of ammonia or have black spots on their shells.

When selecting bivalves (mussels, oysters, clams, scallops, etc.), look for shells that are closed or close when tapped. They should have a clean, briny smell and be heavy for their size, indicating that they contain liquor: a mixture of the animal's own juices and filtered seawater.

Gastropods (periwinkles and whelks) should have intact shells and firm flesh that fills the shell well. Live gastropods should withdraw into their shells when touched.

Fresh sea urchins, sold live, should have mobile, upright spines.

Storing shellfish

Live bivalves should be stored between 39°F and 43°F (4°C–6°C), ideally covered with a damp towel in a non-airtight container. Never immerse them in fresh water. They can be kept for a maximum of 2 days.

If you purchase oysters in a crate or box (*bourriche*), they should be tightly packed and stored flat in a cool place (40°F–59°F/5°–15°C) away from light for up to 5 days. Once the crate has been opened, cover the oysters with a damp towel and a weight to prevent them from losing their liquor; keep them in the refrigerator. (Always check with your supplier for precise storage instructions.) Discard any open shells that do not close when tapped to avoid the risk of food poisoning.

Gastropods (periwinkles and whelks) and sea urchins have similar storage requirements, but sea urchins are particularly fragile and must be kept in the refrigerator in a damp towel and consumed within 24 hours.

Place live crustaceans, such as lobsters and crabs, on the bottom shelf—the coldest part—of the refrigerator wrapped in a damp towel to keep them cool and moist without suffocating them. Never immerse them in fresh water or place them in an airtight container. They will keep for up to 24 hours. In all cases, the sooner you eat crustaceans after purchasing them, the better their texture and taste will be.

Raw or cooked shellfish that have been removed from their shells freeze well. Never freeze live shellfish in their shells. Raw scallops, removed from their shells, can be placed on a tray, frozen individually, and then transferred to a freezer bag.

Preparing and cooking shellfish

Shellfish constantly filter water and accumulate sand and mud, so they must be thoroughly rinsed with cold running water before preparation. Rinse them while sorting them and discard any that are broken or open and do not close when tapped.

Some bivalves (such as cockles, clams, and razor clams) must be soaked to remove any residual sand. To do this, place them in a large bowl and cover them halfway with seawater or heavily salted water—2 generous tablespoons (1¼ oz./35 g) per 4 cups (1 liter) water. Let them soak for at least 4 hours, changing the water once or twice if necessary, depending on the number of shellfish or the amount of sand they expel. Clams tend to squirt a lot of water during this process, so feel free to cover them. Drain and rinse well before cooking.

• Although oysters are usually eaten raw, they first need to be scrubbed to remove any dirt from their shells.

• Mussels are rarely sandy. However, they can be left to soak in fresh water for about 20 minutes, if desired, as they are naturally quite salty.

Shellfish cook quickly: 3–5 minutes over high heat for mussels, and 2–3 minutes for cockles or clams. They should open when cooked, so always discard any that remain closed. Their flavorful cooking juices can be strained and used to make stocks, sauces, or veloutés.

The first step in preparing crustaceans often entails cooking them in court bouillon, then quickly cooling them in ice water to halt the cooking process and preserve the texture of the meat. The specific timing varies, depending on the species and size. Large crustaceans, such as lobster, can be steamed to keep them tender and preserve their delicate taste. Shells, heads, and claws have bold flavors and are perfect for making bisques, stocks, and sauces, so don't let them go to waste!

Glossary of Fish and Shellfish Terms

ANISAKIS: A parasite found in certain fish that must be eliminated in any fish intended for raw consumption by freezing it for at least 24 hours at -4°F (-20°C).

BIVALVE: A mollusk with two shells connected by a hinge, including oysters, mussels, and clams.

BOUQUET GARNI: A bundle of herbs and aromatics added to stocks, sauces, and other dishes during cooking to add flavor. It typically includes parsley, thyme, and bay leaves, often wrapped in a leek green and tied with twine. The components can vary depending on the dish.

BRINING: Soaking fish in a saltwater solution (about 10 percent salt) to firm up the flesh and reduce water loss during cooking.

CORAL: Often called "roe," coral is technically the reproductive organ (gonad) of certain shellfish. In scallops, it is attached to the adductor muscle and varies in color from off-white to orange-red. Most scallops are hermaphroditic, so the coral can contain both male and female parts.

COURT BOUILLON: A broth made with water, vinegar or white wine, vegetables, a bouquet garni, and spices used to poach fish and shellfish.

DARNE: A thick cross-section cut from a round fish such as salmon or tuna that includes skin and bones. Also known as a fish steak.

FILLETING AND FILLET: Removing the fillets of flesh from both sides of the spine. Fillets are boneless, except for the **pin bones.**

FLATFISH: A large group of fish categorized by shape, with flattened bodies and both eyes on the same side of the body (sole, turbot, etc.), as opposed to **round fish.** In France, certain round fish are classed as flatfish, such as John Dory and sea bream (see p. 16).

FUMET: A rich stock made with fish bones and trimmings, or from crustacean heads and shells, used as a base for soups and sauces.

GUTTING: Removing the innards from fish or cephalopods, typically through a ventral cut, leaving only the edible parts.

***IKEJIME* (or *IKE JIME*)**: A traditional Japanese method of slaughtering fish that maintains its quality by reducing stress and preventing the release of lactic acid (see p. 14).

PIN BONES: The thin, flexible intramuscular bones found in the fillets of larger fish, such as salmon. It is recommended to remove them using fish bone tweezers before cooking (see technique p. 52).

POACHING: Cooking fish gently in a simmering, but not boiling, liquid.

REFRESHING: Plunging fish, shellfish, or vegetables into ice water after cooking to stop the cooking process.

ROUND FISH: A large group of fish categorized by shape, with cylindrical bodies and an eye on each side, such as sea bass and cod, as opposed to **flatfish**.

SCALING: The act of removing scales from a fish using a knife or a fish scaler. The French term, *écailler*, also refers to a professional specializing in the preparation and sale of shellfish and crustaceans.

SHELLING: Removing the shell from a crustacean.

SHUCK AND SHUCKING: The shell of a bivalve, such as an oyster or clam, and the action of opening the shell.

SUPREME CUT: A boneless portion of fish cut from a **fillet** (see technique p. 98).

SUSHI- OR SUSHIMI-GRADE: A label used on fish that sellers consider safe to eat raw. Since there are no official standards, it is crucial to buy fish for raw consumption from a trusted source.

TOMALLEY: The culinary term for the hepatopancreas of lobsters and crabs. This soft, green substance inside the body cavity is prized for its intense flavor, but it should be avoided during "red tides" (harmful algal blooms, or extreme algae growth), when toxins can accumulate in it.

TRIMMING: Removing the fins and other inedible parts from a fish to prepare it for cooking.

A FEW NOTES

Unless otherwise specified, all the recipes in this book were made with **fine sea salt**, **unsalted butter**, **all-purpose flour**, **granulated sugar**, **extra-virgin olive oil**, and **hens' eggs** (standard "large" in the US and Canada and "medium" in the UK).

To avoid the risk of infection, purchase fish and shellfish **from trusted sources** and keep your **prep area clean** and your **utensils spotless**.

EQUIPMENT

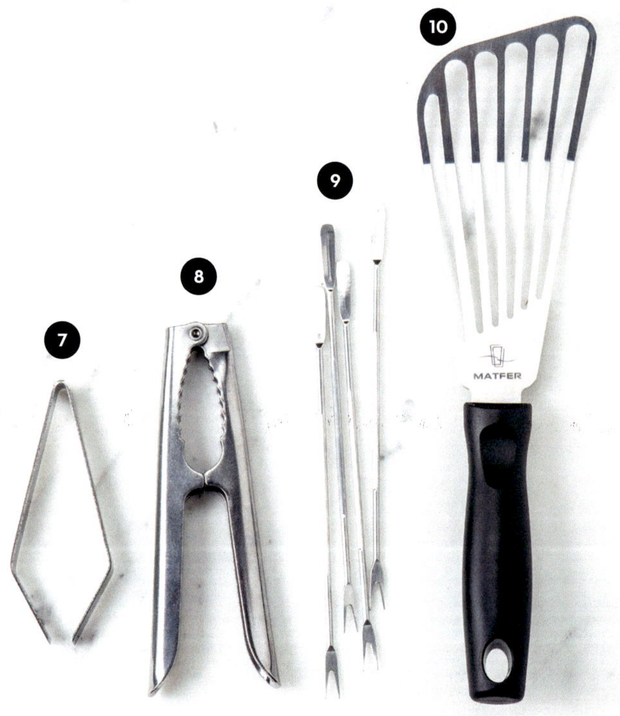

1. Oyster knife with a guard
2. Scallop knife
3. Paring knife
4. Fish filleting (boning) knife
5. Chef's knife
6. Fishmonger's knife

7. Fish bone tweezers
8. Lobster cracker
9. Lobster picks
10. Fish spatula

11. Cutting boards
12. Meat pounder or tenderizer
13. Fish scaler
14. Fish shears

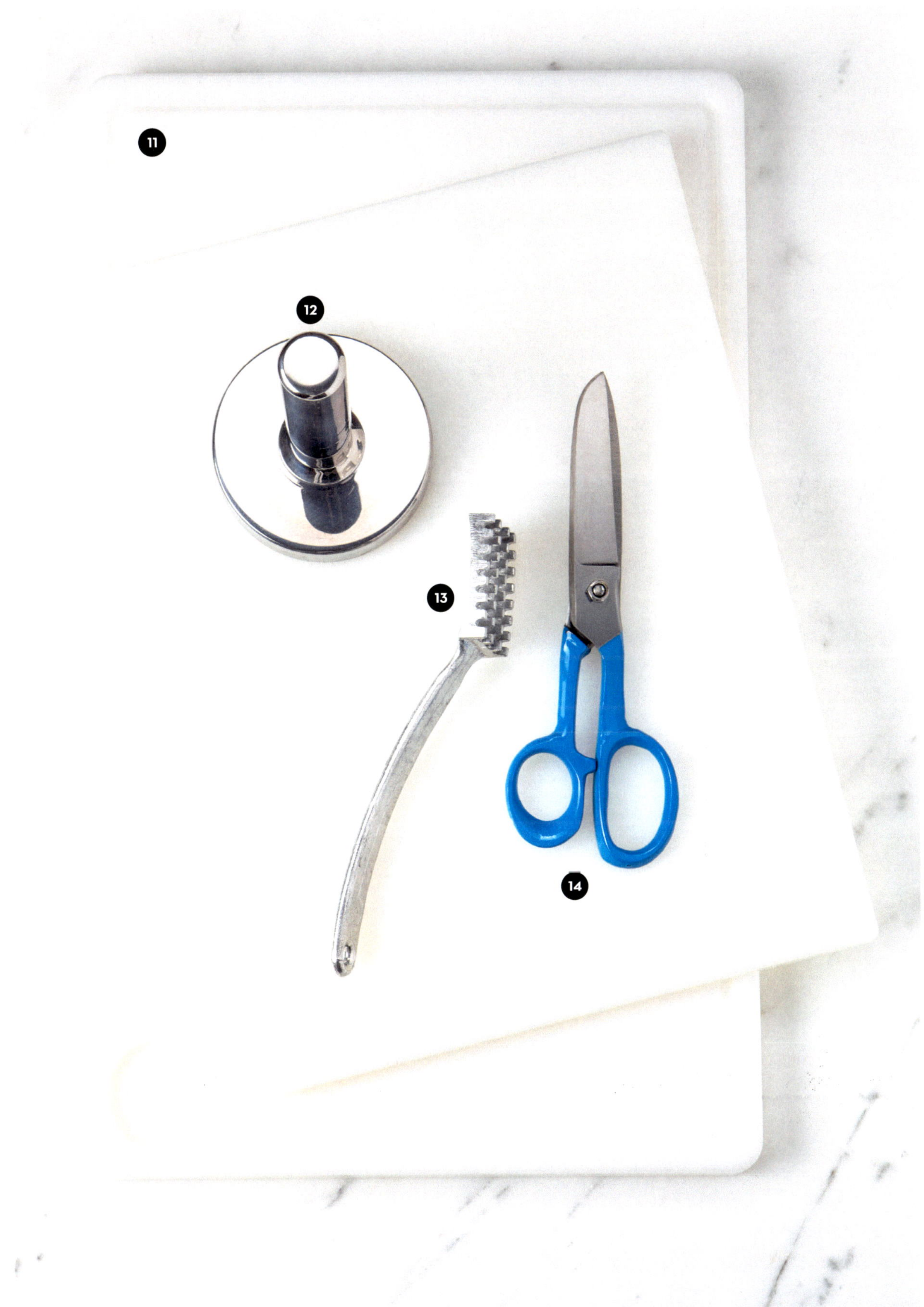
11
12
13
14

TECHNIQUES

PREPARING AND CLEANING

Trimming Trout

Ingredients

Trout or another round fish yielding 2 fillets

Equipment

Cutting board

Fish shears or kitchen scissors

1 • Place the fish on the cutting board, hold it firmly in place, and carefully cut off the dorsal fin using the fish shears or kitchen scissors.

2 • Cut the pectoral fin off the side facing up.

3 • Cut the pelvic fin off the side facing up.

4 • Cut off the anal fin.

5 • Turn the fish over and cut off the pectoral and pelvic fins on the other side.

6 • If serving the fish whole, cut a triangle out of the tail fin to form two pointed tips.

7 • The fish is trimmed.

Trimming Sea Bass

Ingredients

Sea bass or another round fish yielding 2 fillets

Equipment

Fish shears or kitchen scissors

Cutting board

1 • Using the fish shears or kitchen scissors, trim off the dorsal, pectoral, pelvic, and anal fins following the technique for trimming trout (see technique p. 32).

2 • Place the fish on the cutting board. If serving the fish whole, cut a triangle out of the tail fin to form two pointed tips.

3 • The fish is trimmed.

Trimming Sole

Ingredients

Sole or another flatfish yielding 4 fillets

Equipment

Fish shears or kitchen scissors

Cutting board

1 • Place the fish on the cutting board, hold it firmly in place, and carefully cut off the pectoral fin using the fish shears or kitchen scissors.

2 • Hold the tail firmly and cut off the dorsal fin, taking care not to cut into the meat.

3 • Turn the fish over and cut off the anal fin, holding the tail firmly. You can also trim the tail fin slightly, if necessary, to shorten it.

Trimming Sea Bream

Ingredients

Sea bream or another similar fish yielding 2 fillets

Equipment

Fish shears or kitchen scissors

Cutting board

1 • Holding the fish over a bowl, carefully cut off the dorsal fin using the fish shears or kitchen scissors.

2 • Cut the pectoral fin off the side facing up.

3 • Cut off the anal fin.

4 • Cut the pelvic fin off the side facing up, then cut off the fins on the other side.

5 • Place the fish on the cutting board. If serving the fish whole, cut a triangle out of the tail fin to form two pointed tips.

6 • The fish is trimmed.

Scaling Sea Bream

Ingredients

Sea bream or another similar fish yielding 2 fillets, trimmed
(see technique p. 36)

Equipment

Cutting board

Fish scaler

1 • Place the fish on the cutting board and hold it firmly in place at the head end. Using the fish scaler, scrape the fish from the tail toward the head to remove all the scales.

2 • Repeat on the other side, taking care not to tear the skin or flesh.

3 • Rinse and dry the fish.

Scaling Sole

Ingredients

Sole or another flatfish yielding 4 fillets, trimmed
(see technique p. 35)

Equipment

Cutting board

Fish scaler

1 • Place the fish on the cutting board. Holding the fish firmly at the head end, scrape it with the fish scaler to remove all the scales on the side facing up.

2 • Repeat on the other side, taking care not to tear the skin or flesh. Rinse and dry the fish.

Scaling Sea Bass

Ingredients

Sea bass or another round fish yielding 2 fillets, trimmed
(see technique p. 34)

Equipment

Cutting board
Fish scaler

1 • Place the fish on the cutting board and hold it firmly in place.

2 • Using the fish scaler, scrape the fish from the tail toward the head on both sides to remove all the scales, taking care not to tear the skin or flesh. Rinse and dry the fish.

Skinning Fish Fillets Using a Knife

Ingredients

Fish fillet of your choice with the skin on

Equipment

Cutting board
Long knife
Paper towels

1 • Place the fish skin side down on the cutting board and, using the knife, cut across the flesh at the tail end, cutting down to the skin but not through it.

2 • Tilt the knife blade until it is almost parallel with the work surface and slide it between the skin and the flesh.

3 • Hold the skin with a paper towel to prevent it from slipping.

↪

Skinning Fish Fillets Using a Knife (continued)

4 • Carefully move the blade forward slowly to avoid cutting into the flesh.

5 • Grip the skin tightly to make it easier to separate the flesh from it, taking care not to tear it.

6 • Once you reach the middle of the fillet, turn it over and pull the rest of the skin away. It should not have any flesh attached to it.

7 • The fillet is skinned and ready to cook.

Skinning Flatfish by Hand

Ingredients

Flatfish of your choice, trimmed (see technique p. 35)

Equipment

Cutting board

Knife

1 • Place the fish on the cutting board. Using the knife, make a cut across the flesh at the tail end of the fish, cutting down to the skin but not through it.

2 • Hold the tail fin with one hand and start to peel back the skin with the other.

3 • Holding the tail fin firmly, pull the skin away from the flesh, keeping it parallel to the work surface.

↪

Skinning Flatfish by Hand (continued)

4 • Proceed gradually to avoid tearing the skin.

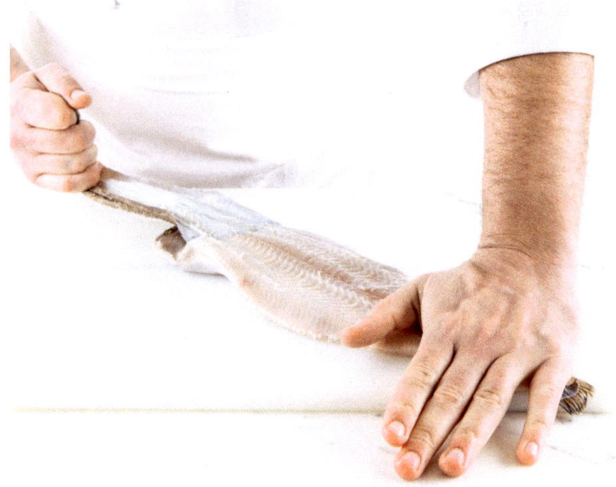

5 • To make it easier, keep the fish as flat as possible using the palm of your hand.

6 • The fish is skinned and ready to cook.

Gutting Sea Bass

Ingredients

Sea bass or another round fish, trimmed and scaled
(see techniques pp. 34 and 40)

Equipment

Fish shears or kitchen scissors

Cutting board

Paring knife

Paper towels

1 • Holding the fish in one hand, insert the bottom blade of the fish shears or kitchen scissors into the anal vent.

2 • Place the fish on the cutting board. Make a shallow cut along the belly of the fish all the way to the base of the head.

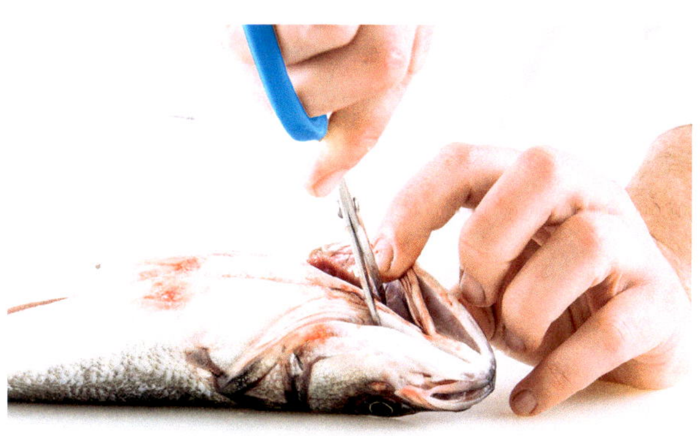

3 • Cut through the attachment at the base of the jaw to release the gills.

↪

Gutting Sea Bass (continued)

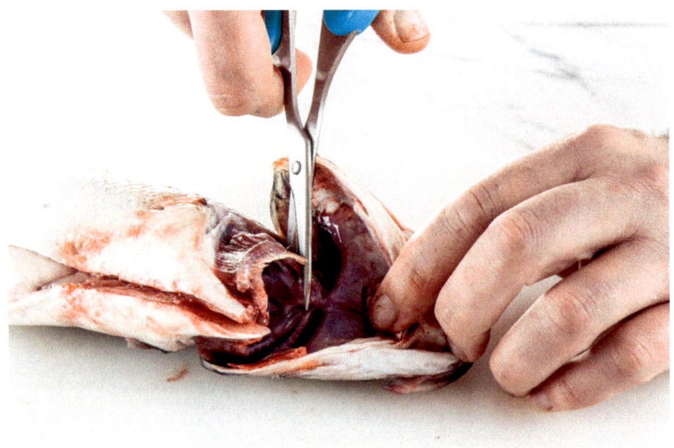

4 • Cut to detach the gills from the head.

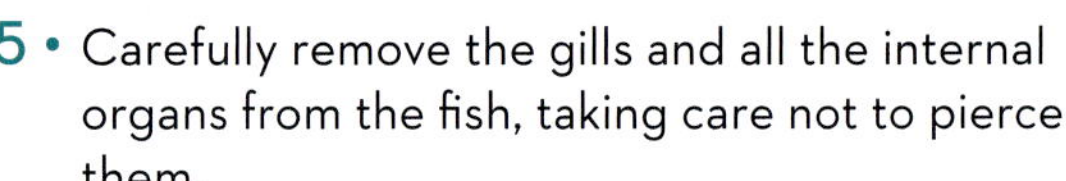

5 • Carefully remove the gills and all the internal organs from the fish, taking care not to pierce them.

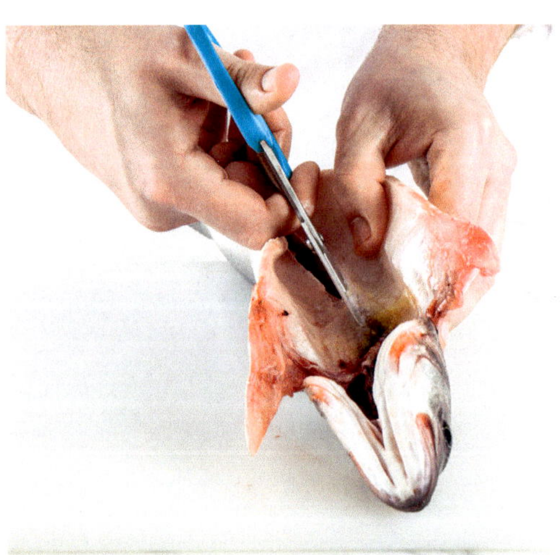

6 • Using the shears or scissors, cut through the wall of the body cavity along the spine.

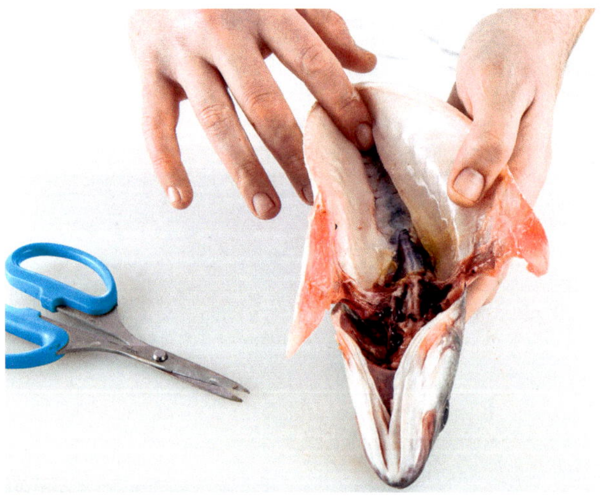

7 • You will see a translucent white membrane.

8 • Using the tip of the paring knife, slit the membrane to access the spine.

9 • Rinse the fish under running water to remove any blood, then dry it thoroughly with paper towels.

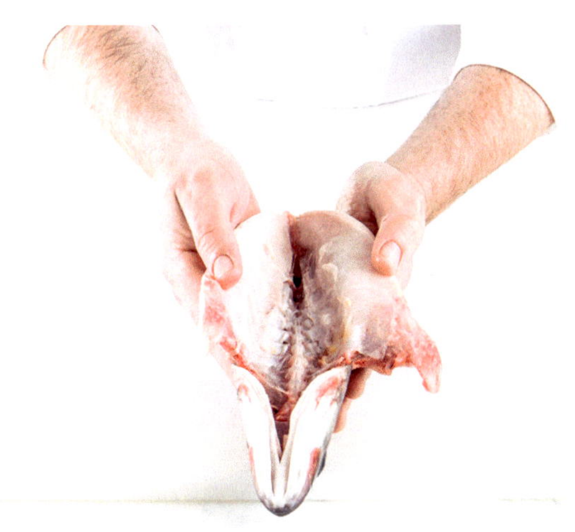

10 • The fish is gutted.

Gutting Sea Bream

Ingredients

Sea bream or another similar fish, trimmed and scaled
(see techniques pp. 36 and 38)

Equipment

Fish shears or kitchen scissors

Paring knife

Paper towels

1 • Holding the fish in one hand, insert the bottom blade of the fish shears or kitchen scissors into the anal vent. Make a shallow cut along the belly of the fish all the way to the base of the head.

2 • Cut to detach the gills from the head.

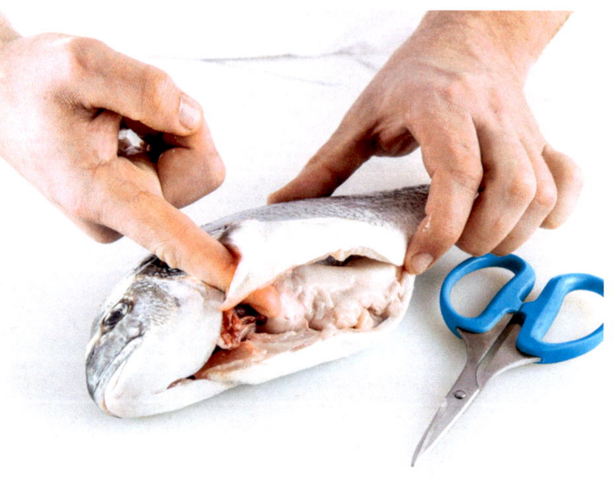

3 • Separate the gills from the body using your index finger.

4 • Carefully remove the gills and all the internal organs from the fish, taking care not to pierce them.

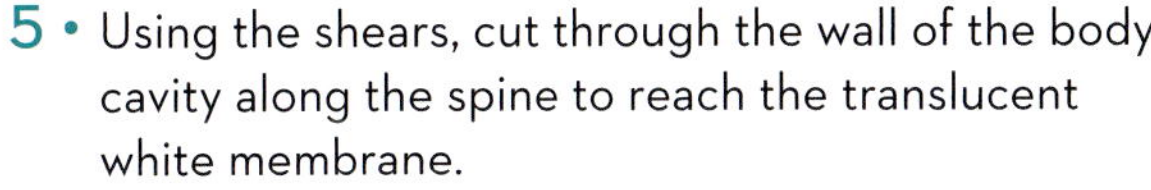

5 • Using the shears, cut through the wall of the body cavity along the spine to reach the translucent white membrane.

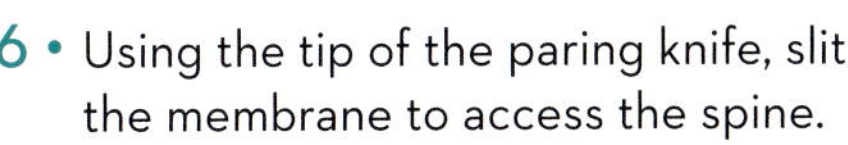

6 • Using the tip of the paring knife, slit the membrane to access the spine.

7 • Rinse the fish under running water to remove any blood, then dry it thoroughly with paper towels.

Gutting Sole

Ingredients

Sole or another flatfish, trimmed and skinned if desired
(see techniques pp. 35 and 43)

Equipment

Cutting board
Knife
Spoon

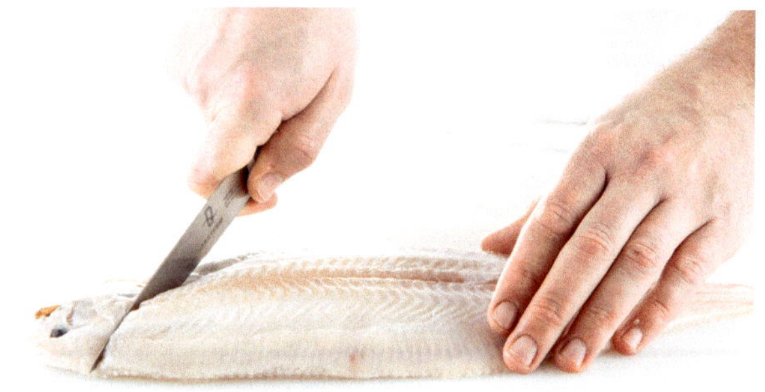

1 • Place the fish on the cutting board. Using the knife, start cutting below the head at an angle.

2 • Finish cutting off the head, taking care to cut just above the belly.

3 • Using your thumb, apply pressure to the fish's belly to push the organs toward the front.

4 • When the organs appear, start to gently pull them out.

5 • Continue pulling the organs out carefully, taking care not to tear them.

6 • Use the end of the spoon handle to remove any blood clots.

7 • The fish is gutted.

Boning Fish Fillets

Ingredients

Fish fillet of your choice

Equipment

Cutting board

Fish bone tweezers

1 • Place the fish on the cutting board. Run your finger along the center of the fillet to locate the pin bones.

2 • Pinch the flesh on both sides of each bone and pull it out using the tweezers.

3 • Repeat this process along the entire length of the fillet until all the pin bones have been removed.

Preparing Monkfish Tails

Ingredients
Monkfish tail

Equipment
Cutting board
Paper towels
Fish shears or kitchen scissors
Fish filleting knife

1 • Place the monkfish tail on the cutting board. Hold the spine of it firmly with one hand and, using the other hand, pull away the skin using a paper towel to help you grip it.

2 • To make it easier, you can gradually work the skin away from the flesh using your fingers.

3 • Remove the skin completely.

↪

Preparing Monkfish Tails (continued)

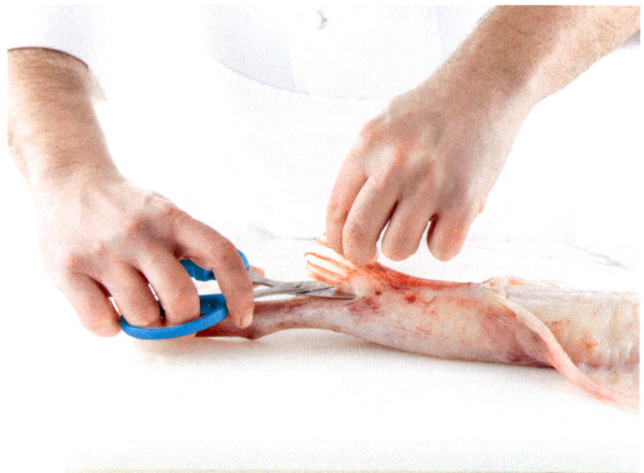

4 • Using the fish shears or kitchen scissors, cut off the dorsal fin.

5 • Using the filleting knife, cut the fatty layer away from the flesh.

6 • Cut away as much fat as possible on both sides.

7 • Turn the tail over and cut to remove the membrane.

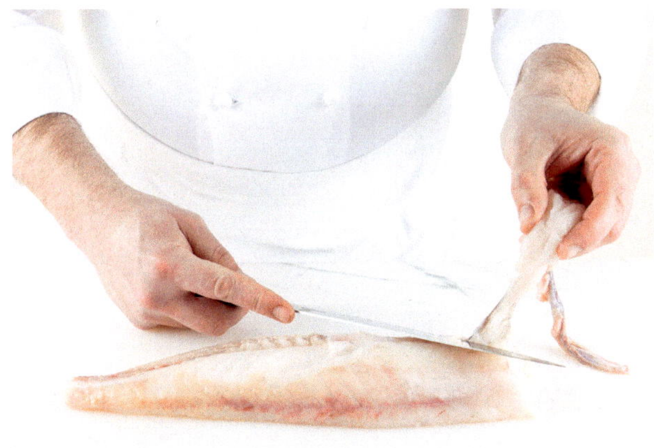

8 • Cut off any bits that remain.

9 • Cut off any bloody parts.

10 • Trim the edges if necessary.

11 • The monkfish tail is now ready to cook.

Deveining Crayfish

Ingredients

Raw crayfish

1 • Pick up and open out the crayfish.

2 • Carefully remove the head from the tail.

3 • Pinch the end of the tail.

4 • Keep pinching, holding the central part of the tail (telson).

5 • Twist the tail back and forth while gently pulling on it.

6 • Slowly pull out the entire "vein" (intestine). The crayfish is now deveined.

Peeling Shrimp (King Prawns)

Ingredients

Raw shrimp or king prawns

Equipment

Wooden toothpick

1 • Pick up and open out a shrimp (king prawn).

2 • Separate the head from the tail.

3 • Slide a finger under the first section of the shell to loosen it. Remove the top part of the shell.

4 • Pull on the pointed part of the tail (telson).

5 • Peel away the rest of the shell.

6 • Using the wooden toothpick, lift up the "vein" (intestine) and pull it away.

7 • The peeled shrimp (king prawns) are ready to be cooked.

Cleaning Mussels

Ingredients

Mussels

Equipment

Paring knife

1 • Wash the mussels in a large bowl of clean water, discarding any that are open and do not close immediately when tapped sharply.

2 • Using the paring knife, scrape the mussels to clean them and remove any barnacles.

3 • Grab the "beard" sticking out from the shell (the byssus threads).

4 • Pull on it firmly to remove it.

5 • The mussels are ready to be cooked.

Shucking Scallops

Ingredients

Scallops in their shells

Equipment

Oyster knife

Paintbrush

Paring knife

1 • Hold the scallop with the rounded shell facing down and the hinge toward you. Slide the tip of the oyster knife between the shell halves on one side.

2 • Make small twisting movements with the knife to pry the shells apart. Scrape the blade along the flat shell to sever the adductor muscle.

3 • Remove the top (flat) shell. Using the knife, begin removing the frill (mantle).

4 • Run the tip of the knife blade beneath the remaining frill to release it.

5 • Remove the rest of the frill and cut off the black stomach sac. Remove everything but the white meat and orange coral (gonad).

6 • If necessary, brush away any sand using the paintbrush dipped in a little water.

7 • Detach the white meat and the coral from the shell.

↪

Shucking Scallops (continued)

8 • Using the paring knife, remove the intestine.

9 • Separate the coral from the white meat.

10 • Cut off the white part of the coral and cut the muscle off the side of the white meat.

11 • The scallops and coral are ready for use.

Shucking Cupped Oysters

Ingredients

Oysters with one cupped shell

Equipment

Oyster knife

Kitchen towel

1 • Hold the oyster in a folded kitchen towel with the rounded side facing down and the hinge toward you. Slide the tip of the oyster knife between the shells on one side.

CHEFS' NOTES

For optimal safety, hold the oysters in a folded kitchen towel or wear special oyster shucking gloves to avoid cutting your hand if the knife slips.

2 • Make small twisting movements with the knife to pry the oyster open. Slide the blade under the upper shell to cut through the adductor muscle.

↪

Shucking Cupped Oysters (continued)

3 • Remove the upper shell.

4 • Working over a bowl to catch the liquor, carefully run the knife around the oyster to release it from the shell, then cut through the muscle holding it.

5 • Holding the oyster in place, pour the liquor into the bowl. Turn the oyster over in the shell.

6 • Remove any shell fragments. The oysters are ready to serve.

Shucking Flat Oysters

Ingredients

European flat oysters (*belons*)

Equipment

Oyster knife

Kitchen towel

1 • Place the oyster in a folded kitchen towel with the flatter side facing up and the hinge toward you. Insert the tip of the oyster knife between the shells at the hinge.

2 • Make small twisting movements with the knife to pry the oyster open.

3 • Slide the blade under the upper shell to cut through the adductor muscle.

4 • Remove the upper shell. Carefully run the knife around the oyster to release it, then cut through the muscle holding it. You can work over a bowl to catch the liquor.

5 • Holding the oyster in place, pour the liquor into a bowl. Turn the oyster over in the shell and remove any shell fragments.

6 • The oysters are ready to serve.

Preparing Sea Urchins

Ingredients

Sea urchin

Equipment

Scissors

Long tweezers

Spoon

CHEFS' NOTES

If you wish, you can wear gloves to protect your hands against the sharp sea urchin spines.

1 • Insert the tip of the bottom scissor blade into the flat part of the sea urchin.

2 • Cut a wide circle around the mouth.

3 • Remove the organs and any other black parts using the tweezers.

4 • Only the orange uni (gonads) should remain.

5 • Using the spoon, carefully remove the 5 lobes of uni attached to the shell.

6 • Rinse them in a bowl of water.

7 • The sea urchin uni is ready for use.

Preparing Squid

Ingredients

Squid

Equipment

Cutting board

Chef's knife

1 • Hold the squid's body firmly.

2 • Pull the tentacles and head away from the body with the innards attached.

3 • Place on the cutting board and cut the innards away from the head.

4 • Separate the head and beak from the tentacles.

5 • Cut to separate the tentacles and arms.

6 • Remove the quill (cartilage) from the body.

7 • Pull off the outer skin and lateral wings (fins).

↪

Preparing Squid (continued)

8 • Turn the body inside out.

9 • Cut off any remaining innards, then return the body back to its original way.

10 • Trim the open end of the body neatly.

11 • The squid is ready to be cooked.

Preparing Cuttlefish

Ingredients
Cuttlefish

Equipment
Cutting board
Fish filleting knife

1 • Place the cuttlefish on the cutting board. Lift the top of the body cavity so that you can insert your hand.

2 • Pull the tentacles and head away from the body with the innards attached.

3 • Cut the tentacles off the head.

↪

Preparing Cuttlefish (continued)

4 • Rinse the tentacles under cold running water, then pat them dry and set aside.

5 • Make a cut along the edge of the body.

6 • Remove the cuttlebone.

7 • Run the knife blade beneath the skin to open it without cutting the flesh.

8 • Detach the membrane.

9 • Pull on the skin to remove it.

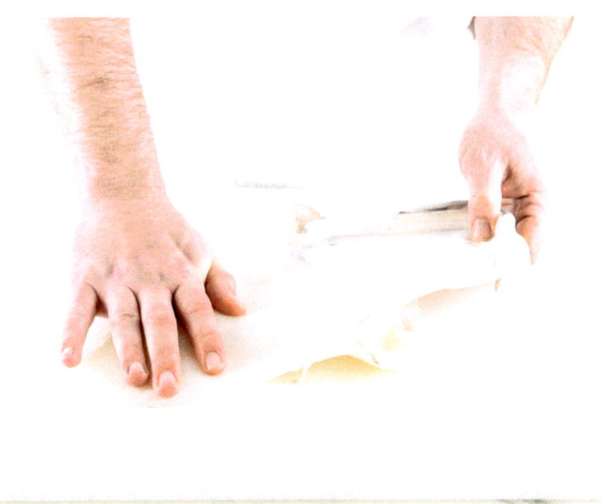

10 • Remove the skin from the other side as well.

11 • The cuttlefish is ready to be cooked.

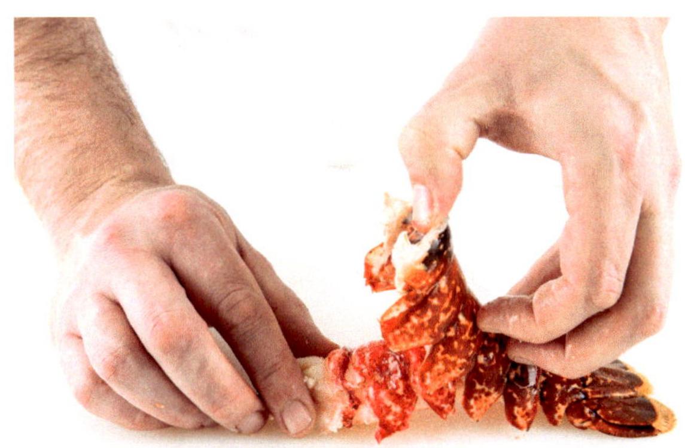

CUTTING

Filleting Sea Bass

Ingredients

Sea bass or another similar round fish yielding 2 fillets, trimmed, scaled, and gutted (see techniques pp. 34, 40, and 45)

Equipment

Cutting board

Fish filleting knife

Scissors

1 • Place the fish on its side on the cutting board. Cut it at an angle below the head on the side facing up.

2 • Make a shallow cut across the fish above the tail fin.

3 • Run the filleting knife along the spine from the cut made at the head to the one at the tail to release the fillet.

4 • Using the scissors, snip through the ribs to detach the fillet.

5 • Turn the fish over, positioning the head so it overhangs the cutting board and remains flat. Cut it at an angle below the head.

6 • Starting at the tail end, run the knife along the spine to release the fillet.

↪

Filleting Sea Bass (continued)

7 • Carefully remove the fillet.

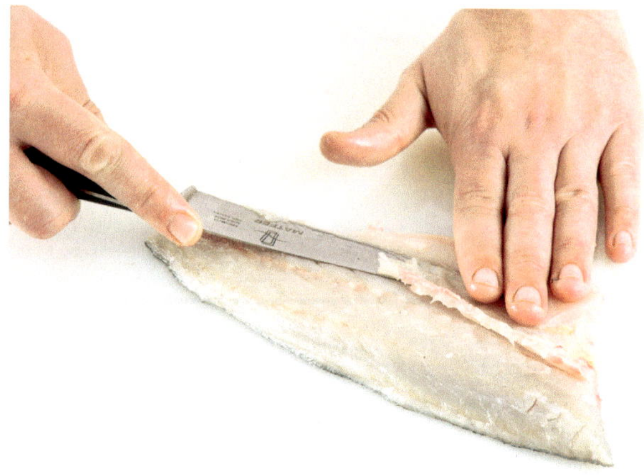

8 • Cut off the bones from the belly section.

9 • Trim the fillet.

10 • Trim off the belly meat.

11 • The fillet (top) is ready for use. The trimmings (center [belly meat] and bottom) can be used to make fish fumet.

Filleting Trout

Ingredients

Trout or another similar round fish yielding 2 fillets, trimmed, scaled, and gutted (see techniques pp. 32, 40, and 45)

Equipment

Cutting board

Fish filleting knife

Scissors

1 • Place the fish on the cutting board. Cut off the head. With the knife horizontal, cut between the spine and the fillet from the head to the tail. Remove the first fillet.

2 • Turn the fish over and work the knife blade between the spine and the fillet at the head end.

3 • Remove the second fillet by cutting along the spine.

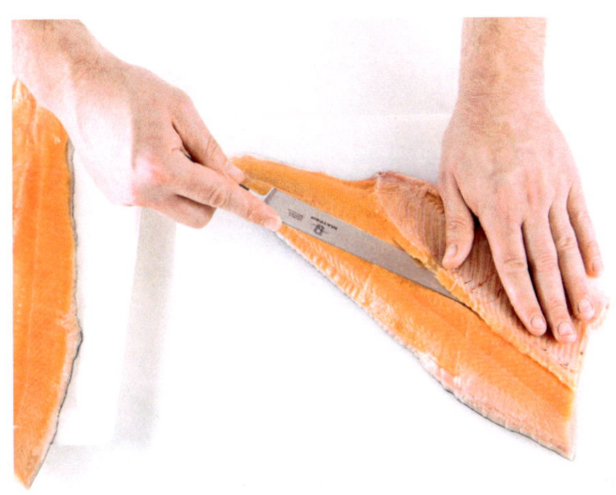

4 • Cut off the rib bones from the belly section.

5 • Cut off the flesh from the belly.

6 • Trim the fillet.

7 • The fillets are ready for use.

Filleting Sea Bream

Ingredients

Sea bream or another similar fish yielding 2 fillets, trimmed, scaled, and gutted (see techniques pp. 36, 38, and 48)

Equipment

Cutting board

Fish shears or kitchen scissors

Fish filleting knife

Chef's knife

1 • Place the fish on the cutting board. Cut off the head using the fish shears or kitchen scissors.

2 • Make a shallow cut along the back from the head to the tail.

3 • Make a shallow cut across the fish above the tail fin.

4 • Run the knife horizontally along the spine and ribs to start removing the fillet.

5 • Continue cutting to separate the bottom of the fillet from the bones.

6 • Using the shears, snip through the ribs to release the fillet.

7 • Turn the fish over and make a shallow cut across the fish above the tail fin.

↪

Filleting Sea Bream (continued)

8 • Make a shallow cut along the back from the tail to the head.

9 • Run the knife flat along the spine to release the fillet.

10 • Continue cutting until the fillet is fully detached.

11 • Trim the fillets.

12 • Lift the ribs away from the flesh.

13 • Cut off the bony part with the ribs.

14 • The fillets are ready for use.

Filleting Sole

Ingredients

Sole or another flatfish yielding 4 fillets, trimmed, scaled, skinned, and gutted (see techniques pp. 35, 39, 43, and 50)

Equipment

Cutting board

Fish filleting knife

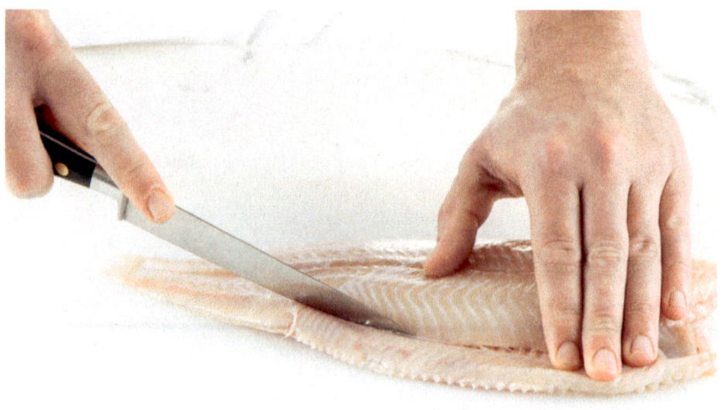

1 • Place the fish on the cutting board. Make a shallow cut into the flesh along the top edge, following the natural curve of the fillet.

2 • Repeat this along the bottom edge of the fillet.

3 • Cut down the center of the fish until you reach the bones.

4 • Run the knife flat along the ribs to separate the fillet.

5 • Turn the fish around so it faces the opposite way and cut off the second fillet.

6 • Turn the fish over and make a shallow cut along the top and bottom edges following the natural curve of the fillets.

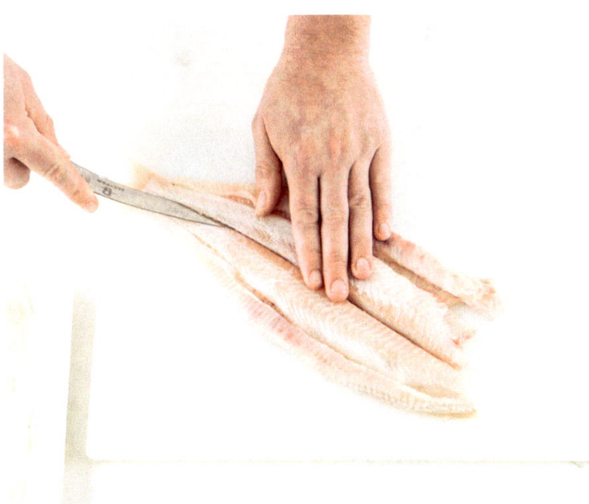

7 • Cut down the center of the fish.

↪

Filleting Sole (continued)

8 • Run the knife flat along the ribs to remove the third fillet.

9 • Turn the fish around so it faces the opposite way and cut off the fourth and final fillet.

10 • Keep cutting until the fillet comes free.

11 • Trim the fillets.

12 • The fillets are ready for use.

Preparing Fish Rib Cuts

Ingredients

Sole or another flatfish, trimmed, scaled, and gutted (see techniques pp. 35, 39, and 50)

Equipment

Large saucepan

Cutting board

Fish filleting knife

1 • Place the fish on the cutting board. Cut off the head and tail, then cut into 2 equal pieces halfway between the head and tail ends. Make a shallow cut lengthwise down the center of 1 piece.

2 • Using the filleting knife, cut off the fillet on one side of the fish.

3 • Turn the fish over and make a cut down the center.

4 • Cut off the fillet from the same side of the fish as before.

5 • Fill the saucepan with water and bring to a boil. Dip the exposed ribs into the boiling water for 5–10 seconds.

6 • Remove the meat from between the bones using your fingers. Repeat steps 1–6 for the second piece of fish.

7 • The fish is ready to be cooked.

Preparing Fish Steaks (*Darnes*)

Ingredients

Whole salmon, trimmed, scaled, and gutted
(see techniques pp. 32, 40, and 45)

Equipment

Cutting board
Chef's knife
Kitchen twine
Scissors

1 • Place the salmon on the cutting board. Cut it crosswise into slices ¾ in. (2 cm) thick.

2 • Using the scissors, cut the rib bone to detach it from the spine.

3 • Trim off the rib bone and fatty parts.

4 • Roll the flaps inward to make a compact round shape.

5 • Wrap a piece of kitchen twine around the outside of each steak.

6 • Tie a knot and cut off the excess twine.

7 • The steaks (*darnes*) are ready to be cooked.

Preparing Supreme Cuts (*Pavés*)

Ingredients

Fish fillet of your choice, skin on or off, pin bones removed (see technique p. 52)

Equipment

Cutting board

Chef's knife

1 • Place the fillet, skin(ned) side down, on the chopping board. Cut it crosswise into equal pieces, making sure the cuts are perfectly straight.

2 • Each piece should weigh between 4½ and 5¼ oz. (125–150 g).

3 • The portions, or *pavés*, are ready to be cooked.

Cutting Fish for Tartare

Ingredients

Thick skinless fish fillet of your choice, pin bones removed (see technique p. 52)

Equipment

Cutting board

Chef's knife

CHEFS' NOTES

When preparing tartare, use fish that is extremely fresh and serve it the day of purchase. Also ensure that your equipment is spotlessly clean.

1 • Place the fillet, skinned side down, on the cutting board. Cut the fillet in half lengthwise and remove any bloody parts.

2 • With the knife blade parallel to the work surface, cut each piece in half horizontally.

3 • Lay the pieces completely flat on the cutting board.

4 • Cut the pieces lengthwise into strips measuring ½ in. (1 cm) in width.

5 • Lay the strips on their side and cut them into ½-in. (1-cm) cubes.

6 • The tartare is ready to serve.

Preparing Fish for Carpaccio

Ingredients

Skinless fish fillet of your choice, pin bones removed (see technique p. 52)

Equipment

Cutting board
Chef's knife
Parchment paper
Meat pounder

CHEFS' NOTES

When preparing carpaccio, use fish that is extremely fresh and serve it the day of purchase. Also ensure that your equipment is spotlessly clean.

1 • Place the fillet on the cutting board. Cut it in half lengthwise.

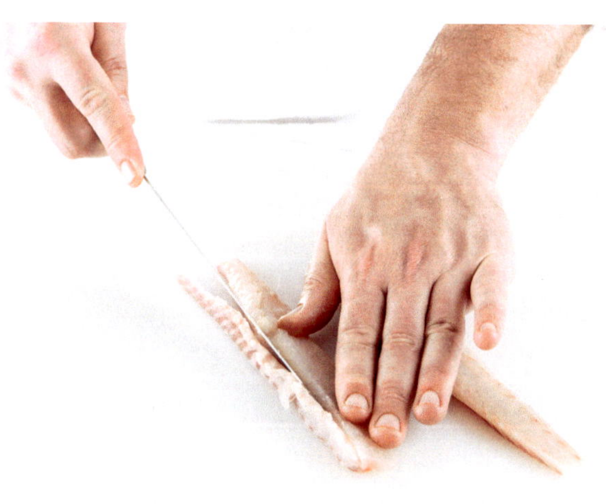

2 • Trim off the bloody parts.

3 • Slice each half as thinly as possible at an angle.

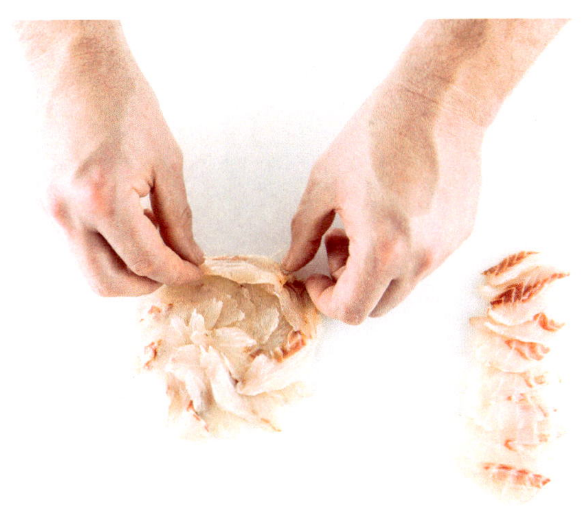

4 • Arrange the slices on parchment paper in an overlapping concentric circle.

5 • Cover with parchment paper.

6 • Using the meat pounder, flatten the fish.

7 • The carpaccio is ready to serve.

Cutting Squid

Ingredients

Squid body, skinned, cleaned, and trimmed (see technique p. 72)

Equipment

Cutting board

Chef's knife

1 • To obtain calamari rings, place the squid body on the cutting board and cut crosswise into ¼-in. (5-mm) slices. The rings are ready to be cooked.

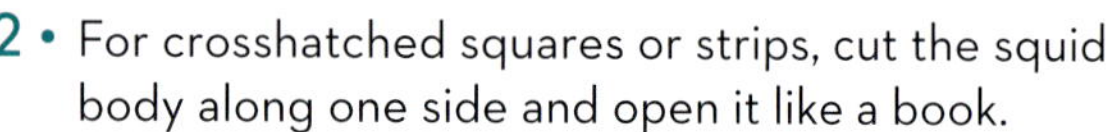

2 • For crosshatched squares or strips, cut the squid body along one side and open it like a book.

3 • Cut the squid body in half.

4 • Score the squid from top to bottom at ¼-in. (5-mm) intervals, taking care not to cut all the way through the flesh.

5 • Score the squid crosswise at ¼-in. (5-mm) intervals to make a crosshatch pattern. To make strips, cut all the way through.

6 • The different cuts of squid are ready to be cooked.

Removing Crab Meat

Ingredients

Spider crab or another crab of your choice

Equipment

Spoon

Scissors

Chef's knife

Wooden skewer

Meat pounder

1 • Cook the crab according to the technique on p. 126. Let cool.

2 • Place the crab on its back and pull off the apron (female crab) or abdominal flap (male crab), using your fingers.

3 • Twist off all the claws and legs.

4 • Remove the body from the shell.

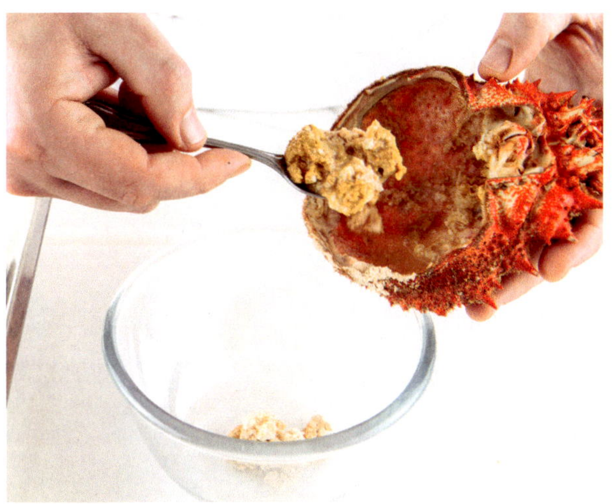

5 • Using the spoon, scoop out the creamy edible meat remaining in the shell.

6 • Using the scissors, cut off all the gills, which are not edible, and discard.

7 • Cut the body into 4 pieces.

↪

Removing Crab Meat (continued)

8 • Remove the meat from the body cavities (this is easiest using a wooden skewer).

9 • Crack the legs and claws using the meat pounder.

10 • Remove the meat from the legs and claws using the wooden skewer.

11 • The crab meat is now ready to serve.

Cutting Raw Lobster

Ingredients

Live lobster (see Chefs' Notes)

Equipment

Cutting board
Chef's knife
Fish bone tweezers
Scissors

1 • Place the lobster the right way up on the cutting board. Hold the chef's knife vertically, with the tip of the blade at the junction between the lobster's head and thorax. Push the knife sharply downward into the lobster to kill it.

2 • Cut through the entire thorax down the center.

3 • Turn the lobster over and start cutting through the body from the head.

↪

Cutting Raw Lobster (continued)

4 • Continue cutting all the way to the tail.

5 • The lobster is now ready to be cleaned.

6 • Using the tweezers, remove any coral (gonad) and the greenish tomalley, or lobster paste.

7 • Remove the digestive tract.

8 • Cut off the antennae.

9 • Hit the claws sharply with the back of the knife blade to crack them.

10 • The lobster is ready to be cooked.

CHEFS' NOTES

This method may seem cruel, but the lobsters are killed instantly (unlike when they are boiled alive). If desired, place them in the freezer for 15 minutes beforehand to sedate them.

You can also ask your fishmonger to kill the lobster, then proceed straight to step 2.

Shelling Cooked Lobsters

Ingredients

Cooked lobster

Equipment

Spoon

Scissors

Rolling pin

Large chef's knife

1 • Pull off the claws and separate the body (cephalothorax, or head and thorax) from the tail.

2 • Scoop out any coral (gonad) and the greenish tomalley, or lobster paste.

3 • Remove the pleopods (swimmerets) from the tail.

4 • Using the scissors, cut along both sides of the softer shell beneath the tail from one end to the other.

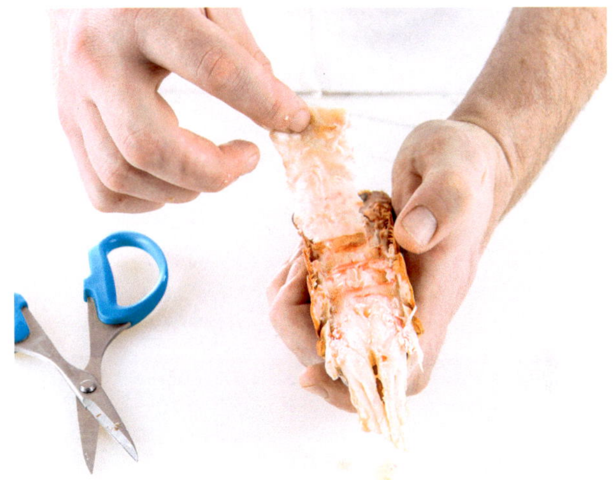

5 • Remove the shell.

6 • Remove the tail meat.

7 • Remove the shell from the body.

↪

Shelling Cooked Lobsters (continued)

8 • Scoop out the stomach sac.

9 • Pull off the legs, then cut off the gills.

10 • Using the rolling pin, roll over each leg to push the meat out.

11 • Pull off the lower part of each claw.

12 • Place each claw on a kitchen towel and firmly tap the shell with the chef's knife to crack it open.

13 • Hold each end of the claw and pull it apart to remove the meat.

14 • Cut open the knuckles with scissors to remove the last small pieces of meat.

15 • The lobster is shelled and ready to serve.

COOKING

Preparing Fish Fumet

Makes 4 cups (1 liter)

Cooking time

45 minutes

Storage

2 days in the refrigerator and 2 months in the freezer

Equipment

Scissors

Dutch oven

Spatula

Skimmer

Conical fine-mesh sieve

Ingredients

500 g (1 lb. 2 oz.) fish trimmings (bones, skin, fins, and fat), preferably white fish

3 tbsp (1¾ oz./50 g) butter

1¾ oz. (50 g) peeled, julienned onion

2 cloves garlic, peeled and julienned

1¾ oz. (50 g) peeled, julienned carrots

1¾ oz. (50 g) julienned celery

1¾ oz. (50 g) julienned leek white

Scant ½ cup (100 ml) dry white wine

2 cups (500 ml) water

Bouquet garni (thyme, bay leaf, and parsley stems tied up in a leek green)

Freshly ground pepper

1 • Using the scissors, cut the fish trimmings into pieces.

2 • Melt the butter in the Dutch oven, then add the julienned vegetables.

3 • Sauté for several minutes, until softened and lightly golden.

4 • Add the fish trimmings, stir to combine, and cook for 15 minutes.

5 • Deglaze with the white wine and reduce by half.

6 • Add the water and bring to a simmer.

7 • Skim any foam from the surface.

↪

Preparing Fish Fumet (continued)

8 • Add the bouquet garni and continue to simmer for an additional 30 minutes.

9 • Season with freshly ground pepper 5 minutes before the end of the cooking time.

10 • Strain the fumet through the conical fine-mesh sieve.

11 • The fish fumet is ready for use.

Poaching

Cooking time
20 minutes

Storage
2 days

Ingredients

Melted butter for the skillet and parchment paper

2/3 oz. (20 g) peeled, finely chopped shallot

2 oz. (60 g) diced tomato

2 turbot supreme cuts (*pavés*), 4½ oz. (125 g) each (see technique p. 98)

3½ tbsp (50 ml) dry white wine

1 cup (250 ml) fish fumet (see technique p. 118)

2 tbsp (1 oz./30 g) butter

3 tsp (3 g) finely chopped parsley

Salt

Equipment

Pastry brush

Oven-safe skillet

Parchment paper

Flexible spatula

Large saucepan

Spoon

Heated plate (for serving)

1 • Preheat the oven to 300°F (150°C/Gas Mark 2). Grease the skillet by brushing a little melted butter over it, then add the shallot and tomato.

2 • Lightly salt the fish.

3 • Cut out a parchment paper disk with the same diameter as the skillet and brush one side with melted butter.

↪

Poaching (continued)

4 • Place the fish in the skillet, then pour in the wine, followed by the fumet.

5 • Cover with the parchment paper disk, buttered side down. Bring to a simmer, then place in the oven for 3 minutes.

6 • Remove the fish from the skillet. Pour the poaching liquid, along with the shallot and tomato, into the large saucepan.

7 • Bring to a boil and cook until the liquid reduces.

8 • Stir in the 2 tbsp (1 oz./30 g) butter and reduce the heat.

9 • Check the consistency—the sauce should coat the back of a spoon.

10 • Stir in the parsley.

11 • Reheat the fish in the sauce and serve immediately on a heated plate.

Cooking Lobster in a Court Bouillon

Makes about 4 qt. (4 liters)

Cooking time

10 minutes

Storage

2 days

Ingredients

4 qt. (4 liters) water

1½ oz. (40 g) coarse gray sea salt

2 onions, peeled and chopped

1 leek, sliced

1 carrot, peeled and sliced

3 cloves garlic, peeled

1 lemon, halved

⅔ cup (150 ml) white wine vinegar

1 bouquet garni (thyme and bay leaf tied up in a leek green)

10 peppercorns

1 tsp (3 g) *piment d'Espelette*

10 coriander seeds

1 tsp (2 g) fennel seeds

1 live lobster weighing 1¼ lb. (600 g)

Equipment

Stock pot

Kitchen twine

Scissors

1 • Place the water, salt, vegetables, lemon, vinegar, bouquet garni, and spices in a stock pot. Bring to a boil and let simmer for 15 minutes.

2 • Kill the lobster (see technique p. 109, step 1). To keep the lobster straight while cooking, pass a piece of twine beneath the rostrum—the sharp, horn-like structure above the eyes.

3 • Wrap the twine beneath the central part of the tail (telson).

4 • Pull the twine taut so it lifts the tail. Tie a knot.

5 • Lower the lobster into the boiling water and simmer for 10 minutes.

6 • Lift the lobster out of the pot using the twine.

7 • Cut the twine.

Cooking Crab in a Court Bouillon

Makes about 4 qt. (4 liters)

Cooking time

15 minutes for a crab weighing 1 lb. 2 oz. (500 g)

20 minutes for a crab weighing 2¼ lb. (1 kg)

Storage

2 days

Ingredients

4 qt. (4 liters) water

1½ oz. (40 g) coarse gray sea salt

2 onions, peeled and chopped

1 leek, sliced

1 carrot, peeled and sliced

3 cloves garlic, peeled

1 lemon, halved

⅔ cup (150 ml) white wine vinegar

1 bouquet garni (thyme and bay leaf tied up in a leek green)

10 peppercorns

1 tsp *piment d'Espelette*

10 coriander seeds

1 tsp (2 g) fennel seeds

1 spider crab (see Chefs' Notes)

Equipment

Large saucepan

Skimmer

1 • Place the water, salt, vegetables, lemon, vinegar, bouquet garni, and spices in a large saucepan. Bring to a boil.

CHEFS' NOTES

To kill a live crab, turn it over onto its back and lift up the flap on the underside to reveal the small hole (anal tract). Thrust the tip of a sharp sturdy knife, skewer, or trussing needle downward through the hole into the crab and move it slightly from side to side to instantly kill it. Alternatively, ask your fishmonger to kill the crab.

2 • Lower the crab into the pan and simmer for 15–20 minutes, depending on the crab's size (see cooking times above).

3 • Lift out the crab using the skimmer.

Preparing Mussels Marinière

Cooking time

10 minutes

Equipment

Dutch oven

Spatula

Ingredients

2 tbsp (1 oz./30 g) butter

3½ oz. (100 g) shallots, peeled and chopped

2 cloves garlic, peeled and finely chopped

1 bouquet garni (5 parsley sprigs, 5 thyme sprigs, and 1 bay leaf tied up in a leek green)

4½ lb. (1.5 kg) mussels, cleaned (see technique p. 60)

2 cups (500 ml) dry white wine

1 tbsp (3 g) finely chopped parsley

1 • Melt the butter in the Dutch oven, then add the shallots and garlic. Cook until softened. Add the bouquet garni.

2 • Add the mussels.

CHEFS' NOTES

This technique can be used for other shellfish, such as cockles or clams.

3 • Pour in the white wine.

4 • Cook for 3–5 minutes over high heat, stirring often.

5 • Cook until all the mussels have opened, then sprinkle in the parsley.

6 • Discard any mussels that remain tightly closed. Serve immediately, with the pan juices spooned over.

Braising Monkfish Tails

Cooking time

20 minutes

Ingredients

1 monkfish tail, skinned and trimmed (see technique p. 53)

4 cloves garlic, peeled and cut lengthwise into quarters

2 sprigs rosemary

¾ cup + 2 tbsp (3½ oz./100 g) all-purpose flour

2 tbsp (30 ml) grape-seed oil

1 tbsp (20 g) + 2 tbsp (1 oz./30 g) butter, cut into pieces

2 cups (500 ml) fish fumet (see technique p. 118)

½ bunch chives

½ lemon

Salt and freshly ground pepper

Equipment

Cutting board

Kitchen twine

Scissors

Skillet

Baking dish slightly bigger than the monkfish tail

Fish spatula

Rack set over a tray

Conical sieve

Medium saucepan

Flexible spatula

Whisk

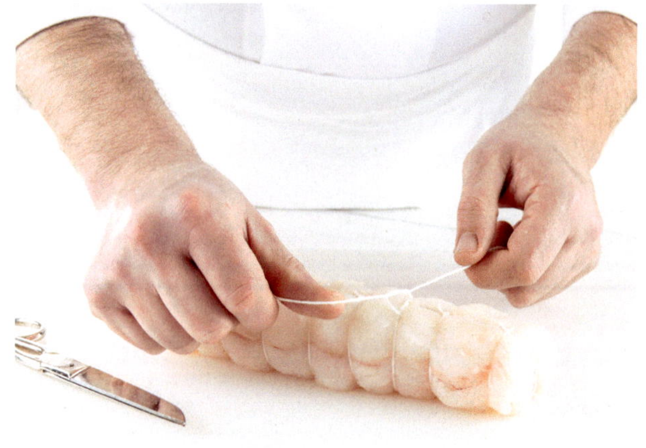

1 • Place the monkfish tail on the cutting board. Tie pieces of twine around it at regular intervals so it keeps its shape during cooking. Preheat the oven to 350°F (180°C/Gas Mark 4).

2 • Using the tip of a knife, make slits in the fish between the twine. Push a piece of garlic and a small piece of rosemary into each slit. Season with salt.

3 • Roll the monkfish tail in the flour to coat and tap it to remove any excess.

4 • Heat the oil and 1 tbsp (20 g) butter in the skillet.

5 • Place the monkfish tail in the skillet and brown it all over, basting it with the fat.

6 • Transfer the fish to the baking dish and pour in the fumet.

7 • Cover the dish with a piece of parchment paper cut to fit snugly inside. Braise in the oven for 15 minutes.

↪

Braising Monkfish Tails (continued)

8 • Using the fish spatula, transfer the monkfish tail to the rack set over a tray.

9 • Strain the fumet through the conical sieve into the medium saucepan.

10 • Bring the fumet to a simmer.

11 • Let the fumet reduce until it is thick and a line drawn through it with a spatula holds its shape.

12 • Remove from the heat and whisk in 2 tbsp (1 oz./30 g) butter until smooth. Season with salt and pepper.

13 • The sauce should coat the back of a spoon.

14 • Drizzle the sauce over the fish.

15 • The braised monkfish tail is ready to be served.

Cooking Fish *en Papillote*

Cooking time

15 minutes

Ingredients

Supreme cuts (*pavés*) of your fish of choice (see technique p. 98)

Lemon segments, diced

1 sprig thyme or another herb of your choice such as parsley, dill, chives, or tarragon, per fillet, chopped

Vegetables of your choice (grated, diced, or sliced)

Olive oil

Salt and freshly ground pepper

Equipment

1 sheet parchment paper per supreme

Oven-safe clip for each packet

1 • Preheat the oven to 300°F (150°C/Gas Mark 2). Season the fish with salt and pepper on both sides and drizzle with olive oil. Arrange the lemon pieces and chopped herbs on top.

2 • For each supreme, fold a sheet of parchment paper in half and make a crease at the fold.

3 • Place a small mound of vegetables in the center of one half of the parchment paper. Top with the fish.

4 • Fold the other half of the parchment paper over the fish, then fold over a corner facing you to make a triangle.

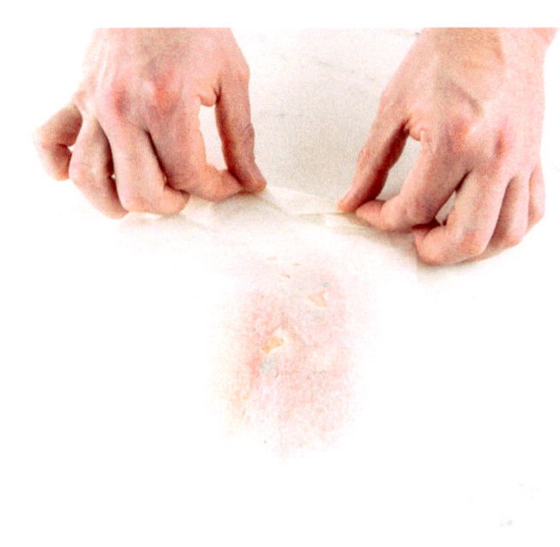

5 • Continue folding like this all the way around to enclose the fish completely.

6 • Secure the packet with the oven-safe clip. Bake in the oven for 10–12 minutes.

7 • Remove the clip from each parcel and carefully open the parchment paper. The fish is ready to serve.

Breading and Frying Fish *Goujons*

Cooking time

5 minutes

Ingredients

Grape-seed oil for deep-frying

Skinless, boneless fish fillets of your choice, cut into long strips

Flour

Eggs, beaten

Dried breadcrumbs

Salt

Equipment

Instant-read thermometer

3 shallow trays or dishes

Tweezers or tongs

High-sided pan for deep-frying

Skimmer

Rack set over a tray

1 • Heat the oil for deep-frying to 355°F (180°C). Season the fish strips with salt.

2 • Dredge the fish strips in the flour to coat and tap them to remove any excess.

3 • Using the tweezers or tongs, dip the flour-coated strips into the beaten egg.

4 • Coat the strips with breadcrumbs.

5 • Carefully lower the breaded fish strips into the oil.

6 • Deep-fry for 4–5 minutes, until crisp and golden brown. Drain using the skimmer and transfer to the rack.

7 • Season the fried fish with salt and serve immediately.

Grilling Fish Supreme Cuts (*Pavés*)

Infusing time
20 minutes

Cooking time
8 minutes

Ingredients
1 lemon slice
A few sprigs thyme, chopped
Grape-seed oil
Skinless salmon supreme cuts (see technique p. 98)
Salt and freshly ground pepper

Equipment
Cutting board
Pastry brush
Cast-iron grill pan
Fish spatula

1 • Combine the lemon and thyme with grape-seed oil in a small bowl and let infuse for 20 minutes. Place the fish skinned side down on the cutting board, season with salt and pepper, and brush with the infused oil.

2 • Turn the fish over, season the skinned side with salt and pepper, and brush with the infused oil.

3 • Heat the grill pan until it is very hot. Place the fish in the pan skinned side uppermost.

4 • Leave until the lower half is cooked (about 2 minutes), rotating the fish 90 degrees to scorch a crosshatch pattern.

5 • Turn the fish over using the fish spatula.

6 • Brush the fish again with the infused oil and continue cooking until it is just cooked through (about 4 minutes).

7 • The fish is ready to serve.

Pan-Roasting

Cooking time

10 minutes

Ingredients

Tronçon (thick, bone-in steak cut) from a large flatfish such as turbot, skin on

Grape-seed oil

2 tbsp (1 oz./30 g) butter

1 clove garlic, unpeeled

1 sprig thyme

Salt and freshly ground pepper

Equipment

Oven-safe skillet

Fish spatula

Spoon

Rack set over a tray

1 • Preheat the oven to 300°F (150°C/Gas Mark 2). Season the fish all over with salt. Heat a little grape-seed oil in the skillet until shimmering, then place the fish skin side down in the pan.

2 • When the skin is deeply golden, turn the fish over.

3 • Add the butter.

4 • Add the garlic and thyme.

5 • Lift the fish away from the skillet to allow the melted butter to soak in underneath.

6 • Generously baste the fish with the butter. Transfer the skillet to the oven and continue cooking for 5–6 minutes, or until cooked to your liking.

7 • Transfer the fish to the rack. It is ready to serve.

Sautéing

Cooking time

6 minutes

Ingredients

Supreme cut (*pavé*) of your fish of choice (see technique p. 98), skin on

Grape-seed oil

1 tbsp (20 g) butter

1 clove garlic, unpeeled

1 sprig thyme

Salt and freshly ground pepper

Equipment

Skillet

Fish spatula

Spoon

Rack set over a tray

1 • Season the skin side of the fish with salt. Heat a little grape-seed oil in the skillet until shimmering.

2 • Place the fish in the skillet skin side down and press down with the spatula so the skin browns evenly.

3 • Check that the skin is golden brown.

4 • Add the butter, garlic, and thyme, and let the butter melt completely.

5 • Turn the fish over. Sauté, basting generously with the melted butter, until cooked to your liking.

6 • Transfer the fish to the rack. It is ready to serve.

RECIPES

ROUND FISH

TROUT GRAVLAX

Gravlax de truite

Serves 4

Active time
45 minutes

Curing time
12 hours

Resting time
Overnight

Cooking time
5 minutes

Equipment
Fish bone tweezers
Food processor
Fine-mesh sieve

Ingredients

Gravlax

- 1 lb. 2 oz. (500 g) trout fillet, skin on
- 10½ oz. (300 g) peeled raw red beets
- 10½ oz. (300 g) salt
- 1 cup (7 oz./200 g) sugar
- 1 generous tbsp (10 g) pink peppercorns
- Zest of 1 lemon
- Scant 1 cup (230 ml) lemon juice

Garnishes

- 1 lb. 2 oz. (500 g) peeled red beets, cooked
- 4 cups (1 liter) aged wine vinegar
- 7 oz. (200 g) peeled raw red beets
- 7 oz. (200 g) peeled raw Chioggia beets
- 4 tsp (20 ml) olive oil
- ¼ bunch lemon thyme
- 1 tsp (5 g) salt

To serve

- 3½ oz. (100 g) trout roe
- 1 handful (10 g) baby beet leaves
- 2 tsp (5 g) beet powder
- ½ tsp (1 g) cracked peppercorns

PREPARING THE GRAVLAX (2 DAYS AHEAD)

Remove the pin bones from the trout fillets (see technique p. 52), leaving the skin on. Place the beets, salt, sugar, peppercorns, and lemon zest and juice in the food processor and process until smooth. Cover the trout with this mixture and let it cure for 12 hours in the refrigerator. The following day, rinse the trout under cold water, then let it rest overnight in the refrigerator.

PREPARING THE GARNISHES

Warm the cooked beets in a large pot of simmering, generously salted water. Drain, then place them in the food processor with the vinegar and process to a vibrant red purée. Strain through the fine-mesh sieve and adjust the seasonings as necessary. Wash and dry the lemon thyme and finely chop the leaves. Cut the raw red and Chioggia beets into ½ × 2½-in. (1 × 6-cm) strips, ⅛ in. (2 mm) thick, using a vegetable peeler. Blanch the strips briefly in boiling water, until just tender, then toss them with the olive oil, lemon thyme, and salt.

TO SERVE

Cut the trout gravlax at a slight angle into ½-in. (1-cm) slices. Place a little beetroot purée on one side of each plate and arrange the beet strips on top. Scatter with trout roe and baby beet leaves, then dust the plate with beet powder. Place slices of trout gravlax on the other side of the plate and sprinkle with cracked peppercorns.

SALMON À *L'UNILATÉRALE* WITH BELUGA LENTILS AND BEURRE BLANC

Pavés de saumon bio cuits à l'unilatérale, lentilles et beurre blanc

Serves 4

Active time
1 hour

Soaking time
4 hours

Cooking time
45 minutes

Ingredients

Beluga lentils

1 cup (7 oz./200 g) Beluga lentils
1 carrot
1 shallot
1 stalk celery
2 cups + 2 tbsp (530 ml) water
1 clove garlic, unpeeled
1 bouquet garni (celery leaves, bay leaf, and thyme)
5¼ oz. (150 g) cured ham end
3 tbsp (1¾ oz./50 g) butter
Salt and freshly ground pepper

Beurre blanc with salmon roe

1½ oz. (40 g) shallots
1 bunch chives
⅓ cup (75 ml) white wine
⅓ cup (75 ml) champagne vinegar
4 tsp (20 ml) heavy cream, min. 35% fat
7 tbsp (3½ oz./100 g) butter, well chilled and diced
Juice of 1 lemon
1¾ oz. (50 g) salmon roe

Salmon à *l'unilatérale*

1 lb. 2 oz. (500 g) thick salmon fillet, preferably organic
2 tbsp (30 ml) grape-seed oil
Salt and freshly ground pepper

Herb salad

2 tbsp (30 ml) olive oil
2 tsp (10 ml) champagne vinegar
¼ bunch dill
¼ bunch cilantro
¼ bunch chervil
Petals of 2 marigold flowers
Salt and freshly ground pepper

PREPARING THE BELUGA LENTILS

Soak the lentils in twice their volume of water for 4 hours. Peel the carrot, shallot, and celery and cut each in half crosswise. Cut one half of the carrot into 3 pieces, then cut the bottom half of the shallot in two lengthwise, keeping the root end intact. Cut one half of the celery stalk in two and add the leaves to the bouquet garni. Finely dice the remaining shallot, carrot, and celery halves and set aside. Drain and rinse the lentils and place in a large saucepan with the water and the large vegetable pieces. Add the garlic and bouquet garni and bring to a boil. Let simmer for 20 minutes, or until the lentils are tender but not mushy. Season with salt and pepper and let cool in the saucepan. Meanwhile, finely dice the cured ham, then sauté it in a skillet with the butter until browned. Add the finely diced vegetables and cook until softened. Adjust the seasonings if necessary, then stir this mixture into the cooked lentils.

PREPARING THE BEURRE BLANC WITH SALMON ROE

Peel and finely chop the shallots. Finely chop the chives. Place the shallots, wine, and vinegar in a small saucepan and reduce until all the liquid has evaporated. Add the cream and bring to a gentle simmer. Over very low heat, whisk in the butter piece by piece, waiting until each piece has melted before adding the next. Whisking continuously, cook until the beurre blanc is pale and thick. Stir in a little lemon juice, to taste, then add the chives. Remove from the heat, add the salmon roe, and gently stir to coat.

PREPARING THE SALMON À L'UNILATÉRALE

Cut the salmon fillet into 4 equal portions (see technique p. 98) and season both sides with salt and pepper. Warm the grape-seed oil in a sauté pan over medium heat. Place the salmon in the pan skin side down and increase the heat to medium-high. Cook for 10–15 minutes, until the skin is crisp and golden and the tops of the fillets are warm but still raw. Transfer to a rack.

PREPARING THE HERB SALAD

To make a vinaigrette, whisk together the olive oil and vinegar and season with salt and pepper. Wash and dry the dill, cilantro, and chervil and remove the stems. Place the herbs in a bowl with the marigold petals and lightly dress with the vinaigrette.

TO SERVE

For each serving, ladle lentils into a shallow bowl and top with a salmon portion, skin side up. Arrange a little herb salad over one half of the fish, then drizzle the other half with beurre blanc.

TUNA TATAKI WITH HORSERADISH ICE CREAM AND MARINE GARNISHES

Tataki de thon, navet green meat, saveurs iodées

Serves 4

Active time

1½ hours

Cooking time

2¼ hours

Chilling time

1 hour

Equipment

Immersion blender

Fine-mesh sieve

Ice cream maker

Mandoline

Ingredients

Horseradish ice cream

2 cups (500 ml) whole milk (reserve 1 tbsp/5 ml, well chilled, for the agar-agar powder)

Scant ½ cup (100 ml) heavy cream, min. 35% fat

¼ cup (1¾ oz./50 g) sugar

1½ tbsp (1 oz./30 g) glucose syrup

2¼ tsp (5 g) agar-agar powder

1¾ oz. (50 g) grated horseradish

Scant ½ tsp (2 g) salt

Seaweed chips

1¾ oz. (50 g) fresh dulse seaweed

Canola oil

Tuna tataki

Neutral oil

1 lb. 2 oz. (500 g) sashimi-grade red tuna fillet

Radish shavings

1 Green Meat or Red Meat radish

Samphire

⅓ oz. (10 g) fresh samphire

Vinaigrette

3 tsp (15 ml) toasted sesame oil

1 tsp (5 ml) sweet soy sauce

1 tsp (5 ml) rice vinegar

¼ tsp (2 g) ginger paste

To serve

12 borage flowers

4 Mertensia (oyster plant) leaves

2 tsp (10 g) black sesame seeds

PREPARING THE HORSERADISH ICE CREAM

Place the milk, minus the reserved 1 tbsp (5 ml), in a large saucepan. Stir in the cream, sugar, and glucose syrup and bring to a boil. Dissolve the agar-agar powder in the reserved milk and add to the hot milk mixture. Return to a boil, stirring continuously with a spatula. Add the horseradish and salt, then remove from the heat and process with the immersion blender until smooth. Strain through the fine-mesh sieve and adjust the seasonings if necessary. Chill until cold, then churn in the ice cream maker according to the manufacturer's instructions. Freeze until serving.

PREPARING THE SEAWEED CHIPS

Preheat the oven to 160°F (70°C/Gas on the lowest setting). Rinse the dulce seaweed, then wrap it in a dish towel to dry thoroughly. Brush the seaweed with canola oil, spread it across a baking sheet, and bake for 2 hours, or until dry and crisp.

PREPARING THE TUNA TATAKI

Heat a little neutral oil in a skillet until shimmering, then add the tuna and sear it for 1 minute on all sides, until lightly golden. Remove the tuna from the skillet and let it rest for 1 hour in the refrigerator.

PREPARING THE RADISH SHAVINGS

Wash and peel the radish, then cut it into 1/16-in. (1-mm) slices crosswise using the mandoline.

PREPARING THE SAMPHIRE

Place the samphire in a saucepan with water and bring to a boil. Drain and immediately cool in cold water.

PREPARING THE VINAIGRETTE

Whisk together all the vinaigrette ingredients.

TO SERVE

Cut the tuna tataki into thin slices, about ⅛ in. (3–4 mm) thick. Brush the slices with vinaigrette, then arrange them in slightly overlapping rows on each serving plate. Top with a quenelle of horseradish ice cream and garnish with borage flowers, Mertensia leaves, seaweed chips, radish shavings, and samphire. Sprinkle with black sesame seeds.

MACKEREL RILLETTES WITH LIME

Rillettes de maquereau citronné

Serves 4

Active time
25 minutes

Cooking time
10 minutes

Storage
3 days

Equipment
Fish filleting knife
Fish bone tweezers
Microplane grater

Ingredients
1 lb. 2 oz. (500 g) mackerel
2 tsp (10 ml) white vinegar
Olive oil
½ bunch chives
¼ bunch dill
1 lime
Scant ½ cup (3½ oz./100 g) mascarpone
Salt and freshly ground pepper
Toasted baguette slices

Using the fish filleting knife, fillet the mackerel (see technique p. 80) and remove any pin bones (see technique p. 52).

Soak the fillets skin side down in the vinegar for 10 minutes, then gently remove the skin.

Fry the fillets in a skillet with a little olive oil over medium heat until the flesh is just cooked through but soft. Place in a bowl and mash with a fork until broken up.

Snip the chives into small pieces, finely chop the dill, and finely grate the zest of the lime. Add all three to the mackerel and stir to combine.

Stir in the mascarpone to loosen, then drizzle with a little olive oil and season with salt and pepper. Stir to blend.

Serve in an empty sardine tin, if you wish, with toasted baguette slices on the side.

TARAMASALATA WITH PITA BREAD

Tarama

Serves 4

Active time
30 minutes

Rising time
1 hour 20 minutes

Cooking time
2–3 minutes

Storage
1 day

Equipment
Blender
Stand mixer + paddle beater

Ingredients

Taramasalata
- 7 oz. (200 g) smoked cod roe
- 10½ oz. (300 g) day-old white sandwich bread
- 2 cups (500 ml) grape-seed oil
- Scant ½ cup (100 ml) olive oil
- Zest and juice of 2 lemons
- Salt

Pita bread
- 4 cups (1 lb. 2 oz./500 g) all-purpose flour
- 1¼ tsp (5 g) sugar
- 1 tsp (5 g) salt
- ⅔ oz. (20 g) fresh yeast
- 1¼ cups (300 ml) water
- 2 tsp (10 ml) olive oil

To serve
- 1 tsp (5 g) ground sumac
- Finely grated zest of 1 lemon
- 2 tsp (10 ml) olive oil

PREPARING THE TARAMASALATA

Remove the outer membrane from the cod roe sac. Remove the crust from the bread. Moisten the bread with a little water, then squeeze it to remove excess moisture. Place it in the blender with the cod roe and process until smooth. With the motor running, gradually drizzle in both the grape-seed oil and the olive oil until emulsified. Add the lemon zest and juice, and salt to taste.

PREPARING THE PITA BREAD

Place the flour, sugar, and salt in the stand mixer bowl. Crumble in the fresh yeast, ensuring it does not come into direct contact with the salt. Make a well in the center, add the water and olive oil, and knead on medium speed until the dough is smooth and supple. Let rise for 1 hour at room temperature. Divide the dough into 12 equal pieces, then roll each piece into a 4-in. (10-cm) disk, ¼ in. (5 mm) thick, and place on a baking sheet lined with parchment paper. Let rise for 20 minutes at room temperature. Meanwhile, preheat the oven to 430°F (220°C/Gas Mark 7). Bake the pitas for 2–3 minutes, or just until they are puffed and lightly golden.

TO SERVE

Serve the taramasalata in a bowl dusted with ground sumac and sprinkled with finely grated lemon zest. Make a small well in the center and pour in a little olive oil. Serve the fresh-baked pita bread on the side.

HAKE CEVICHE WITH PICKLED BERRIES AND BUCKWHEAT TUILES

Ceviche de merlu aux fruits rouges, pickles, oseille et sarrasin

Serves 4

Active time
1½ hours

Cooking time
15 minutes

Macerating time
12 hours

Infusing time
2 hours

Marinating time
20 minutes

Equipment
Food processor
Fine-mesh sieve
Microplane grater
Silicone baking mat with a floral motif of your choice

Ingredients

Pickled red berries
Scant ½ cup (100 ml) water
¼ cup (1¾ oz./50 g) sugar
⅔ cup (150 ml) spirit vinegar
2¾ oz. (75 g) raspberries
2¾ oz. (75 g) red currants

Garnishes
⅕ oz. (5 g) dried hibiscus flowers
1½ tbsp (25 ml) canola oil
3½ oz. (100 g) lovage
Salt

Leche de tigre marinade
1¾ oz. (50 g) red onion
½ bird's eye chili pepper
⅔ oz. (20 g) fresh ginger
½ stalk lemongrass
1 oz. (25 g) cilantro
Juice and finely grated zest of 2 limes
Generous ¾ cup (200 ml) buttermilk
2½ tsp (10 g) sugar
Salt

Hake ceviche
1 lb. 2 oz. (500 g) skinless, boneless hake fillet, previously frozen for at least 24 hours (see Chefs' Notes)
Leche de tigre marinade (see above)

Buckwheat tuiles and popcorn
Scant ½ cup (3½ oz./100 g) egg white (about 3 whites)
Scant ½ tsp (2 g) salt
½ cup (2 oz./60 g) all-purpose flour
2 tbsp (20 g) buckwheat flour
3 tbsp (1¾ oz./50 g) butter, melted
2 tsp (10 ml) canola oil
2¾ oz. (80 g) kasha (toasted buckwheat groats)

To serve
Red-veined sorrel leaves

CHEFS' NOTES

Freeze the fish at -4°F (-20°C) for a minimum of 24 hours prior to use to eliminate parasites, such as anisakis.

PREPARING THE PICKLED RED BERRIES (1 DAY AHEAD)
Bring the water, sugar, and vinegar to a boil in a small saucepan; stir to dissolve the sugar. Let cool completely in the refrigerator. Cut the raspberries in half and place them in an airtight container with the red currants. Pour the cooled vinegar mixture over the berries, close the container, and let macerate for 12 hours in the refrigerator.

PREPARING THE GARNISHES
Place the dried hibiscus flowers in the food processor and process to a very fine powder. Set aside. Clean the food processor bowl, then add the oil, lovage, and a little salt and process until smooth. Strain through the fine-mesh sieve into a bowl and let infuse for 2 hours in the refrigerator, allowing the clear green oil to rise to the surface.

PREPARING THE LECHE DE TIGRE MARINADE
Peel the red onion, then thinly slice a quarter of it, and reserve for garnish; finely chop the rest and place in a large bowl. Wash the chili pepper, remove the seeds, and chop it finely; add to the bowl. Peel the ginger and lemongrass and grate them into the bowl using the Microplane grater. Wash, dry, and roughly chop the cilantro, then add it to the bowl, followed by the lime juice and zest, buttermilk, and sugar. Season with salt and stir until well combined. Adjust the seasonings if necessary.

PREPARING THE HAKE CEVICHE
Cut the hake fillet into ¼-in. (5-mm) dice and place in a large bowl. Add the *leche de tigre* marinade and let marinate for 20 minutes in the refrigerator.

PREPARING THE BUCKWHEAT TUILES AND POPCORN
To prepare the tuiles, preheat the oven to 325°F (160°C/Gas Mark 3) and place the silicone baking mat with a floral motif on a baking sheet. Whisk together the egg white, salt, all-purpose flour, and buckwheat flour in a medium bowl, then whisk in the melted butter. Let the batter cool to room temperature, then fill the silicone mold cavities and bake for 6–8 minutes, depending on the mold. Turn the tuiles out onto a rack and let them cool completely. To prepare the buckwheat popcorn, heat the canola oil in a skillet until shimmering, then add the kasha and reduce the heat to medium. Cover and cook for 2–3 minutes, until the groats pop like popcorn.

TO SERVE
Spoon ceviche into the center of each serving plate and scatter with the pickled berries, buckwheat popcorn, and reserved red onion slices. Garnish with red-veined sorrel leaves, then dust with hibiscus powder and drizzle with lovage-infused oil. Top each serving with a buckwheat tuile and place a pickled red currant in the center.

SEAFOOD PÂTÉ EN CROÛTE

Pâté en croûte de la mer

Serves 8

Active time
6 hours

Chilling time
5 hours

Marinating time
3 hours

Freezing time
3 hours

Cooking time
3 hours

Storage
2 days

Equipment
Bowl scraper
7 × 4 ½-in. (18 × 11-cm) oval pâté en croûte mold, 3 in. (7.5 cm) deep
Pie crimper
Pie weights
Steam oven (or steamer)
Instant-read thermometer
Silicone baking mat
Coffee filter

Ingredients

Pâté en croûte pastry
2½ cups (10½ oz./300 g) all-purpose flour
2½ tbsp (25 g) potato starch
1 tbsp (18 g) salt
⅓ cup (75 ml) water
¾ tsp (4 ml) white vinegar
⅔ cup (5 oz./150 g) lightly beaten egg (3 eggs)
1 stick + 5 tbsp (6½ oz./185 g) butter, softened
1 egg, lightly beaten, for the egg wash

Filling
5¼ oz. (150 g) monkfish liver
1 pinch sugar
1 pinch ground black pepper
1 tsp cognac
3 tsp (16 g) salt, divided
1 sheet nori seaweed
10½ oz. (300 g) boneless, skinless sea trout fillets
10½ oz. (300 g) boneless, skinless monkfish fillets
10½ oz. (300 g) boneless, skinless brill fillets
2 tsp (10 ml) Noilly Prat vermouth
¾ tsp (2 g) *piment d'Espelette*
2 tbsp (10 g) finely chopped parsley leaves

Scallop topping
3½ oz. (100 g) shucked scallops
4 tsp (20 ml) olive oil
4 sheets (8 g) gelatin (200 Bloom)
2 cups (500 ml) fish fumet (see technique p. 118)
3 egg whites
1 lemon
½ zucchini
10 chervil leaves
Salt

Garnish
1¾ oz. (50 g) trout roe

PREPARING THE PÂTÉ EN CROÛTE PASTRY

Combine the flour and potato starch in a medium bowl. In a separate bowl, dissolve the salt in the water and vinegar, then whisk in the 2/3 cup (5 oz./150 g) lightly beaten egg. Place the butter in a large bowl and add the wet ingredients along with half the dry ingredients. Using the bowl scraper, work the ingredients together. Add the remaining dry ingredients and work them in until you have a smooth dough. Shape the dough into a ball and flatten it into a disk, 1/2 in. (1 cm) thick. Cover with plastic wrap and let rest for 1 hour in the refrigerator. Roll the dough to a thickness of about 1/8 in. (4 mm), then return it to the refrigerator and let it rest for an additional 30 minutes. Cut the dough into 2 pieces: a 4½ × 12-in. (11 × 30-cm) rectangle and a 5½ × 7-in. (14 × 18-cm) oval. Wrap the rectangle around the inside edge of the mold, pressing it against the sides to make it stick. Place the oval in the base of the mold and press the edges to seal them well. Crimp all the way around the top edge using the pie crimper. Let the dough rest for an additional 1 hour in the refrigerator. Meanwhile, preheat the oven to 285°F (140°C/Gas Mark 1). Place the pie weights in the base of the mold and blind-bake the pastry for 1¼ hours. Remove the weights and return the pastry to the oven for an additional 5–10 minutes, until it is cooked through and golden. Brush the inside of the pastry with the egg wash and return to the oven for 2 minutes to seal. Let cool to room temperature.

PREPARING THE FILLING

Preheat the steam oven to 160°F (70°C/Gas on the lowest setting). Remove the large veins from the center of the monkfish liver using a knife. Combine the sugar, pepper, cognac, and a generous 1/2 tsp (3 g) of the salt in a bowl. Add the monkfish liver and let it marinate for 2 hours in the refrigerator. Place a piece of plastic wrap on a cutting board and set the nori seaweed on top. Drain the monkfish liver, place it in the center of the nori, and roll the nori up to make a roll with a 1¼-in. (3-cm) diameter, using the plastic wrap to help. Keep the plastic wrap on the roll to maintain its shape and cook it in the steam oven (or steamer) until the internal temperature reaches 145°F (63°C). Immediately place in the freezer and freeze for 2 hours. Meanwhile, cut the trout, monkfish, and brill into 3/4 × 1½-in. (2 × 4-cm) pieces and place in a bowl with the vermouth, *piment d'Espelette*, parsley, and remaining 2½ tsp (13 g) salt. Stir to coat and let marinate for 1 hour in the refrigerator.

ASSEMBLING AND BAKING THE PÂTÉ EN CROÛTE

Preheat the oven to 250°F (130°C/Gas Mark ½). Place half of the marinated fish mixture in the blind-baked pastry. Remove the plastic wrap from the monkfish liver roll and place it in the center. Cover with the remaining fish mixture, leaving a ½-in. (1-cm) gap at the top of the mold. Cut a piece of parchment paper to fit just inside the pastry and place it over the filling. Bake for 25–30 minutes, until the internal temperature reaches 131°F (55°C). Let the pâté en croûte cool at room temperature for 10 minutes, then transfer it to the refrigerator and let it cool completely.

PREPARING THE SCALLOP TOPPING

Preheat the oven to 250°F (130°C/Gas Mark ½) and line a rimmed baking sheet with parchment paper. Cut the scallops into 1/8-in. (3-mm) slices. On the prepared baking sheet, arrange the slices in overlapping rows to form an oval shape the size of the mold (you will trim them later). Drizzle the scallops with the olive oil and season them lightly with salt. Cover with the silicone baking mat and bake for 3–5 minutes. Immediately place the baking sheet with the scallops in the freezer and freeze for 1 hour to firm them up. Meanwhile, soak the gelatin in a bowl of cold water until softened. Remove the scallops from the freezer and trim them so that they fit perfectly inside the pastry edges; place them over the filling. Bring the fish fumet to a boil in a large saucepan. In a bowl, whisk the egg whites until foamy. Whisk the whites into the fumet, then remove from the heat and let them set. Strain the fumet through the coffee filter to obtain a clear consommé, then measure out 1⅔ cups (400 ml) of the still-warm liquid and place in a bowl. Squeeze the gelatin to remove excess liquid and stir it into the consommé until dissolved. Let the mixture cool at room temperature until it begins to thicken but is not fully set (it should still be pourable). Meanwhile, wash the lemon and zucchini. Remove the zest from the lemon in strips, place in a saucepan with cold water, and bring to a boil to blanch. Refresh the zest in cold water, then cut it into small diamonds with ¼-in. (6-mm) sides. Peel the zucchini and blanch the skin in boiling salted water for 1 minute. Cool the skin in ice water, then cut it into small diamonds with ¼-in. (6-mm) sides. Scatter the lemon and zucchini diamonds and chervil leaves over the scallops. As soon as the fish fumet jelly has a wobbly consistency, pour it over the scallops. Chill for 2 hours, or until fully set.

GARNISH AND SERVE

When the scallop topping has set, garnish the pâté en croûte with the trout roe. Serve sliced.

GURNARD AND WEEVER BOUILLABAISSE WITH SAFFRON AIOLI AND GARLIC CROUTONS

Bouillabaisse de vive et de grondin, biscotte d'aïoli

Serves 12

Active time

2 hours

Cooking time

2½ hours

Resting time

30 minutes

Storage

2 days

Equipment

Food mill

Fine-mesh sieve

Ingredients

Fish soup

9 lb. (4 kg) assorted rockfish of your choice

4 onions

3 leeks, white parts only

½ bunch celery

2 bulbs fennel

1¾ lb. (800 g) tomatoes

3 heads garlic

⅔ cup (150 ml) olive oil

Scant ½ cup (100 ml) pastis

5 tbsp (2½ oz./75 g) tomato paste

4 qt. (4 liters) fish fumet (see technique p. 118) or water

20 saffron threads

3 tbsp (20 g) Spigol spice mix

Fish

4 weevers, poisonous spines removed

4 gurnards

2¼ lb. (1 kg) conger eel

Garlic croutons

1 baguette

Olive oil

2 cloves garlic, peeled and halved

Saffron aioli

1–2 heads garlic (to obtain 2 tbsp cooked garlic)

1½ oz. (40 g) sandwich bread

10 saffron threads

2 egg yolks

Scant ½ cup (100 ml) olive oil

⅔ cup (150 ml) grapeseed oil

Juice and finely grated zest of ¼ lemon

1 tbsp (15 g) harissa (optional)

Vegetables

6 waxy potatoes, preferably Charlotte

4 cups (1 liter) fish fumet (see technique p. 118)

12 bulbs mini fennel

To serve

Leaves of 1 bunch Motti Cress or baby lovage

PREPARING THE FISH SOUP

Trim, scale, and gut the rockfish (see techniques pp. 32–40, 45–50), then cut them crosswise into pieces. Rinse them well under cold running water and set aside. Peel and thinly slice the onions, leek whites, celery, and fennel. Wash and roughly chop the tomatoes. Separate the garlic cloves, then peel and roughly crush them. Heat the olive oil in a large pot and sweat the onions, leeks, celery, and fennel for 10 minutes, until softened but not browned. Add the rockfish and sweat for 10–15 minutes. Deglaze with the pastis, then stir in the tomatoes and tomato paste. Pour in the fish fumet or water to cover, then add the garlic, saffron, and Spigol spice mix. Bring to a boil quickly, skimming any foam from the surface. Let simmer for 25 minutes. Pass the soup through the food mill, then strain it through the fine-mesh sieve into a large clean saucepan. Reduce over low heat for 20 minutes, skimming frequently, until the soup has a deep color and a syrupy consistency. Adjust the seasonings if necessary.

PREPARING THE FISH

Trim, scale, and gut the weavers and gurnards (see techniques pp. 32, 34, 40, and 45), then fillet them (see techniques pp. 80–84). Cut the fillets in half. Cut the conger eel into 6 pieces.

PREPARING THE GARLIC CROUTONS

Preheat the oven to 300°F (150°C/Gas Mark 2). Cut the baguette into 12 slices, ½ in. (1 cm) wide. Place the slices on a baking sheet, drizzle them with olive oil, and dry them in the oven for 6–7 minutes, or until golden and crisp. As soon as you remove the croutons from the oven, rub both sides with the cut ends of the garlic cloves.

PREPARING THE SAFFRON AIOLI

Preheat the oven to 350°F (180°C/Gas Mark 4). Cut the garlic head(s) in half crosswise and wrap them in parchment paper, sealing the edges well. Roast for 25 minutes. Meanwhile, soak the bread in a little water to soften it. Peel the roasted garlic cloves and mash them to obtain 2 tbsp. Squeeze the excess water from the bread and place the bread in a bowl with the garlic and saffron; mash to a purée. Whisk in the egg yolks. Whisking continuously, gradually drizzle in the olive and grapeseed oils in a thin, steady stream until the mixture is pale, thick, and emulsified. Whisk in the lemon juice and zest, followed by the harissa, if using. Adjust the seasonings if necessary.

PREPARING THE VEGETABLES

Peel the potatoes and cut them into oval, soap bar-like shapes (*savonnettes*). Place them in a large saucepan with the fish fumet, bring to a simmer, and cook until they are just tender, then remove them from the pan. Peel the outer layer off the fennel bulbs and cook them until just tender in the fish fumet. Remove from the pan, set aside, and keep warm. Reduce the fumet to a glaze and add it to the fish soup.

TO SERVE

Just before serving, reheat the fish soup and cook the weevers, gurnards, and conger eel in it. Place the fish and vegetables in shallow serving bowls. Place the fish soup in a pitcher and pour it over the fish and vegetables at the table. Scatter with Motti Cress leaves. Serve the garlic croutons and saffron aioli on the side.

SALT COD SPREAD

Brandade de morue

Serves 4

Active time

30 minutes

Soaking time

48 hours

Cooking time

1 hour

Storage

3 days

Equipment

Mortar + pestle

Potato masher

1½-in. (4-cm) round cookie cutter

Mandoline

4-in. (10-cm) round cake pan, 2½ in. (6 cm) deep

4-in. (10-cm) stainless steel ring

Ingredients

Salt cod

14 oz. (400 g) salt cod

Salt cod spread

1 bunch flat-leaf parsley

Desalted and rehydrated salt cod (see above)

2 cups (500 ml) whole milk

1 bay leaf

5 cloves garlic, unpeeled

Generous ¾ cup (200 ml) olive oil

2¼ lb. (1 kg) waxy potatoes, preferably Charlotte

Salt and freshly ground pepper

Pommes Anna

1 lb. 2 oz. (500 g) small waxy potatoes, preferably Belle de Fontenay

7 tbsp (3½ oz./100 g) clarified butter

2 tsp (10 g) salt

To serve

6 flat-leaf parsley leaves

¼ tsp (1 g) fleur de sel

DESALINATING AND REHYDRATING THE SALT COD (2 DAYS AHEAD)

To desalinate and rehydrate the salt cod, soak it in water for 48 hours, changing the water 5 or 6 times.

PREPARING THE SALT COD SPREAD

Wash the parsley and remove the leaves from the stems, reserving them both. Drain the cod and place it in a large pot with the milk, parsley stems, and bay leaf. Roughly crush the garlic cloves and add them to the pot. Simmer for 15 minutes, then remove the cod and garlic cloves and set the milk aside. Flake the cod into the mortar, saving a few larger pieces for garnishing. Peel the garlic cloves and add them to the mortar with the cod. Pound to a coarse purée, gradually incorporating the olive oil to obtain an emulsion. Peel the potatoes, cut them into large dice, and cook them in a large pot of boiling salted water for about 20 minutes, or until tender. Drain the potatoes, place them in a large bowl, and mash them using the potato masher, adding a little of the reserved milk to thin them out. Add the cod mixture to the bowl and stir to combine. Finely chop the parsley leaves, reserving 6 whole leaves for garnishing, and stir them in. Add more salt if necessary, then season with freshly ground pepper.

PREPARING THE POMMES ANNA

Preheat the oven to 400°F (200°C/Gas Mark 6). Peel the potatoes and cut them into cylinders with a 1½-in. (4-cm) diameter using the cookie cutter. Cut the cylinders into 1⁄16-in (1-mm) slices using the mandoline to ensure uniformity. Melt the clarified butter in a saucepan and brush a layer over the base of the 4-in. (10-cm) round cake pan (see Chefs' Notes). Arrange potato slices in a tight, overlapping circle in the center. Season with salt, then work outward in a clockwise direction, layering the potato slices in overlapping concentric circles until you reach the edge of the pan. Drizzle with clarified butter, then add another layer of potato slices in the opposite direction. Season with salt and drizzle with butter. Repeat this process for two more layers, alternating directions each time. Cover with aluminum foil and bake for 15 minutes, then remove the foil and bake for an additional 10 minutes, until cooked through and golden. Turn the pommes Anna out of the pan and set aside.

TO SERVE

Place the 4-in. (10-cm) stainless steel ring in the center of a serving plate and fill it with salt cod spread. Remove the ring and place the pommes Anna on top, then form a 1½-in. (4-cm) circle of salt cod spread in the center. Arrange the reserved cod pieces around the circle, interspersing them with the parsley leaves. Sprinkle with fleur de sel.

CHEFS' NOTES

To prevent the pommes Anna from sticking to the pan, place a parchment paper disk on the bottom of the pan and brush it with clarified butter.

NORDIC-STYLE FISH AND CHIPS WITH TARTAR SAUCE AND WAFFLE CHIPS

"Fish and chips" nordique, sauce tartare et pommes gaufrettes

Serves 4

Active time
2 hours

Cooking time
15 minutes

Equipment
Mandoline + crinkle or waffle blade
Deep fryer
Instant-read thermometer

Ingredients

Hake
1¼ lb. (600 g) skinless, boneless hake fillet
Salt

Beer batter
1 cup (4 oz./120 g) all-purpose flour
⅓ cup (2 oz./60 g) cornstarch
1 tsp (5 g) salt
2 tsp (5 g) paprika
1½ tsp (4 g) curry powder
1¼ tsp (5 g) baking powder
1 egg
Scant ¾ cup (170 ml) blonde beer

Tartar sauce
2 egg yolks
1 tbsp (15 ml) lemon juice
1 generous tbsp (20 g) Dijon mustard
1 cup (250 ml) grape-seed oil
½ bunch parsley
1½ oz. (40 g) shallots
1½ oz. (40 g) capers
1½ oz. (40 g) cornichons
5 drops Worcestershire sauce
Salt and freshly ground pepper

Waffle chips and fried parsley leaves
2¼ lb. (1 kg) floury potatoes, preferably Agria
8 cups (2 liters) oil for deep-frying
15 parsley leaves
Salt

To cook and serve
Flour
Salt

PREPARING THE HAKE

Cut the hake fillet lengthwise into approximately 5 × 1½-in. (12 × 4-cm) pieces. Season with salt and reserve in the refrigerator.

PREPARING THE BEER BATTER

Place the flour in a large bowl and add the cornstarch, salt, paprika, curry powder, and baking powder. Whisk until well combined. Make a well in the center, add the egg, and whisk gently, gradually incorporating the flour. Pour in the beer, whisking continuously to avoid lumps.

PREPARING THE TARTAR SAUCE

Whisk together the egg yolks, lemon juice, and mustard in a large bowl. Whisking continuously, gradually drizzle in the grape-seed oil in a thin, steady stream until the mixture is pale, thick, and emulsified. Wash and dry the parsley, remove the stems, and finely chop the leaves, reserving 15 whole leaves for garnishing. Peel and finely chop the shallots, then chop the capers and cornichons. Stir the parsley, shallots, capers, and cornichons into the mayonnaise, then add the Worcestershire sauce and adjust the seasonings if necessary.

PREPARING THE WAFFLE CHIPS AND FRIED PARSLEY LEAVES

Peel and rinse the potatoes. Fit the mandoline with the crinkle blade and set it to a thickness of 1⁄16 in. (2 mm). Take one potato and cut off the first slice. Turn the potato 90 degrees to the right and cut a second slice to obtain a crosshatch pattern. Turn the potato 90 degrees to the left and cut again. Continue slicing, rotating the potato one-quarter turn before each slice, and regulating the thickness as necessary. Rinse the slices several times under running water to remove excess starch. Dry the potatoes thoroughly and place on paper towels. Heat the oil for deep-frying to 300°F (150°C) and deep-fry the waffle chips for 4 minutes, or until they are golden. Place on paper towels and season immediately with salt. Deep-fry the reserved parsley leaves at 300°F (150°C) for 3 minutes. Place on paper towels and season immediately with salt.

TO COOK AND SERVE

Heat the oil for deep-frying to 355°F (180°C). Dredge the hake pieces in flour, shaking off the excess. Dip them in the beer batter and immediately place them in the oil. Deep-fry for 5 minutes, then drain on paper towels and season with salt. Serve the fish alongside the waffle chips with tartar sauce in a bowl on the side. Garnish with the fried parsley leaves.

SALT COD FRITTERS WITH SWEET-AND-SOUR CHILI SAUCE

Accras de morue, sauce aigre-douce au piment oiseau

Serves 4

Active time
30 minutes

Cooking time
5 minutes

Equipment
Deep fryer
Instant-read thermometer

Ingredients

Sweet-and-sour chili sauce
1 bird's eye chili pepper
1 clove garlic
⅓ cup (80 ml) water
⅓ cup (2½ oz./70 g) sugar
⅓ cup (80 ml) rice vinegar
1½ tsp (5 g) cornstarch
2 tbsp cold water

Salt cod fritters
Scant 2½ cups (600 ml) whole milk, divided
10½ oz. (300 g) salt cod, soaked for 48 hours in 5–6 changes of water
1½ oz. (40 g) yellow onion
½ oz. (15 g) parsley
1 scallion
1¾ cups (8 oz./225 g) all-purpose flour
1 egg
2 tsp (5 g) sweet paprika
1¼ tsp (5 g) baking soda

PREPARING THE SWEET-AND-SOUR CHILI SAUCE

Wash the chili pepper, remove the seeds, and finely chop it. Peel and finely chop the garlic. Place the chili pepper and garlic in a saucepan with the ⅓ cup (80 ml) water, sugar, and vinegar, and bring to a boil. In a small bowl, combine the cornstarch and 2 tbsp cold water. Add this mixture to the saucepan and whisk until the sauce thickens.

PREPARING THE SALT COD FRITTERS

Place 2 cups (500 ml) of the milk in a large saucepan, add the cod, and bring to a simmer. Poach for 10 minutes, then drain. Flake the cod using a fork. Peel and finely chop the onion. Wash, dry, and chop the parsley. Wash and thinly slice the scallion at an angle, reserving a small amount for garnishing. In a large bowl, whisk together the flour, egg, and remaining scant ½ cup (100 ml) of milk. Add the cod, onion, parsley, paprika, baking soda, and scallion, reserving a little of the green part for garnish. Using a spatula, stir until well combined. Heat the oil for deep-frying to 355°F (180°C). Using two soup spoons, scoop up a small amount of batter and drop it into the hot oil. Deep-fry for about 3 minutes, or until golden and crisp. Drain on paper towels.

TO SERVE

Place the fritters in a bowl and sprinkle with the reserved scallion. Serve with the sweet chili sauce in a bowl on the side for dipping.

FLEMISH-STYLE FISH SOUP

Waterzoi

Serves 4

Active time
1½ hours

Resting time
10 minutes

Cooking time
1½ hours

Storage
2 days

Equipment
Fish scaler
Fish bone tweezers
Fine-mesh sieve
Griddle
Food processor

Ingredients

Fish and shellfish
- ¾ lb. (350 g) pollock
- 7 oz. (200 g) coarse sea salt
- 2 smoked herring fillets (*hareng saur*)
- 4 scallops with the coral (roe) attached
- 1 stick + 2 tbsp (5¼ oz./150 g) butter, divided
- 8 cups (2 liters) water
- 3½ oz. (100 g) fresh seaweed of your choice
- Generous ¾ cup (200 ml) white wine
- 8 cockles (*coques*), soaked in 2–3 changes of salted water (see p. 21)
- 8 mussels, cleaned (see technique p. 60)

Sauce
- 1 lb. 2 oz. (500 g) fish bones (ask your fishmonger for some to complement those from the pollock)
- 3½ oz. (100 g) celery
- 1¾ oz. (50 g) shallot
- 2¾ oz. (75 g) button mushrooms
- 7 tbsp (3½ oz./100 g) butter, divided
- ⅓ oz. (10 g) parsley stems
- 1 cup (250 ml) white wine
- 2 cups (500 ml) heavy cream, min. 35% fat

Vegetables
- 4 baby leeks
- 4 spring carrots
- 8 stalks celery
- 2 cloves garlic, unpeeled
- 5 tbsp (2½ oz./75 g) butter
- ⅔ cup (150 ml) fish fumet (see technique p. 118)
- ¼ bunch thyme

Celery oil
- 12 celery leaves
- 1¼ cups (300 ml) neutral oil

PREPARING THE FISH AND SHELLFISH

Cover the pollock with the coarse salt and let sit for 10 minutes, then rinse thoroughly under cold, running water. Remove the skin (see techniques pp. 41–43) and cut the fish into pieces weighing 2¾ oz. (80 g) each. Remove any pin bones (see technique p. 52). Cut the smoked herring fillets in half at an angle. Dry the scallops thoroughly. Melt 5 tbsp (2½ oz./75 g) of the butter in a sauté pan over low heat, then add the pollock and cook for 5 minutes. Melt the remaining butter in a separate skillet over medium-high heat, add the scallops, and sear them quickly on both sides, until lightly golden. Place the water, seaweed, and wine in a large saucepan and simmer for 30 minutes. Add the cockles and mussels and cook for 10 seconds, just long enough for them to open. Discard any that remain closed.

PREPARING THE SAUCE

Cut the fish bones into 2½-in. (6-cm) pieces. Peel and finely dice the celery and shallot. Wipe and thinly slice the mushrooms. Heat half the butter in a skillet and sweat the vegetables and parsley stems until softened but not browned, then add the fish bones and sweat for an additional 5 minutes. Deglaze with the white wine and reduce until the liquid has thickened. Add enough water to just cover the ingredients and let simmer for 25 minutes. Strain the fish stock through the fine-mesh sieve into a large clean saucepan and reduce until it thickens slightly. In a small saucepan, reduce the cream by three-quarters. Add the cream to the reduced fish stock, then remove from the heat and whisk in the remaining butter.

PREPARING THE VEGETABLES

Cook the leeks on an ungreased griddle or in an ungreased skillet until they are completely charred. Remove the outer layers and cut the insides at an angle into 2-in. (5-cm) pieces. Peel the carrots and celery and cut both at an angle into 2-in. (5-cm) pieces. Roughly crush the garlic. Melt the butter in a large saucepan and cook the leeks, celery, and carrots with the garlic, fumet, and thyme for 7–8 minutes, covered. Check for doneness using the tip of a paring knife—the vegetables should be meltingly soft.

PREPARING THE CELERY OIL

Wash and dry the celery leaves, then place them in the food processor with the oil and process for 10 minutes. Strain through the fine-mesh sieve.

TO SERVE

Warm the sauce, add the smoked herring, and let simmer for 5 minutes. Add the remaining fish and shellfish to the sauce and cook until warmed through. Reheat the vegetables. Divide the sauce, fish, shellfish, and vegetables evenly among four shallow bowls and drizzle with celery oil.

PIKE QUENELLES WITH NANTUA SAUCE

Quenelles de brochet, sauce nantua

Serves 10

Active time
1 hour

Cooking time
1 hour

Chilling time
2 hours

Storage
2 days

Equipment
Food processor
Fine-mesh drum sifter
Fine-mesh conical sieve

Ingredients

Panada
- ½ cup (125 ml) whole milk
- 1 tbsp (20 g) butter
- 5 tsp (25 g) salt
- 1¾ tsp (4 g) ground white pepper
- 3 tbsp (1 oz./30 g) all-purpose flour, sifted
- 2 egg yolks

Pike farce
- 2¼ lb. (1 kg) pike meat, well chilled
- 3 eggs, well chilled
- Panada (see above), well chilled
- 1½ sticks (6 oz./180 g) butter, at room temperature and diced
- Scant 1 cup (220 ml) heavy cream, min. 35% fat, well chilled
- Salt and freshly ground pepper

Nantua sauce
- 1 onion
- 3 shallots
- 2 cloves garlic
- 4 tomatoes
- 3½ tbsp (50 ml) olive oil
- 3½ lb. (1.5 kg) crayfish carcasses
- 1 tbsp (15 g) tomato paste
- Scant ½ cup (100 ml) cognac
- Scant ½ cup (100 ml) Noilly Prat vermouth
- 2 cups (500 ml) fish fumet (see technique p. 118)
- 1 tsp (3 g) *piment d'Espelette*
- ½ bunch tarragon tied together with twine
- 2 cups (500 ml) heavy cream, min. 35% fat
- Salt and freshly ground pepper

Shimeji mushrooms
- 10½ oz. (300 g) shimeji mushrooms
- 3 tbsp (1¾ oz./50 g) butter
- Salt and freshly ground pepper

To serve
- 30 shrimp, cooked and peeled
- 10 garlic flowers

PREPARING THE PANADA
Place the milk, butter, salt, and white pepper in a large saucepan and bring to a boil. Remove from the heat and add the flour. Stirring continuously with a spatula, cook the mixture over high heat until it is no longer sticky to the touch. Still stirring, reduce the heat to low and incorporate the egg yolks one at a time. Immediately transfer the panada to a tray and press plastic wrap over the surface. Let it cool for 1 hour in the refrigerator.

PREPARING THE PIKE FARCE
Place the pike meat and eggs in the food processor and process until smooth. Mix in the panada, followed by the butter. Pass the farce through the fine-mesh drum sifter into a clean bowl, stir in the cream, and season with salt and pepper. Cover the bowl and chill for 1 hour.

PREPARING THE NANTUA SAUCE
Peel the onion, shallots, and garlic and cut all three into ¼-in. (7-mm) dice. Wash the tomatoes and cut them into ¼-in. (7-mm) dice as well. Heat the olive oil in a sauté pan until shimmering, then add the crayfish carcasses and cook until browned. Add the vegetables and cook for 10 minutes, until softened and browned. Stir in the tomato paste, then deglaze with the cognac. Add the vermouth, followed by the fish fumet, *piment d'Espelette*, and tarragon, and let simmer for 30 minutes. Strain the sauce through the fine-mesh sieve, reserving the crayfish heads for garnish, if desired. Stir in the cream and adjust the seasonings if necessary.

PREPARING THE SHIMEJI MUSHROOMS
Quickly sauté the shimeji mushrooms in a skillet over high heat with the butter and a little water, until tender and lightly browned. Season with salt and pepper.

ASSEMBLING AND COOKING THE PIKE QUENELLES
Preheat the oven to 350°F (180°C/Gas Mark 4) and dust a tray with flour. Shape the pike farce into large quenelles weighing 5¼ oz. (150 g) each and gently set them on the prepared tray. Pour the Nantua sauce into a baking dish just large enough to hold the quenelles. Poach the quenelles in simmering, salted water for 4 minutes on each side. Using a skimmer, carefully transfer the quenelles to a clean dish towel to drain. Place the quenelles in the baking dish with the sauce and bake for 8 minutes, until puffed.

TO SERVE
For each serving, place shimeji mushrooms in the base of a shallow bowl and top with a pike quenelle. Arrange the shrimp and garlic flowers around the quenelle and garnish with a crayfish head, if desired. Coat the quenelles with the Nantua sauce and serve immediately.

BUTTERFLIED TROUT WITH GREEN BEANS AND ALMONDS

Truite de l'Éclimont aux amandes

Serves 4

Active time

1 hour

Cooking time

20 minutes

Equipment

Fish scaler

Fish bone tweezers

Ingredients

Green beans and lemons

7 oz. (200 g) green beans

8 cups (2 liters) water

1½ oz. (40 g) coarse sea salt

2 lemons

Trout

4 trout, weighing 8¾ oz. (250 g) each

¾ cup + 2 tbsp (3½ oz./100 g) all-purpose flour

3½ tbsp (50 ml) grapeseed oil

4 tbsp (2 oz./60 g) butter

Scant 1 cup (2¾ oz./80 g) slivered almonds

Salt and freshly ground pepper

To serve

A few sprigs chervil

Trout pan juices (see above)

2 lemons, halved

PREPARING THE GREEN BEANS AND LEMONS

Trim the ends off the green beans and wash the beans thoroughly. Place the water and salt in a large pot and bring to a boil. Blanch the beans for 5 minutes, then remove them with a skimmer and immediately plunge them into ice water. When the beans have cooled completely, drain them and set them aside. Peel the lemons, removing all the bitter white pith. Remove the segments and cut them into ¼-in. (6-mm) dice.

PREPARING THE TROUT

Trim, scale, and gut the trout (see techniques pp. 32, 40, and 45), then dry them with paper towels. To butterfly the trout, cut each one open along the belly, from head to tail, as if to fillet it (see technique p. 84), but leave the fish intact. Using a filleting knife, slice the ribs free on both sides. Cut off the bones from the belly section, then, using the fish bone tweezers, carefully remove the pin bones (see technique p. 52). Season the open side of each trout with salt, then dredge the skin side in the flour to coat it lightly. Heat the oil in a large nonstick skillet over medium heat, then place the trout in the pan, skin side down, working in batches if necessary. When the skin is crisp and golden brown, add the butter and continue cooking on the same side, basting the fish regularly with the melted butter. When the fish are cooked through, remove from the skillet. Place the almonds in the pan and cook them in the same butter until deeply golden. Drain the almonds on paper towels and reserve the pan juices.

TO SERVE

Wash and dry the chervil and remove the stems. Reheat the green beans in a skillet with a little of the reserved trout pan juices, then add the toasted almonds and a squeeze of lemon juice. Cook over low heat, stirring often, until the beans are warmed through and well coated. Place a trout skin side up on each serving plate. Arrange the green beans and almonds alongside the fish and scatter them with the diced lemon segments. Garnish with a few fresh chervil leaves and serve with the remaining pan juices and lemon halves on the side.

STUFFED TROUT WITH MATELOTE SAUCE

Darnes de truite

Serves 6

Active time

1½ hours

Cooking time

2 hours

Chilling time

Overnight

Equipment

Steam oven (or steamer)

Fish scaler

Fish bone tweezers

Food processor

Kitchen twine

Fine-mesh sieve

Ingredients

Stuffed trout

1 trout, weighing 4½ lb. (2 kg)

7 oz. (200 g) cooked foie gras

3½ oz. (100 g) button mushrooms

3 tbsp (1¾ oz./50 g) butter

1 tsp (5 g) salt

10½ oz. (300 g) skinless, boneless whiting fillet

Scant ½ cup (100 ml) heavy cream, min. 35% fat

Matelote sauce

1 lb. 2 oz. (500 g) trout or other fish bones (see above or ask your fishmonger, if necessary)

1¾ oz. (50 g) leek whites

3½ oz. (100 g) shallots

2¾ oz. (75 g) button mushrooms

3 tbsp (1¾ oz./50 g) butter, divided

2 cups (500 ml) red wine

1 bouquet garni (bay leaf and parsley stems tied up in a leek green)

Garnishes

14 oz. (400 g) celery root (celeriac)

2 cloves garlic

3 tbsp (1¾ oz./50 g) salted butter

¼ bunch lemon thyme

1¾ cups (450 ml) vegetable stock, divided

6 button mushrooms

1 tbsp (20 g) unsalted butter

Juice of ½ lemon

12 cooked chestnuts

2 tsp (10 ml) chicken jus

To serve

18 sprigs tarragon

PREPARING THE STUFFED TROUT (1 DAY AHEAD)

Preheat the steam oven to 140°F (60°C/Gas on the lowest setting). Trim, scale, and gut the trout (see techniques pp. 32, 40, and 45). Cut open along the belly, as if to fillet it (see technique p. 84), but leave the fish intact. Using a filleting knife, slice the ribs free on both sides. Cut off the bones from the belly section, then, using the fish bone tweezers, carefully remove the pin bones (see technique p. 52). Reserve the bones in the refrigerator for the matelote sauce. Cover the cooked foie gras with plastic wrap and shape it into a log, 1½ in. (4 cm) in diameter and the same length as the trout. Wipe the mushrooms and cut them in half from top to bottom, then cut each half at a slight angle into 4–6 slices. Heat the butter in a skillet and sauté the mushrooms with the salt until tender and browned, then chop them finely. Remove any pin bones from the whiting fillet, cut it into pieces, and process in the food processor with the cream until smooth. Combine the whiting mixture with the mushrooms and spread over the boned trout to a thickness of 1⁄16 in. (2 mm). Remove the plastic wrap from the foie gras log and place it in the center, then close the trout, cover it with plastic wrap, and shape it into a log. Cook in the steam oven (or steamer) for 45 minutes. Let rest overnight in the refrigerator.

PREPARING THE MATELOTE SAUCE

Cut the fish bones into 2½-in. (6-cm) pieces. Finely dice the leek whites. Peel and finely dice the shallots. Wipe and thinly slice the mushrooms. Heat half the butter in a large saucepan and sweat the leek, shallots, and mushrooms until softened, then add the fish bones and sweat until they turn white. Deglaze with the wine, adding one-third at a time and reducing it to a glaze after each addition. Add the bouquet garni and enough water to just cover the ingredients and let simmer for 25 minutes. Strain through the fine-mesh sieve into a clean saucepan and reduce until thickened. Remove from the heat and whisk in the remaining butter.

PREPARING THE GARNISHES

Peel the celery root and cut it into small dice. Peel and finely chop the garlic. Heat the salted butter in a sauté pan and sweat the celery root with the garlic and lemon thyme until softened but not browned. Finish cooking it as you would a risotto, gradually adding 1 cup (250 ml) of the vegetable stock a ladleful at a time. Cut grooves into the mushroom caps at regular intervals to turn, or tournée, them. Heat the unsalted butter in a saucepan and sweat the mushrooms, then add the lemon juice and the remaining vegetable stock. In a separate small saucepan, heat the chestnuts with the chicken jus until the jus reduces to a glaze.

TO SERVE

Preheat the oven to 250°F (120°C/Gas Mark ½). Cut the trout into 1½-in. (4-cm) thick slices and reheat in the oven for 5 minutes. Serve over a little sauce, with the garnishes, scattered with tarragon, and remaining sauce alongside.

PICKLED HERRING WITH MUSTARD VINAIGRETTE AND HARLEQUIN VEGETABLES

Harengs marinés, vinaigrette moutardée et harlequin de légumes

Serves 4

Active time
1 hour

Marinating time
5 hours

Cooking time
30 minutes

Storage
3 days

Equipment
Fish scaler
Fine-mesh sieve

Ingredients

Pickled herring
4 fresh herring
Scant 1/2 tsp (2 g) smoked salt
3/4 tsp (2 g) coarsely ground pepper
3 1/2 oz. (100 g) sweet onions
4 tsp (20 ml) white vinegar
3 1/2 tbsp (50 ml) white wine
1 tsp (3 g) mustard seeds
1 whole clove
2 bay leaves
4 sprigs thyme
Generous 3/4 cup (200 ml) neutral oil

Mustard vinaigrette
2/3 oz. (20 g) shallot
3 1/2 tbsp (50 ml) white vinegar
1/4 tsp (1 g) salt
2 tbsp (1 oz./30 g) wholegrain mustard
2/3 cup (150 ml) sunflower oil

Vegetables
3 1/2 oz. (100 g) waxy potatoes, preferably Charlotte
3 1/2 oz. (100 g) carrots
3 1/2 oz. (100 g) red onions
Generous 3/4 cup (200 ml) neutral oil
Scant 1/2 tsp (2 g) salt
Herring heads and bones (see above)
4 cups (1 liter) water

To serve
2 scallions
8 borage flowers

PREPARING THE PICKLED HERRING

Trim, scale, and gut the herring (see techniques pp. 32, 40, and 45), reserving the heads for the herring stock. Fillet the herring (see technique p. 84), leaving the skin on, then remove the bones and reserve them for the stock. Cut each fillet into two pieces at an angle and season with the smoked salt and coarsely ground pepper. Peel the onions and cut them crosswise into 1/8-in. (2-mm) slices. Place the slices in a large saucepan with the vinegar, wine, mustard seeds, clove, bay leaves, and thyme. Bring to a boil, then stir in the oil. Place the herring pieces in a dish, pour the vinegar mixture over them, and cover. Let marinate for 5 hours at room temperature.

PREPARING THE MUSTARD VINAIGRETTE

Peel the shallot, chop it very finely, and place in a small bowl with the vinegar and salt. Let marinate for about 5 minutes, then stir in the wholegrain mustard. Whisking continuously, drizzle in the oil in a slow, steady stream to obtain an emulsion.

PREPARING THE VEGETABLES

Peel the potatoes, carrots, and red onions and cut them into 5 × 1/2-in. (2 × 1-cm) diamond shapes, 1/16 in. (1 mm) thick. Reserve all the trimmings for the herring stock. Heat the neutral oil in a large skillet and cook the vegetables separately with the salt until coated and softened, but not browned. Remove the skillet from the heat. Place the herring heads and bones in a pot with the water and bring to a boil, skimming any foam from the surface. Add the potato, carrot, and onion trimmings and simmer for 20 minutes. Strain the stock through the fine-mesh sieve, then measure out a generous 3/4 cup (200 ml), add it to the vegetables in the skillet, and bring to a gentle simmer. Cook until the vegetables are tender but not falling apart.

TO SERVE

Remove the herring from the marinade and pat dry with paper towels. Wash the scallions and slice them thinly at an angle. Place pickled herring on one side of each serving plate and arrange the vegetables in a harlequin pattern on the other side. Generously drizzle with the mustard vinaigrette and garnish with the scallions and borage flowers.

BRETON SEAFOOD STEW

Cotriade

Serves 4

Active time
1¼ hours

Cooking time
1½ hours

Storage
3 days

Equipment
Fish scaler
Fine-mesh sieve

Ingredients

Seafood
1 lb. 2 oz. (500 g) red gurnard
10½ oz. (300 g) conger eel
8 sardines
4 langoustines

Fish soup
1½ lb. (750 g) small rockfish (*bouilles*)
3½ oz. (100 g) onions
4½ oz. (125 g) fennel
½ head garlic
8¾ oz. (250 g) tomatoes
Scant ½ cup (100 ml) canola oil
¼ bunch thyme
1 cup (250 ml) hard apple cider
3 qt. (3 liters) water
Prepared red gurnard, sardines, conger eel, and langoustines (see above)

Vegetables
8 spring carrots
10½ oz. (300 g) waxy potatoes, preferably Charlotte
4 baby leeks
5 scallions
Strained fish soup (see above)

To serve
½ bunch garlic flowers

PREPARING THE SEAFOOD

Trim and scale the fish as needed (see techniques pp. 32 and 40), then gut them (see technique p. 45). Cut the red gurnard into pieces weighing 1¾ oz. (50 g) each. Fillet the eel, then cut the fillets into pieces weighing 1¾ oz. (50 g) each. Remove the fillets from the sardines without separating them at the belly. Shell the langoustines (see technique p. 58), reserving the heads for garnishing. Poach the heads in boiling water for 5 minutes to sterilize them, then set them aside until serving.

PREPARING THE FISH SOUP

If the rockfish are small, cut them into pieces without gutting them. If they are large, gut them to prevent a bitter taste in the soup (see technique p. 45), then cut them into pieces. Peel and thinly slice the onion and fennel. Separate the garlic cloves and roughly crush them, leaving them unpeeled. Wash the tomatoes and cut them crosswise into ½-in. (1-cm) slices. Heat the canola oil in a Dutch oven and sweat the onions and fennel until softened but not browned. Add the garlic and thyme. Gently set the pieces of rockfish over the vegetables and reduce the heat to low—do not stir at all from this point on. Cover and cook for about 5 minutes, then place the tomato slices over the fish and continue cooking with the lid on for an additional 15–20 minutes. Deglaze with cider and reduce by half, then add the water and simmer for 20–30 minutes, without stirring. Set the fine-mesh sieve over a large clean saucepan and gently ladle the fish soup into it, taking care not to stir the ingredients too much. Bring the strained fish soup to a simmer, add the red gurnard, sardines, eel, and langoustines, and poach for 5 minutes. Remove with a skimmer and set aside.

PREPARING THE VEGETABLES

Peel the carrots and potatoes and cut them in half lengthwise, then cut the halves into 2¾-in. (7-cm) pieces at an angle. Peel the outer layer off the leeks and cut them into 2¾-in. (7-cm) pieces at an angle. Trim the green parts off the scallions, leaving ¾ in. (2 cm), then cut them in half lengthwise. Poach the vegetables in the fish soup until just tender, checking for doneness with the tip of a paring knife. Remove with a skimmer and keep the fish soup hot.

TO SERVE

Cut the garlic flowers into 2¾-in. (7-cm) pieces. Place the vegetables in the base of a Dutch oven for serving, then add the fish and langoustines. Carefully pour in the fish soup. Garnish with the reserved langoustine heads and garlic flowers.

LE CREUSET
LE CREUSET

ZUKE-STYLE BONITO NIGIRI

Sushi nigiri à la bonite façon "zuke"

Serves 4

Active time
4 hours

Infusing time
8 hours

Marinating time
4 hours

Cooking time
30 minutes

Resting time
32 minutes

Equipment
Fine-mesh sieve
Microplane grater

Ingredients

Nikiri (sweet soy sauce)
- 3/4 cup (180 ml) soy sauce (shoyu or koikuchi)
- Scant 1/3 cup (2 oz./60 g) sugar
- 2 tbsp + 1 tsp (35 ml) saké
- 2/3 oz. (20 g) kombu seaweed
- 1/3 oz. (10 g) dried bonito flakes (katsuobushi)

Zuke-style bonito
- 1 lb. 2 oz. (500 g) boneless bonito (skipjack tuna) fillets
- 8 cups (2 liters) water
- 1 1/4 cups (300 ml) mirin
- 1 1/4 cups (300 ml) soy sauce (shoyu or koikuchi)

Sushi rice
- 2 cups (14 oz./400 g) sushi rice
- Scant 1 1/2 cups (360 ml/400 g) mineral water
- 6 drops sesame oil
- 2 1/2 tbsp (1 oz./30 g) demerara sugar
- 3 tsp (15 g) salt
- Generous 1/3 cup (90 ml) rice vinegar

Garnishes
- 1 3/4 oz. (50 g) fresh ginger
- 2/3 oz. (20 g) chives
- 12 shiso leaves

To serve
- 1/4 cup (60 ml) water
- 2 tsp (10 ml) unseasoned rice vinegar

PREPARING THE NIKIRI (SWEET SOY SAUCE; 1 DAY AHEAD)
Warm the soy sauce, sugar, and saké in a saucepan until the sugar dissolves, then bring to a boil. Remove from the heat and let cool to room temperature. Stir in the kombu and dried bonito flakes and let infuse for 8 hours in the refrigerator. The following day, strain the nikiri through the fine-mesh sieve into a clean container.

PREPARING THE ZUKE-STYLE BONITO
Remove the skin from the bonito fillets (see technique p. 41) and cut off any dark or black parts. Cut each fillet into 4 equal pieces. Bring the water to a boil and place a large bowl of ice water on the countertop alongside. Blanch the fish for 3 seconds in the boiling water, then immediately plunge them into the ice water to cool them quickly. Drain the fish and place in a dish. Whisk together the mirin and soy sauce, pour over the fish, and let marinate for 4 hours in the refrigerator.

PREPARING THE SUSHI RICE
To remove excess starch, rinse the rice several times under running water, until the water runs clear. Let the rice drain for 10 minutes in a colander, then transfer it to a large saucepan and add the mineral water and the sesame oil. Let soak for 10 minutes off the heat. Cover and cook over high heat for 10 minutes, then reduce the heat to low and continue cooking for an additional 10 minutes, still covered. It is crucial to keep the pan covered throughout the cooking time. Remove the rice from the heat and let it sit in the pan for 10 minutes, keeping the lid on. Meanwhile, in a small bowl, dissolve the sugar and salt in the rice vinegar. While the rice is still hot, transfer it to a large bowl and sprinkle the vinegar mixture over it. Using a spatula, gently lift the rice grains from the bottom to incorporate the liquid. Take care not to crush the rice, which will make it gummy. Let rest for 2 minutes, then lift the rice again and turn it over to distribute the vinegar more evenly. Place a damp paper towel over the rice and let it sit at room temperature until serving.

PREPARING THE GARNISHES
Peel the ginger and finely grate it using the Microplane grater. Wash and finely chop the chives. Wash and dry the shiso leaves.

TO SERVE
Drain the bonito fillets and pat them dry with paper towels. Cut them crosswise into slices about 1/3 in. (8 mm) thick. Arrange the shiso leaves on serving plates. Whisk together the water and rice vinegar in a bowl. For each nigiri, moisten your hands with the water-vinegar mixture, then take a small amount of the sushi rice and gently squeeze it into an oval shape slightly smaller than the fish pieces. Place a bonito slice on top of each rice mound and brush the fish with nikiri to glaze it. Set the nigiri over the shiso leaves and garnish with a little grated ginger and a sprinkling of chives.

PISSALADIÈRE

Serves 4

Active time
30 minutes

Rising time
1 hour

Cooking time
1 hour

Storage
3 days

Equipment
Kitchen torch (or gas burner)

Ingredients

Dough

- 2½ cups (10½ oz./300 g) all-purpose flour
- Generous ½ tsp (3 g) salt
- ⅔ oz. (20 g) fresh yeast
- Generous ¾ cup (200 ml) water, divided
- 4 tsp (20 ml) olive oil

Onion compote

- 1 lb. 2 oz. (500 g) onions
- 1 clove garlic
- 10 salt-packed anchovies
- Leaves of ¼ bunch thyme
- ¼ bunch rosemary
- Scant ½ cup (100 ml) olive oil

To assemble

- 12 anchovies
- 12 Taggiasca olives
- 12 rosemary leaves

PREPARING THE DOUGH

Sift the flour into a large bowl, then whisk in the salt. Dissolve the yeast in 3½ tbsp (50 ml) of the water. Make a well in the flour and pour in the yeast mixture, the remaining water, and the olive oil. Stir until the mixture comes together into a smooth dough. Shape the dough into a ball, place it in a lightly oiled bowl, and cover with a dish towel. Let rise for 1 hour at room temperature.

PREPARING THE ONION COMPOTE

Peel and thinly slice the onions. Peel and chop the garlic. Chop the anchovies and thyme. Singe the rosemary using the kitchen torch (or a gas burner), then chop the leaves. Warm the olive oil in a skillet over low heat, then add the onions, garlic, anchovies, rosemary, and thyme. Cook until the onions are fall-apart tender and lightly golden. Adjust the seasonings if necessary.

ASSEMBLING AND BAKING THE PISSALADIÈRE

Preheat the oven to 400°F (200°C/Gas Mark 6). Cut the anchovies at an angle into 1¼-in. (3-cm) pieces. Drain the olives and chop them if necessary. Roll the dough into a 12-in. (30-cm) disk, ¼ in. (5 mm) thick, and place it on a baking sheet lined with parchment paper. Spread the onion compote across the dough, leaving an approximate ¾-in. (1.5-cm) border all the way around. Bake the pissaladière for 15 minutes, then remove it from the oven and arrange the anchovies, olives, and rosemary leaves on top in staggered rows. Return to the oven and bake for an additional 5 minutes.

DOGFISH SKEWERS WITH ENDIVE SALAD

Brochettes de saumonette

Serves 4

Active time
1 hour

Infusing time
2 hours

Cooking time
40 minutes

Equipment
Instant-read thermometer
8 metal skewers
Oven-safe skillet
Microplane grater

Ingredients

Coffee-infused oil
- Scant 1/2 cup (100 ml) neutral oil
- 2 tsp (5 g) instant coffee

Glazed dogfish
- 14 oz. (400 g) skinless dogfish (rock salmon)
- Generous 3/4 cup (200 ml) red wine
- Generous 3/4 cup (200 ml) port wine
- Generous 3/4 cup (200 ml) sour cherry juice
- 1 2/3 cups (400 ml) fish fumet (see technique p. 118)

Dogfish skewers
- 8 large cloves garlic
- 3 1/2 tbsp (50 ml) olive oil
- 1/4 bunch thyme
- 1 1/2 tsp (5 g) black peppercorns
- 1 tomato
- Glazed dogfish (see above)

Endive salad
- 10 young yellow (Belgian) endives
- Coffee-infused oil (see above)

To serve
- 4 coffee beans

PREPARING THE COFFEE-INFUSED OIL
Heat the neutral oil to 176°F (80°C) in a small saucepan. Stir in the instant coffee and let it infuse for 2 hours, maintaining the temperature.

PREPARING THE GLAZED DOGFISH
Preheat the oven to 400°F (200°C/Gas Mark 6). Cut the dogfish into 16 pieces weighing just under 1 oz. (25 g) each. Combine the red wine and port wine in a medium saucepan and bring to a boil. In a separate large saucepan, reduce the sour cherry juice and fish fumet until thickened, then add the wine and port mixture. To glaze the dogfish, evenly coat the pieces with the sauce and bake in the oven for 10 minutes, turning and recoating them with sauce every 2 minutes.

PREPARING THE DOGFISH SKEWERS
Peel the garlic cloves and cook them in a small saucepan with the olive oil, thyme, and peppercorns until tender. Peel the tomato, cut into 8 wedges, and remove the seeds. To assemble the skewers, start with a piece of glazed dogfish, then add a tomato piece followed by a second piece of dogfish. Finish with a garlic clove.

PREPARING THE ENDIVE SALAD
Cut the endives into feather shapes, then toss them with the coffee-infused oil to coat.

TO SERVE
Preheat the oven to 400°F (200°C/Gas Mark 6). Just before serving, place the dogfish skewers in the oven-safe skillet and reheat them in the oven for about 1 minute. Arrange endive salad on each serving plate and finely grate the coffee beans over it using the Microplane grater. Place 2 dogfish skewers over the salad on each plate.

RED MULLET WITH FRIED ARTICHOKES AND CHORIZO CREAM SAUCE

Rouget barbet et crème de chorizo

Serves 4

Active time

1½ hours

Cooking time

1 hour

Equipment

Food processor

Fine-mesh sieve

2 sauce bottles

Fish scaler

Fish bone tweezers

Deep fryer

Instant-read thermometer

Melon baller

Oven-safe skillet

Ingredients

Chorizo chips

3½ oz. (100 g) sweet Spanish chorizo

Chorizo cream sauce

2 oz. (60 g) shallots

4 tsp (20 ml) neutral oil

4½ oz. (130 g) spicy Spanish chorizo

2½ tbsp (40 ml) white wine

1½ tbsp (25 ml) sherry vinegar

Generous ¾ cup (200 ml) white stock

Generous ¾ cup (200 ml) heavy cream, min. 35% fat

Salt

Toum

4½ oz. (125 g) heads garlic

6½ tbsp (3 oz./90 g) egg white (3 whites)

2 tbsp (30 ml) lemon juice

4 tsp (20 g) Dijon mustard

Generous ¾ cup (200 ml) canola oil

2 tsp (10 ml) whole milk

Stuffed red mullet

8¾ oz. (250 g) boneless, skinless red mullet fillets, diced

1½ oz. (40 g) spicy Spanish chorizo, diced

2 tbsp (1 oz./30 g) egg white (1 white)

Generous ¾ cup (200 ml) heavy cream, min. 35% fat

4 whole red mullet, weighing 7–8¾ oz. (200–250 g) each

Salt

Fried artichokes

Oil for deep-frying

2 small purple artichokes (*artichauts poivrade*)

To serve

Neutral oil

Marigold petals

PREPARING THE CHORIZO CHIPS AND CREAM SAUCE

To prepare the chips, preheat the oven to 250°F (130°C/Gas Mark ½). Cut the sweet chorizo into 1⁄16-in. (1-mm) slices, spread over a baking sheet in a single layer, and bake for 15–20 minutes, until crisp. To prepare the cream sauce, peel and finely chop the shallots and sweat them in a large saucepan with the neutral oil until softened but not browned. Cut the spicy chorizo into ½-in. (1-cm) dice and add to the pan. Deglaze with the white wine and sherry vinegar, and reduce until all the liquid has evaporated. Add the white stock, followed by the cream, and cook over low heat for 15 minutes. Process the sauce in the food processor until smooth, then strain it through the fine-mesh sieve and season with salt. Transfer to one of the sauce bottles.

PREPARING THE TOUM

Separate the garlic cloves, peel them, and briefly blanch them whole in a pot of boiling water. Drain and place in the food processor with the egg white, lemon juice, and mustard. Process until smooth. With the motor running, drizzle in the oil in a thin, steady stream, then pour the milk down the feeder tube to obtain a creamy texture. Transfer to the second sauce bottle.

PREPARING THE STUFFED RED MULLET

Place the diced red mullet and chorizo in the food processor and process until very finely chopped. Mix in the egg white, then add the cream and process until smooth. Season with salt. Trim, scale, and gut the whole red mullet (see techniques pp. 34, 40, and 45), then cut each one open along its back, leaving the base intact. Remove the heads. Using a filleting knife, slice the ribs free on both sides. Cut off the bones from the belly section, then, using the fish bone tweezers, remove the pin bones (see technique p. 52). Season the insides of the fillets with salt, and stuff with the red mullet-chorizo mixture. Close the fish around the stuffing.

PREPARING THE FRIED ARTICHOKES

Heat the oil for deep-frying to 320°F (160°C). Remove the tough outer leaves of the artichokes and use a melon baller to scoop out the choke. Cut the artichokes in half and immediately lower into the hot oil to prevent browning. Deep-fry for 2–3 minutes, just until tender. Drain on paper towels.

TO SERVE

Preheat the oven to 350°F (180°C/Gas Mark 4). Warm a little neutral oil in the oven-safe skillet over high heat and sear the stuffed red mullet for 1–2 minutes on each side. Finish cooking the fish in the oven for 4–5 minutes. Squeeze a little chorizo cream sauce onto one side of each serving plate and top with a fried artichoke half. Squeeze a little toum into the center and scatter with marigold petals. Arrange the chorizo chips like scales over the stuffed fish and place one on each plate.

POACHED SARDINES IN SICHUAN PEPPER-INFUSED OIL

Sardines confites à l'huile infusée à la baie de Sichuan

Serves 4

Active time
30 minutes

Cooking time
30 minutes

Resting time
15 minutes

Chilling time
1–2 hours

Storage
3 days

Equipment
Channel knife
Instant-read thermometer

Ingredients

Quick-cured sardines
- 12 sardines, gutted
- 9 oz. (250 g) coarse sea salt

Oil-poached sardines
- 1 carrot
- 2/3 oz. (20 g) preserved lemon
- 1 2/3 cups (400 ml) olive oil
- 1 tsp (2 g) Sichuan peppercorns
- 12 quick-cured sardines (see above)
- 2 bay leaves
- 2 sprigs thyme

PREPARING THE QUICK-CURED SARDINES
Remove the heads from the sardines, if desired. Rinse the fish, then cover them completely in the coarse salt and let them sit for 15 minutes. Rinse well and dry with paper towels.

PREPARING THE OIL-POACHED SARDINES
Preheat the oven to 147°F (64°C/Gas on the lowest possible setting). Peel the carrot, then cut lengthwise grooves in it at regular intervals using the channel knife. Slice the carrot thinly. Remove the preserved lemon peel and cut it into thin strips. Place the olive oil and Sichuan peppercorns in a small saucepan and heat to 140°F (60°C). Place the quick-cured sardines in a baking dish, ensuring they fit snugly. Add the carrot, preserved lemon peel, bay leaves, and thyme. Pour the hot oil over the sardines and poach them in the oven for 30 minutes. Let cool for 1–2 hours in the refrigerator before serving.

POLLEN-CRUSTED MACKEREL

Maquereau pané au pollen

Serves 4

Active time
1 hour

Cooking time
25 minutes

Soaking time
25 minutes

Equipment
Juicer
Immersion blender
Mandoline
Fish scaler
Fish bone tweezers
Kitchen torch

Ingredients

Fennel mayonnaise
1 bulb fennel
1 tbsp (15 g) tarragon mustard
Scant 1/2 tsp (2 g) salt
Scant 1/2 tsp (1 g) ground white pepper
1 egg yolk
Scant 1/2 cup (100 ml) neutral oil

Garnishes
7 oz. (200 g) sea spaghetti (*Himanthalia elongata*)
3 tbsp (1¾ oz./50 g) butter
8¾ oz. (250 g) fennel
1/3 oz. (10 g) rock samphire (*Crithmum maritimum*)
2 tsp (10 ml) linseed oil
1/2 tsp (2 g) fleur de sel

Pollen-crusted mackerel
2 mackerel, weighing about 10 oz. (300 g) each
2/3 cup (3½ oz./100 g) cornstarch
Generous 1/2 tsp (3 g) salt
Scant 1/2 cup (3½ oz./100 g) egg white (about 3½ whites)
3½ oz. (100 g) pollen
2/3 cup (150 ml) olive oil

To serve
1/3 oz. (10 g) finger lime
A few sprigs rock samphire

PREPARING THE FENNEL MAYONNAISE
Wash the fennel, then juice it using the juicer. In a small saucepan, reduce the fennel juice over high heat until thickened to a glaze-like consistency. Let cool completely. Place the fennel glaze, tarragon mustard, salt, white pepper, and egg yolk in a small bowl. Add the oil and blend using the immersion blender until the mixture emulsifies.

PREPARING THE GARNISHES
Soak the sea spaghetti in cold water for 10 minutes to remove some of the salt. Drain and pat dry. Heat the butter in a large saucepan until it browns and has a nutty aroma, then add the sea spaghetti and cook until tender. Remove the skillet from the heat, leaving the sea spaghetti inside. Remove the outer layer of the fennel, cut the fennel into ¼-in. (5-mm) slices using the mandoline, and let soak in ice water for 15 minutes. Drain the fennel, place it in a bowl with the rock samphire, and toss with the linseed oil and fleur de sel.

PREPARING THE POLLEN-CRUSTED MACKEREL
Trim, scale, and gut the mackerel (see techniques pp. 32, 40, and 45), then fillet them and remove the pin bones (see techniques pp. 84 and 52). Trim the 4 fillets at a slight angle. Combine the cornstarch and salt in a shallow dish, whisk the egg whites in a second shallow dish, and place the pollen in a third dish. Dip the mackerel fillets, flesh side only, into each dish in the same order as above. Warm the olive oil in a skillet over very low heat, then add the mackerel with the pollen-crusted side down. Cook for 2 minutes, or until the crust is golden, then transfer to a rack with the skin side facing up. Use the kitchen torch to char the skin side.

TO SERVE
Preheat the oven to 325°F (160°C/Gas Mark 3). Remove the caviar-like pulp from the finger lime. Reheat the sea spaghetti in the brown butter. Reheat the mackerel in the oven for 2 minutes, or until cooked to your liking. Place a mackerel fillet on each serving plate with the pollen-crusted side facing up. Arrange the fennel and rock samphire salad and the sea spaghetti attractively around the fish. Add a quenelle of fennel mayonnaise and dot with the finger lime pulp and a few rock samphire sprigs.

ALBACORE TUNA BURGER WITH SOCCA FRIES

Burger de thon albacore, frites de socca

Serves 4

Active time

1 hour

Cooking time

3½ hours

Chilling time

1 hour

Marinating time

1 hour

Equipment

Immersion blender

12 × 16-in. (30 × 40-cm) silicone mold, ½ in. (1 cm) deep

Deep fryer

Instant-read thermometer

4 × 4-in. (10-cm) hamburger rings

Ingredients

Oven-dried tomatoes

8 Roma tomatoes

2 cloves garlic, peeled and thinly sliced

8 sprigs thyme

2½ tbsp (40 ml) olive oil

1 pinch sugar

Salt and freshly ground pepper

Socca fries

2 cups (500 ml) water

2 cups (6 oz./170 g) chickpea flour

1 tsp (5 g) salt

Albacore tuna burgers

1¼ lb. (600 g) skinless, boneless albacore tuna fillet

Scant ½ cup (100 ml) soy sauce

Leaves of ½ bunch cilantro

1 oz. (30 g) fresh ginger, peeled and chopped

Finely grated zest and juice of 1 lime

Generous ¾ cup (200 ml) olive oil

Wasabi mayonnaise

1 egg yolk

1 tbsp rice vinegar

3 tbsp wasabi paste

⅔ cup (160 ml) grape-seed oil

Salt and freshly ground pepper

Garnishes

4 lettuce leaves

7 oz. (200 g) carrots

Salt and freshly ground pepper

To serve

Oil for deep-frying

Salt and freshly ground pepper

4 burger buns

PREPARING THE OVEN-DRIED TOMATOES
Preheat the oven to 195°F (90°C/Gas on the lowest setting). To peel the tomatoes, score a cross on each base and briefly immerse them in boiling water; remove the skin. Cut the tomatoes crosswise into 4 equal slices, remove the seeds, and place on a rimmed baking sheet with the sliced garlic and thyme. Drizzle with the olive oil, sprinkle with the sugar, and season with salt and pepper. Dry in the oven for 3 hours.

PREPARING THE SOCCA FRIES
Preheat the oven to 250°F (130°C/Gas Mark ½) and place a bowl of water on the bottom rack, to prevent the socca from drying out. Place the water, chickpea flour, and salt in a large bowl and blend until smooth using the immersion blender. Pour the batter into the silicone mold and bake for 20–25 minutes, just until the socca is set and firm to the touch. Let rest for 5 minutes at room temperature, then press plastic wrap over the surface and refrigerate for about 1 hour, or until completely cooled.

PREPARING THE ALBACORE TUNA BURGERS
Cut the tuna into ½-in. (1-cm) dice and place in a bowl set over a larger bowl filled with ice. Place the soy sauce, cilantro leaves, ginger, lime zest and juice, and olive oil in a bowl and blend until smooth using the immersion blender. Pour this mixture over the tuna, reserving a little for the carrots. Let marinate for 1 hour in the refrigerator.

PREPARING THE WASABI MAYONNAISE
Whisk together the egg yolk and rice vinegar in a large bowl. Whisk in the wasabi paste, adjusting the amount according to your desired heat level. Whisking continuously, gradually drizzle in the grape-seed oil in a thin, steady stream, as if preparing a classic mayonnaise. Keep whisking until the mixture is thick, glossy, and emulsified. Season with a pinch of salt and reserve in the refrigerator.

PREPARING THE GARNISHES
Wash and dry the lettuce. Peel the carrots, julienne them finely, and toss them with the reserved tuna marinade.

TO COOK
To cook the socca fries, heat the oil for deep-frying to 355°F (180°C). Remove the plastic wrap from the socca mold and turn the socca out onto a work surface. Cut it into 3 equal strips, then cut each strip into long fry-like sticks. Deep-fry until deeply golden, then drain and season with salt and pepper. To cook the tuna burgers, fill the hamburger rings with the marinated tuna, pressing down gently to form compact patties. Warm a nonstick skillet over high heat, then add the tuna patties in the rings and sear each side briefly until the outsides are caramelized, but the centers remain pink. Remove from the skillet and remove the rings. Toast the buns and spread wasabi mayonnaise over the cut sides.

TO SERVE
Place the tuna burgers on the bun bases and top with the oven-dried tomato slices, lettuce, and the seasoned julienned carrots. Cover with the bun lids and serve with the socca fries and remaining wasabi mayonnaise on the side.

BRAISED GARLIC-STUDDED MONKFISH TAIL WITH KALE AND MASHED POTATOES

Gigot de lotte braisé piqué d'ail, chou kale, purée de pommes de terre

Serves 4

Active time

2 hours

Cooking time

1 hour

Equipment

Kitchen twine

12 × 6-in. (30 × 16-cm) earthenware baking dish, 4 in. (10 cm) deep

Fine-mesh sieve

Food mill

Ingredients

Monkfish tail

1 monkfish tail, weighing 2½ lb. (1.2 kg)

4 cloves garlic

2 sprigs rosemary

¾ cup + 2 tbsp (3½ oz./100 g) all-purpose flour

2 tbsp (30 ml) grape-seed oil

2 cups (500 ml) fish fumet (see technique p. 118)

1 tbsp (20 g) butter

½ bunch chives, finely chopped

Juice of ½ lemon

Salt and freshly ground pepper

Mashed potatoes

1 lb. 2 oz. (500 g) waxy potatoes, preferably Bintje

Coarse sea salt

Scant ½ cup (100 ml) whole milk

5 tbsp (2½ oz./75 g) butter, diced

Kale

15¾ oz. (450 g) kale

1 oz. (30 g) shallot

2 tbsp (1 oz./30 g) butter

Salt and freshly ground pepper

To serve

Parsley microgreens

Fleur de sel

PREPARING THE MONKFISH TAIL

Preheat the oven to 350°F (180°C/Gas Mark 4). Peel and trim the monkfish tail (see technique p. 53), then tie it like a roast using the kitchen twine (see technique p. 130). Peel the garlic, remove the germs, and cut each clove into 6 pieces. Using the tip of a paring knife, make slits in the fish on both sides, between the pieces of twine. Push a piece of garlic and some rosemary into each slit. Season the monkfish tail very lightly with salt, then roll it in the flour to coat. Heat the grape-seed oil in a sauté pan and sear the monkfish tail on all sides until pale golden brown all over. Transfer the tail to the earthenware baking dish. Bring the fish fumet to a boil and pour enough into the dish to cover the monkfish tail halfway. Cover the dish with a piece of parchment paper cut to fit snugly inside and bake for 15–20 minutes, until a metal skewer inserted into the center meets no resistance. Remove the twine and transfer the monkfish tail to a rack. Lower the oven temperature to 160°F (70°C/Gas on the lowest setting). Strain the pan juices through the fine-mesh sieve into a clean saucepan and reduce to a glaze. Remove the sauce from the heat and whisk in the butter, chives, and lemon juice. Coat the monkfish tail with the sauce and keep it warm in the oven.

PREPARING THE MASHED POTATOES

Peel and rinse the potatoes and cut them into approximately 1½-in. (4-cm) cubes. Place in a large saucepan, cover with cold water, and bring to a boil. Reduce the heat, season with coarse sea salt, and let simmer for 30 minutes, or until completely tender. In a separate saucepan, bring the milk to a boil. Drain the potatoes. While they are still warm, pass them through the food mill back into the saucepan. Stirring with a spatula, gradually stir in the butter and hot milk. Make sure the potatoes stay warm. Adjust the consistency by adding a little more milk, if necessary. Adjust the seasonings as needed.

PREPARING THE KALE

Remove the stems from the kale and blanch it in boiling salted water for 3 minutes, or until tender. Cool it in a bowl of ice water, then dry it well with paper towels. Peel and finely chop the shallot and sweat it in a large saucepan with the butter. Add the kale and stir to coat. Season with salt and pepper.

TO SERVE

Make a bed of kale on a large serving dish and place the monkfish tail on top. Scatter with parsley microgreens and sprinkle with fleur de sel. Serve the mashed potatoes in a bowl on the side.

FRIED GUDGEONS WITH CAPERS AND SAUCE VERTE

Goujons frits, câpres et sauce verte

Serves 4

Active time
1 hour

Cooking time
1 hour 10 minutes

Equipment
Food processor
Instant-read thermometer
Muslin
Deep fryer
Drum sieve

Ingredients

Parsley powder
½ bunch parsley

Sauce verte
1 bunch parsley
½ bunch watercress
½ bunch tarragon
3½ tbsp (50 ml) cold water
2 egg yolks
2 tsp (10 g) Dijon mustard
3½ tbsp (50 ml) lime juice
1 cup (250 ml) canola oil
Salt

Fried gudgeons
¾ cup + 2 tbsp (3½ oz./100 g) all-purpose flour
¼ cup (1½ oz./40 g) finely ground semolina flour
1 tsp (2 g) garlic powder
2 tsp (5 g) onion powder
¾ tsp (2 g) ground coriander
¾ tsp (2 g) sweet paprika
1¼ lb. (600 g) gudgeons
Salt

PREPARING THE PARSLEY POWDER

Preheat the oven to 120°F (50°C/Gas on the lowest setting). Wash and dry the parsley, remove the stems, and spread the leaves over a rimmed baking sheet. Dry them in the oven for 1 hour, then grind them to a fine powder in the food processor.

PREPARING THE SAUCE VERTE

Wash and dry the parsley, watercress, and tarragon, then purée them with the cold water in the food processor. Transfer the purée to a small saucepan and warm to 160°F (70°C). Maintain this temperature until the chlorophyll rises to the surface, then skim this thick layer off and strain it through the muslin, letting it drain for several minutes. In a large bowl, whisk together the egg yolks, mustard, and lime juice; season with salt. Whisking continuously, gradually drizzle in the canola oil in a thin, steady stream until the mixture is pale, thick, and emulsified. Whisk in the chlorophyll.

PREPARING THE FRIED GUDGEONS

Combine the all-purpose flour, semolina flour, garlic powder, onion powder, ground coriander, and paprika in a large bowl. Rinse the gudgeons, dry them with paper towels, and coat them with the flour mixture, then place them in the drum sieve and shake gently to remove any excess. Heat the oil for deep-frying to 355°F (180°C) and fry the gudgeons for about 3 minutes, or until golden and crisp. Season immediately with salt.

TO SERVE

Serve the fried gudgeons with the sauce verte on the side, dusted with parsley powder.

LET US SHARE GOOD MOMENTS

WHITEFISH WITH CELERY ROOT RISOTTO AND SEVRUGA CAVIAR CREAM SAUCE

Féra cuite à basse température, risotto de céleri et crème de sevruga

Serves 4

Active time

1¼ hours

Cooking time

2½ hours

Soaking time

25 minutes

Equipment

¾-in. (2-cm) round cookie cutter

Mandoline

Fish scaler

Fish bone tweezers

Fine-mesh sieve

Steam oven (or steamer)

Instant-read thermometer

4¾-in. (12-cm) stainless-steel ring

Ingredients

Garnishes

4 slices smoked bacon

2 thin slices sandwich bread

2 tbsp (1 oz./30 g) clarified butter

1 white zucchini, weighing 5¼ oz. (150 g)

1 tbsp (20 g) unsalted butter

2 pearl onions

Salt and freshly ground pepper

Celery root risotto

14 oz. (400 g) celery root (celeriac)

1¾ oz. (50 g) shallots

3 tbsp (1½ oz./40 g) butter

1¼ cups (300 ml) fish fumet (see technique p. 118) or water

Scant ¼ cup (1¾ oz./50 g) crème fraîche

½ cup (1¾ oz./50 g) grated Parmesan

Finely grated zest and juice of 1 lemon

Salt and freshly ground pepper

Whitefish

2 freshwater whitefish (*féra*), weighing 1¼ lb. (600 g) each

4 cups (1 liter) cold water

4 tsp (20 g) salt

White wine cream sauce

Heads and bones of 2 whitefish (see above)

3½ oz. (100 g) shallots

1¾ oz. (50 g) celery

2 cloves garlic

3 tbsp (1¾ oz./50 g) butter

Generous ¾ cup (200 ml) dry white wine

2 cups (500 ml) water

1 bouquet garni (thyme and bay leaf)

1 tsp (3 g) black peppercorns

Scant ½ cup (3½ oz./100 g) crème fraîche

To serve

½ bunch chives

1½ oz. (40 g) Sevruga caviar

Pea shoots

PREPARING THE GARNISHES

Preheat the oven to 300°F (150°C/Gas Mark 2). Place the bacon on a rimmed baking sheet lined with parchment paper. Cover with another sheet of parchment paper, then place a second baking sheet on top to keep the bacon flat. Bake for 25 minutes, until very crisp, then drain on paper towels. Raise the oven temperature to 340°F (170°C/Gas Mark 3) and place the sandwich bread on a baking sheet. Melt the clarified butter and brush it over the bread, coating it lightly. Bake for 10 minutes, until deeply golden, then cut out small disks using the cookie cutter. Wash the zucchini, cut it into 1½-in. (4-cm) pieces, and cut each piece into quarters. Trim the edges to give each quarter an oval shape. Place in a large saucepan with the unsalted butter and add enough water to cover halfway. Cook until the zucchini is tender and the liquid has reduced to a glaze. Peel the pearl onions and slice them very thinly. Immediately place them in ice water and let soak for 10 minutes to make them crisp. Drain the onion slices, then dry them on paper towels.

PREPARING THE CELERY ROOT RISOTTO

Wash and peel the celery root, then cut it into ⅛-in. (2-mm) dice using the mandoline. Peel and finely chop the shallots. Melt the butter in a medium saucepan over low heat and sweat the shallots for 5 minutes, until softened but not browned. Add the celery root, then add the fish fumet or water one ladleful at a time, waiting until the liquid is partially absorbed before adding the next. Ensure the celery root is never fully submerged in liquid. Continue until the celery root has an al dente texture. Remove from the heat and stir in the crème fraîche and grated Parmesan. Add a little lemon zest and a dash of lemon juice, then season with salt and pepper to taste. Set aside.

PREPARING THE WHITEFISH

Trim, scale, and gut the whitefish (see techniques pp. 34, 40, and 45), then rinse them well under running water. Fillet and skin the fish and remove the pin bones (see techniques pp. 80, 41–43, and 52). Reserve the heads and bones for the sauce. Place the cold water and salt in a large bowl and stir until the salt has dissolved completely. Place the whitefish fillets in the brine and let them soak for 12 minutes. Drain the fillets and pat them dry with paper towels, then fold each fillet in half lengthwise. Make a cut along the fold on the outer-facing side, without cutting all the way through. This keeps the fish folded and ensures a neater finish. Cover each folded fillet tightly with plastic wrap to give it an even shape. Set aside at room temperature.

PREPARING THE WHITE WINE CREAM SAUCE

Remove the gills and eyes from the reserved whitefish heads, then roughly chop the heads and bones and rinse them thoroughly under running water. Peel and finely chop the shallots, celery, and garlic. Melt the butter in a medium saucepan and sweat the shallots, celery, and garlic over medium-low heat, covered, for 10–15 minutes. Add the heads and bones, return the lid, and cook over medium heat for 5–10 minutes. Deglaze with white wine and reduce by two-thirds. Add the water, bouquet garni, and peppercorns and gently simmer for about 25 minutes, regularly skimming any foam from the surface. Strain the sauce through the fine-mesh sieve into a clean saucepan and reduce it to a glaze that coats the back of a spoon. Stir in the crème fraîche, bring to a boil, and remove from the heat.

COOKING THE WHITEFISH

Preheat the steam oven to 130°F (55°C/Gas on the lowest setting). Cook the whitefish fillets in the steam oven (or steamer) for about 20 minutes, or until the internal temperature reaches exactly 115°F (46°C). Remove the plastic wrap and place the fillets on a rack.

TO SERVE

Wash and finely chop the chives. Reheat the celery root risotto and stir in the chives just before serving. Gently reheat the white wine cream sauce, then remove it from the heat and stir in the caviar. Arrange the zucchini, bacon, toasted sandwich bread disks, and pearl onion slices attractively over the whitefish fillets and scatter with pea shoots. For each serving, place the stainless-steel ring in the center of the plate and pour an even circle of white wine cream sauce around the inside edge. Carefully fill the center of the wine-sauce ring with celery root risotto. Remove the ring and top the risotto with a garnished whitefish fillet.

COD AND LOBSTER SAUSAGES WITH COCKLES, ARTICHOKES, AND CAULIFLOWER MOUSSELINE

Boudin de cabillaud, homard et crêtes de coques, mousseline de chou-fleur

Serves 6

Active time

2 hours

Cooking time

1 hour

Marinating time

Overnight

Infusing time

10 minutes

Equipment

Fine-mesh sieve

Kitchen twine

Food processor

Pastry bag + large plain round tip

Steam oven (or steamer)

Melon baller

Ingredients

Pickled cauliflower

Generous 3/4 cup (210 ml) water

Scant 1/3 cup (70 ml) white vinegar

3/4 cup (5 oz./140 g) sugar

3 tsp (15 g) salt

3½ oz. (100 g) small yellow cauliflower florets

3½ oz. (100 g) small purple cauliflower florets

Shallot confit

1½ oz. (40 g) French gray shallots

2½ tbsp (40 ml) Noilly Prat vermouth

4 tsp (20 ml) mineral water

Infused milk

1¾ oz. (50 g) leek greens

1 clove garlic, unpeeled

1 tbsp (20 g) butter

1 cup (250 ml) whole milk

1 sprig thyme

1 sprig tarragon

1 whole clove

Cod and lobster sausages

2 lobsters

5¼ oz. (150 g) skinless, boneless cod fillets

3½ oz. (100 g) chicken breast

1 oz. (30 g) shallot confit (see left)

Scant ½ cup (100 ml) infused milk (see left)

2/3 cup (150 ml) heavy cream, min. 35% fat, well chilled

1½ tsp (7 g) salt

Scant ½ tsp (1 g) *piment d'Espelette*

½ bunch tarragon

6½ ft. (2 meters) pork casing, 32/34 mm

Cauliflower mousseline

½ head cauliflower

8 cups (2 liters) water

4 tsp (20 ml) white vinegar

Scant 1 oz. (25 g) coarse sea salt

Generous 3/4 cup (200 ml) whole milk

Generous 3/4 cup (200 ml) heavy cream, min. 35% fat

Artichokes

3 small purple artichokes

1 lemon, halved

Generous 3/4 cup (200 ml) water

1¼ tsp (5 g) sugar

3 tbsp (1¾ oz./50 g) butter, well chilled

2 tbsp (30 ml) olive oil

Cockles marinière

4¼ oz. (120 g) shallots

1/5 oz. (5 g) flat-leaf parsley

2 tbsp (1 oz./30 g) butter

2¼ lb. (1 kg) cockles, soaked in salted water

Generous 3/4 cup (200 ml) white wine

3½ tbsp (50 ml) heavy cream, min. 35% fat

PREPARING THE PICKLED CAULIFLOWER (1 DAY AHEAD)

Warm the water, vinegar, sugar, and salt in a saucepan until the sugar and salt dissolve, then bring to a boil. Place the yellow and purple cauliflower florets in two separate bowls. Pour the boiling brine over them, then cover and let marinate overnight in the refrigerator.

PREPARING THE SHALLOT CONFIT

Peel and finely chop the shallots and place them in a small saucepan with the vermouth and mineral water. Cook, covered, until all the liquid has evaporated and the shallots are fall-apart tender.

PREPARING THE INFUSED MILK

Wash and thinly slice the leek greens and sweat them in a saucepan with the garlic and butter over low heat, until softened but not browned. Add the milk and let simmer for 5 minutes, then remove from the heat and add the thyme, tarragon, and clove. Cover the saucepan with plastic wrap and let infuse for 10 minutes. Strain the milk through the fine-mesh sieve and chill until cold.

PREPARING THE COD AND LOBSTER SAUSAGES

Cook the lobsters (see technique p. 124), placing them in the pot claw side down—the tails should cook for 2 minutes, and the claws for 8 minutes. Plunge the lobsters into ice water to cool them quickly. Cut the cod and chicken breast into pieces, place in the food processor with the shallot confit, and process until smooth. Add the infused milk, followed by the cream, salt, and *piment d'Espelette*. Process again until smooth. Shell the lobsters (see technique p. 112). Weigh out 8¾ oz. (250 g) of the claw meat and cut it into small dice. Reserve the lobster tails for serving. Wash, dry, and finely chop the tarragon. Fold the diced lobster meat and tarragon into the cod and chicken mixture, then transfer it to the pastry bag. Pipe the filling into the pork casing and tie a knot at the end. Shape into 6 individual sausages weighing 3½ oz. (100 g) each, twisting in opposite directions between each one to separate them well. Poach the sausages in simmering water for 10 minutes. Alternatively, cook them in the steam oven at 176°F (80°C) for 10 minutes.

PREPARING THE CAULIFLOWER MOUSSELINE

Wash the cauliflower and cut it into ½-in. (1-cm) pieces. Bring the water, vinegar, and salt to a boil in a large saucepan. Add the cauliflower and cook for 10 minutes, or until fall-apart tender. In a separate saucepan, bring the milk and cream to a boil. Drain the cauliflower, place it in the food processor, and process with enough of the milk and cream mixture to obtain a smooth purée. Adjust the seasonings if necessary.

PREPARING THE ARTICHOKES

Cut the stems off the artichokes about 2 in. (4–5 cm) below the base, trim the tops, and pull off the outer leaves. Peel the stems, then trim around the hearts using a paring knife. Cut the artichokes in half and scoop out the chokes using the melon baller. Rub with the lemon and reserve in a bowl of water until cooking. Place the artichokes in a sauté pan with the generous ¾ cup (200 ml) water, sugar, butter, and olive oil, and cook at a gentle simmer for 10 minutes.

PREPARING THE COCKLES MARINIÈRE

Peel and chop the shallots. Finely chop the parsley. Melt the butter in a Dutch oven and sweat the shallots until softened but not browned. Add the cockles and the wine and cook for 3–5 minutes over high heat, stirring often, until all the shells have opened. Remove the cockles from their shells and reserve them in a saucepan with 4 tbsp of the pan juices and the parsley. Strain the remaining pan juices through the fine-mesh sieve into a clean saucepan, add the cream, and bring to a boil. Blend in the food processor to obtain a foam.

TO SERVE

Preheat the steam oven to 175°F (80°C/Gas on the lowest setting). Place the sausages and reserved lobster tails in a baking dish, cover with plastic wrap, and reheat in the steam oven (or steamer) for 10 minutes. Reheat the artichokes and cockles together in the same saucepan with the 4 tbsp of pan juices. Cut each sausage at an angle into 3 pieces and cut each lobster tail lengthwise into 3 pieces. Place a little cauliflower mousseline in the center of each serving plate. Arrange the sausage, artichokes, cockles, pickled cauliflower florets, and lobster around the mousseline, then add a few mounds of cockle foam.

SEA BASS WITH EINKORN RISOTTO AND PORCINI MUSHROOMS

Bar et risotto de petit épeautre aux cèpes

Serves 4

Active time

2½ hours

Cooking time

4–5 hours

Equipment

Mandoline

Fine-mesh sieve

Food processor

Oven-safe skillet

Ingredients

Candied porcini slices

Generous ¾ cup (200 ml) water

¼ cup (2¾ oz./80 g) glucose syrup

Scant ½ tsp (2 g) salt

3½ oz. (100 g) fresh porcini mushrooms

Toasted hazelnuts

⅓ cup (1¾ oz./50 g) hazelnuts

Einkorn risotto

5¼ oz. (150 g) einkorn berries, soaked in water for 12 hours at room temperature

1¾ oz. (50 g) shallots

2 tbsp (25 g) butter

2 tsp (10 ml) white wine

4 cups (1 liter) vegetable broth or white stock

Generous ½ cup (2 oz./60 g) grated Parmesan

2 tsp (10 ml) heavy cream, min. 35% fat

Salt

Mushroom jus

3½ oz. (100 g) onions

1 lb. 2 oz. (500 g) button mushrooms

1 clove garlic

3½ tbsp (50 ml) sunflower oil

Scant ⅓ cup (2¾ oz./80 g) teriyaki sauce

⅓ oz. (10 g) black garlic

4 cups (1 liter) mushroom or vegetable stock

1 bouquet garni (bay leaf and thyme tied up in a leek green)

Mushroom powder

3½ oz. (100 g) dried mushrooms

Porcini mushrooms

1 clove garlic

8¾ oz. (250 g) fresh porcini mushrooms

3 tbsp (1½ oz./40 g) clarified butter

1 sprig thyme

Salt

Sea bass with crispy scales

1¼ lb. (600 g) boneless, skin-on sea bass fillet, left unscaled

2 tsp (10 ml) canola oil

2 tsp (10 g) butter, browned and melted

Salt

To serve

Marigold petals

Micro anise hyssop leaves

PREPARING THE CANDIED PORCINI SLICES

Preheat the oven to 115°F (45°C/Gas on the lowest setting) and line a rimmed baking sheet with parchment paper. Heat the water, glucose syrup, and salt in a saucepan and boil to obtain a syrup. Let cool. Use a soft brush to clean the porcini mushrooms, removing any dirt or debris, then cut them into approximately 1⁄16-in. (1-mm) slices using the mandoline. Immerse the slices in the syrup to coat, then place them on the prepared baking sheet in a single layer. Dry in the oven for 2–3 hours, or until completely dry.

PREPARING THE TOASTED HAZELNUTS

Preheat the oven to 325°F (160°C/Gas Mark 3). Spread the hazelnuts over a rimmed baking sheet lined with parchment paper and toast them in the oven for 8 minutes. Let cool slightly, then chop roughly.

PREPARING THE EINKORN RISOTTO

Place the soaked einkorn berries in a large pot of cold water and bring to a boil. Blanch for 5 minutes, then drain. Peel and finely chop the shallots and sweat them in a large skillet with the butter. Add the einkorn berries, then deglaze with the wine and cook until all the liquid has evaporated. Add the broth one ladleful at a time, waiting until the einkorn absorbs all the liquid before adding the next, gradually adjusting the amount as needed. Cook for about 40 minutes in total. Remove from the heat and stir in the Parmesan, followed by the cream. Adjust the seasonings if necessary.

PREPARING THE MUSHROOM JUS

Peel and finely chop the onions. Wipe and thinly slice the mushrooms. Peel and roughly crush the garlic. Heat the sunflower oil in a large saucepan over medium-high heat and sweat the onions, mushrooms, and garlic until softened, then increase the heat to high and cook until browned. Deglaze with the teriyaki sauce, then add the black garlic and let reduce for 2 minutes. Deglaze with the stock, add the bouquet garni, and let simmer for 45 minutes. Strain the jus through the fine-mesh sieve into a clean saucepan and reduce it again until syrupy and glossy.

PREPARING THE MUSHROOM POWDER

Grind the dried mushrooms to a fine powder in the food processor.

PREPARING THE PORCINI MUSHROOMS

Peel the garlic clove and cut it in half. Use a soft brush to clean the porcini mushrooms, removing any dirt or debris, then cut them in half lengthwise. Heat the clarified butter in a skillet and add the porcini cut side down. Add the garlic and thyme and cook until the cut sides are evenly golden brown. Turn the mushrooms over and season them with salt. Cook until just tender, then remove from the heat.

PREPARING THE SEA BASS WITH CRISPY SCALES

Preheat the broiler. Cut the sea bass fillet into 4 equal pieces, pat them dry on both sides with paper towels, and season them with salt. Heat the oil in the oven-safe skillet and pan-fry the fish fillets skin side down for about 1½ minutes, then turn the fillets over and brush the skin with the browned butter. Place under the broiler for 1–2 minutes, or until the scales turn crisp and flake away from the skin.

TO SERVE

Dust one end of each serving plate with mushroom powder and place a sea bass fillet alongside, skin side up. Make a rectangle of einkorn risotto opposite the sea bass and arrange the sautéed and candied porcini mushrooms on top. Garnish with toasted hazelnuts, marigold petals, and micro anise hyssop leaves. Drizzle a little mushroom jus in the center of each plate and serve the rest in a small jug on the side.

ANCHOÏADE TARTINES WITH VEGETABLES AND PICKLED MUSTARD SEEDS

Tartine d'anchoïade, légumes crus et graines de moutarde

Serves 4

Active time
1 hour

Cooking time
10 minutes

Storage
3 days

Equipment
Sterilized 1-cup (250-ml) jar
Food processor
Mandoline
Fine-mesh sieve

Ingredients

Pickled mustard seeds
2/3 cup (150 ml) spirit vinegar
Scant 1/2 cup (100 ml) water
1/4 cup (1 3/4 oz./50 g) sugar
1/3 cup (2 oz./60 g) mustard seeds

Anchoïade
1 sprig lovage
1 sprig parsley
1 clove garlic
1 3/4 oz. (50 g) onion
1 1/4 tsp (5 g) sugar
8 3/4 oz. (250 g) oil-packed anchovies
Generous 3/4 cup (200 ml) olive oil
1 ice cube

Vegetables
3 1/2 oz. (100 g) red radishes
3 1/2 oz. (100 g) cucumber
1/3 oz. (10 g) fennel
1 yellow carrot
1 stalk celery
3 1/2 oz. (100 g) fresh peas in their pods
Scant 1/2 cup (100 ml) olive oil
3 1/2 tbsp (50 ml) apple cider vinegar
1/2 tsp (2 g) sugar
Salt

Tartine bases
1 clove garlic
Generous 3/4 cup (200 ml) olive oil
4 slices country bread

To serve
2 sheets nori, finely julienned
Nasturtium flowers and leaves

PREPARING THE PICKLED MUSTARD SEEDS

Warm the vinegar, water, and sugar in a saucepan until the sugar dissolves, then bring to a boil. Add the mustard seeds and let simmer for 2 minutes. Pour the mixture into the 1-cup (250-ml) jar and let cool to room temperature.

PREPARING THE ANCHOÏADE

Wash and dry the lovage and parsley. Peel and roughly chop the garlic and onion. Place all four in the food processor with the sugar and process until smooth. Add the anchovies and process again until smooth. With the motor running, gradually pour the oil down the feeder tube to emulsify. Blend in the ice cube at the end to firm up the mixture.

PREPARING THE VEGETABLES

Wash the radishes and cut them crosswise into 1/16-in. (1-mm) slices using the mandoline. Wash the cucumber, fennel, and carrot, and cut each one lengthwise into strips, 1/16 in. (1 mm) thick, using the mandoline. Place the cucumber strips in a colander, sprinkle them with salt, and let them sit until they begin to release their water. Dry the cucumber strips in a clean dish towel, then roll them. Wash, peel, and finely dice the celery, reserving the central leaves for garnishing. Shell the peas and blanch them in boiling salted water. Let cool. Whisk together the olive oil, apple cider vinegar, and sugar to make a vinaigrette.

PREPARING THE TARTINE BASES

Peel the garlic clove and cut it in half crosswise. Warm the olive oil in a skillet and brown the country bread slices for 2 minutes on each side. Rub one side of each slice with the garlic.

TO SERVE

Spread the anchoïade over the garlic-rubbed sides of the tartine bases. Toss the vegetables with the vinaigrette and arrange them attractively over the anchoïade. Add a few spoonfuls of pickled mustard seeds, then garnish with the julienned nori, reserved celery leaves, and nasturtium flowers and leaves.

COD CONFIT WITH MISO-GLAZED BUTTERNUT SQUASH MILLEFEUILLES

Cabillaud confit et butternut au miso

Serves 4

Active time
1½ hours

Cooking time
1½ hours

Cooling time
1 hour

Soaking time
10 minutes

Equipment
- Mandoline
- 8 × 2¾-in. (20 × 7-cm) loaf pan, 3 in. (8 cm) deep
- 1½-in. (4-cm) round cookie cutter
- Instant-read thermometer
- Food processor
- Sauce bottle or pastry bag with a plain round tip
- Large oven-safe saucepan
- Kitchen torch

Ingredients

Miso-glazed butternut squash millefeuilles
- 3 tbsp (1¾ oz./50 g) clarified butter
- 1½ tsp (10 g) brown (genmai) miso
- 1 lb. 2 oz. (500 g) butternut squash

Fried rice paper tuiles
- Generous ¾ cup (200 ml) oil for deep-frying
- 2 sheets rice paper

Sesame-egg yolk sauce
- 4 egg yolks, left whole
- 2 cups (500 ml) olive oil
- 2 tsp (10 g) tahini
- ¾ tsp (5 g) brown (genmai) miso

Cod confit
- 4 cups (1 liter) water
- Scant ½ cup (3½ oz./100 g) salt
- 1¼ lb. (600 g) boneless, skinless cod fillet
- 2 cups (500 ml) olive oil (reserved from above)
- ⅕ oz. (5 g) dried bonito flakes (katsuobushi)

To serve
- 1 tbsp (15 g) butter, melted
- 1½ tsp (5 g) gomasio
- ⅓ oz. (10 g) dried bonito flakes (katsuobushi)
- 4 shiso microgreens

PREPARING THE MISO-GLAZED BUTTERNUT SQUASH MILLEFEUILLES
Preheat the oven to 350°F (180°C/Gas Mark 4). Melt the clarified butter in a saucepan and stir in the miso. Peel the butternut squash, remove the seeds, and cut it crosswise into 1⁄16-in. (1-mm) slices using the mandoline. Place the slices in a large bowl and pour the miso butter over them. Stir to coat. Arrange the slices in layers in the loaf pan, cover with a piece of parchment paper, and place an oven-safe weight over the top to act as a press. Bake for 45 minutes, then let cool for 1 hour at room temperature. Cut out the millefeuilles using the cookie cutter.

PREPARING THE FRIED RICE PAPER TUILES
In a high-sided skillet, heat the oil for deep-frying to 355°F (180°C). Deep-fry the rice paper sheets until curled and crisp. Drain on paper towels and season with salt.

PREPARING THE SESAME-EGG YOLK SAUCE
Carefully place the egg yolks in a saucepan, taking care not to break them. Cover them with the olive oil and poach them at 154°F (68°C) for 30 minutes. They should have a creamy texture. Transfer the yolks to the food processor, reserving the oil for cooking the cod. Add the tahini and miso to the food processor and process until smooth. Transfer to a sauce bottle or pastry bag fitted with a plain round tip.

PREPARING THE COD CONFIT
Preheat the oven to 175°F (80°C/Gas on the lowest setting). Place the water and salt in a large bowl and stir until the salt has dissolved completely. Cut the cod fillet into 4 equal pieces, place it in the brine, and let it soak for 10 minutes in the refrigerator. Drain the fish and pat it dry with paper towels. Place the reserved olive oil and dried bonito flakes in the large oven-safe saucepan and heat to 176°F (80°C). Carefully lower the cod into the oil, then place the saucepan in the oven and let poach for about 10 minutes, or until the cod's internal temperature reaches 124°F (51°C).

TO SERVE
Char the butternut squash millefeuilles using the kitchen torch, then brush with the melted butter to give them a glossy sheen. Place a piece of confit cod on each serving plate, skin side up. Place a butternut squash millefeuille next to the fish and top it with a fried rice paper tuile. Add several mounds of sesame-egg yolk sauce of different sizes and sprinkle with gomasio. Garnish with a small handful of dried bonito flakes and shiso microgreens.

HADDOCK AND MUSSEL BLANQUETTE

Blanquette de la mer au haddock

Serves 4

Active time

1½ hours

Soaking time

2–3 hours

Cooking time

1 hour

Equipment

Fine-mesh sieve

Ingredients

Haddock

- 14 oz. (400 g) smoked haddock fillets
- 1 cup (250 ml) whole milk
- 3 cups (750 ml) fish fumet (see technique p. 118)
- 10½ oz. (300 g) skinless, boneless fresh haddock fillet

Mussels marinière

- 1 tbsp (15 g) butter
- 1¾ oz. (50 g) shallots, chopped
- 1 clove garlic, finely chopped
- 1 bouquet garni (2 parsley sprigs, 2 thyme sprigs, and 1 bay leaf wrapped in a leek green)
- 1½ lb. (750 g) mussels, cleaned (see technique p. 60)
- 1 cup (250 ml) dry white wine
- 1 tbsp (3 g) finely chopped parsley

Vegetables

- 8¾ oz. (250 g) baby leeks
- 3½ tbsp (50 ml) olive oil, divided
- 7 oz. (200 g) peas in their pods, shelled
- 8¾ oz. (250 g) button mushrooms
- 8¾ oz. (250 g) scallions
- 5¼ oz. (150 g) snow peas
- Scant ½ cup (100 ml) water
- 4 tsp (20 ml) lemon juice
- Salt

Sauce

- Reserved poaching liquid (see left)
- 2½ tbsp (1½ oz./40 g) egg yolk (2 yolks)
- ⅔ cup (150 ml) crème fraîche
- 3 tbsp (1¾ oz./50 g) butter
- Scant ½ cup (1¾ oz./50 g) all-purpose flour
- Reserved mussels marinière liquid (see left)

PREPARING THE HADDOCK

Cover the smoked haddock with cold water and let it soak for 2–3 hours to remove excess salt. Drain the smoked haddock and cut it into 1¼–1½-in. (3–4-cm) cubes. Place in a large saucepan with the milk and fish fumet (both should be at room temperature or cold) and bring to a boil. Poach the smoked haddock for 2 minutes, then remove it with a slotted spoon and let both the fish and the poaching liquid cool to room temperature. Cut the fresh haddock into 1¼–1½-in. (3–4-cm) cubes, place it in the cooled poaching liquid, and bring to a boil. Let poach for 2 minutes, then remove with a slotted spoon and let cool. Reserve the poaching liquid for the sauce.

PREPARING THE MUSSELS MARINIÈRE

Melt the butter in a Dutch oven, then add the shallots and garlic and cook until softened. Add the bouquet garni, mussels, and white wine. Cook for 3–5 minutes over high heat, stirring often, or until all the mussels have opened. Add the parsley. Remove the mussels from their shells and strain the liquid through the fine-mesh sieve, reserving it for the sauce.

PREPARING THE VEGETABLES

Preheat the oven to 350°F (180°C/Gas Mark 4). Wash and trim the leeks, then wrap them in an aluminum foil packet with 4 tsp (20 ml) of the olive oil and a little salt. Roast in the oven for 20 minutes. Clean the mushrooms. Thinly slice the scallions. Cook the shelled peas in a large pot of boiling salted water until just tender, then transfer to a bowl of ice water using a slotted spoon. Cook the snow peas in the same pot until they are crisp-tender, then plunge into ice water. Place the mushrooms in a sauté pan with the remaining olive oil, water, and lemon juice and cook, covered, for 8 minutes. Cut the roasted leeks at an angle into approximately ½-in. (1-cm) pieces.

PREPARING THE SAUCE

Reheat the haddock poaching liquid. Whisk together the egg yolk and crème fraîche in a medium bowl. To make a white roux, melt the butter in a large saucepan until foamy, then whisk in the flour until smooth. Whisking continuously, cook for a couple of minutes until slightly thickened, but not browned. Gradually whisk in 4 cups (1 liter) of the hot poaching liquid and cook over low heat for 3 minutes, whisking continuously. Whisk in the strained mussels marinière liquid, then remove from the heat. While the sauce is still hot, whisk a little into the egg yolk and crème fraîche mixture to temper the yolks, then whisk this mixture into the sauce. Do not let the sauce boil after this, or the yolks will curdle. Adjust the seasonings and consistency as necessary, then strain through the fine-mesh sieve into a Dutch oven.

TO SERVE

Gently reheat the sauce, if necessary. Add the fish, mussels, and vegetables, scatter over the scallion greens, and serve directly from the pot.

TROUT PITHIVIERS

Pithiviers à la truite

Serves 4

Active time

3 hours

Soaking time

15 minutes

Cooking time

1½ hours

Chilling time

1 hour

Resting time

1 hour

Storage

2 days

Equipment

Fish bone tweezers

6-in. (16-cm) round pastry cutter

Food processor

8-in. (20-cm) nonstick skillet

8½-in. (22-cm) round pastry cutter

6-in. (16-cm) tart ring

Instant-read thermometer

Ingredients

Trout layer

1¼ lb. (600 g) trout fillet, slightly over 6 in. (16 cm) wide

4 cups (1 liter) water

Scant ¼ cup (1¾ oz./50 g) salt

Beluga lentil layer

1¼ cups (8¾ oz./250 g) Beluga lentils

1¾ oz. (50 g) carrots

1¾ oz. (50 g) onion

1 tbsp (20 g) butter

1 bouquet garni (parsley, bay leaf, and thyme tied up in a leek green)

2 whole cloves

4 cups (1 liter) white stock, at room temperature or cold

Salt and freshly ground pepper

Mushroom duxelles

1¾ oz. (50 g) shallots

1½ lb. (750 g) button mushrooms

2 tbsp (25 g) butter

Herb crêpes

½ bunch parsley

¼ bunch chives

¼ bunch lovage

2 eggs

Scant ½ tsp (2 g) salt

1 cup (4½ oz./125 g) all-purpose flour

1 cup (250 ml) whole milk

Neutral oil

Spinach omelets

3½ oz. (100 g) fresh spinach

1¾ oz. (50 g) sorrel

2 tbsp (25 g) butter

3 eggs

Scant ½ tsp (2 g) salt

Neutral oil

To assemble

1¼ lb. (600 g) puff pastry dough, store-bought or homemade

1 egg yolk

4 tsp (20 ml) whole milk

PREPARING THE TROUT LAYER

Remove the skin and pin bones from the trout fillet (see techniques pp. 41 and 52). Place the water and salt in a large bowl and stir until the salt has dissolved completely. Place the trout in the brine and let soak for 15 minutes. Drain the fish, then cut out a 6-in. (16-cm) disk using the pastry cutter. Reserve the remaining fish for another recipe.

PREPARING THE BELUGA LENTIL LAYER

Rinse the lentils. Peel and roughly chop the carrots and onion. Melt the butter in a large pot and sweat the carrots and onion until softened but not browned. Add the lentils, bouquet garni, cloves, and stock and bring to a boil. Let simmer for 10 minutes, or until the lentils are just tender but not falling apart. Remove three-quarters of the lentils using a slotted spoon, let them drain and set aside. Cook the remaining lentils for an additional 10 minutes, then drain them, reserving the stock. Remove the vegetables, bouquet garni, and cloves and place the remaining lentils in the food processor. Add a little stock and process until smooth. Fold in the reserved lentils and season with salt and pepper.

PREPARING THE MUSHROOM DUXELLES

Peel and finely chop the shallots. Peel and finely chop the mushrooms. Melt the butter in a large saucepan and sweat the shallots until softened but not browned. Add the mushrooms and cook over low heat until the mushrooms release their liquid and it evaporates. Season with salt.

PREPARING THE HERB CRÊPES

Wash and dry the parsley, chives, and lovage, place them in the food processor, and process until smooth. Whisk together the eggs in a large bowl, then whisk in the chopped herbs and salt. Gradually whisk in the flour, followed by the milk; whisk until smooth. Warm the 8-in. (20-cm) nonstick skillet over medium-low heat, brush it with a little neutral oil, then add half the batter, tilting the pan to coat the base evenly. Cook for a few minutes on each side, until set. Repeat this process with the remaining batter.

PREPARING THE SPINACH OMELETS

Wash and drain the spinach and sorrel and remove the stems. Melt the butter in a large saucepan over low heat, without letting it brown. Add the spinach and sorrel and cook for a few minutes, until they wilt. Drain in a colander, pressing down to release as much liquid as possible. Whisk together the eggs and salt in a large bowl, then stir in the spinach and sorrel. Grease the 8-in. (20-cm) nonstick skillet with a little neutral oil. Pour in a small amount of the omelet mixture to obtain a thickness of 1⁄16–1⁄8 in. (2–3 mm). Cook until the surface is just set, then remove the omelet from the pan. Repeat this process to cook a second omelet.

ASSEMBLING AND BAKING THE PITHIVIERS

Roll the pastry dough to a thickness of about 1⁄8 in. (4 mm) and cut out two disks using the 8½-in. (22-cm) pastry cutter. Place one pastry disk on a baking sheet lined with parchment paper, then set the tart ring in the center, leaving an even border all the way around. Cut the herb crêpes into disks using the 6-in. (16-cm) pastry cutter and place one over the dough in the ring. Cover with half the lentils, top with a spinach omelet, and then add half the mushroom duxelles, spreading it evenly. Add the trout, then repeat the layers in reverse order to obtain a symmetrical appearance. Remove the tart ring, then brush water around the pastry border to moisten it. Cover with the second pastry disk and press down to seal the edges well without leaving visible marks on the dough. Crimp all the way around. Whisk together the egg yolk and milk to make an egg wash, brush it over the pithiviers, and chill for 1 hour. Preheat the oven to 400°F (200°C/Gas Mark 6). Brush the pithiviers again with the egg wash and decorate the top as you wish using the tip of a paring knife. Make a hole (chimney) in the center to allow steam to escape. Bake for 10 minutes at 400°F (200°C/Gas Mark 6), then lower the oven temperature to 340°F (170°C/Gas Mark 3) and continue baking for about 30 minutes, or until the internal temperature reaches 113°F (45°C). Serve warm.

YELLOWTAIL CARPACCIO WITH DANMUJI, CUCUMBER GELÉE, AND PONZU EMULSION

Carpaccio de sériole, émulsion de ponzu, danmuji et gelée de concombre

Serves 4

Active time
1 hour

Cooking time
5 minutes

Chilling time
Overnight + 4 hours

Blending time
30 minutes

Setting time
2 hours

Equipment
Mandoline
Sterilized 4-cup (1-liter) jar
Blender
Instant-read thermometer
Coffee filter
Fine-mesh sieve
½-in. (15-mm) diamond-shaped cookie cutter
Immersion blender
Sauce bottle

Ingredients

Danmuji
7 oz. (200 g) long turnip or daikon radish
1 cup + 4 tsp (270 ml) water
¾ cup (180 ml) rice vinegar
⅓ cup (2½ oz./70 g) sugar
2 tbsp (30 ml) soy sauce
2 star anise pods
1½ tsp (5 g) peppercorns
2 tsp (5 g) ground turmeric

Chive oil
4 bunches chives
Generous ¾ cup (200 ml) grape-seed oil

Cucumber gelée
2 sheets (4 g) gelatin (200 Bloom)
1 cucumber
4 tsp (20 ml) rice vinegar
Scant ½ tsp (2 g) salt

Red onion
½ red onion

Yellowtail
14 oz. (400 g) yellowtail (hamachi) fillet
2½ tbsp (40 ml) ponzu sauce
Fleur de sel

Ponzu-ginger emulsion
Scant 1 oz. (25 g) fresh ginger
3 tbsp + 1 tsp (1½ oz./45 g) egg white (1½ whites)
1 tbsp (15 ml) lime juice
1 tbsp (15 ml) ponzu sauce
Scant ½ tsp (2 g) salt
¾ cup (180 ml) grape-seed oil
4 tsp (20 ml) water

To serve
Shiso microgreens
Petals of 2 marigold flowers

PREPARING THE DANMUJI (1 DAY AHEAD)

Peel the turnip or radish and cut it crosswise into slices approximately ⅛-in. (4-mm) thick using the mandoline. Place the slices in the 4-cup (1-liter) jar. Heat the water, vinegar, sugar, soy sauce, star anise, peppercorns, and turmeric in a saucepan until the sugar dissolves, then bring to a boil. Immediately pour the hot liquid over the turnip or radish, then close the jar and let cool to room temperature. Let sit overnight in the refrigerator.

PREPARING THE CHIVE OIL

Wash and dry the chives and place them in the blender with the grape-seed oil. Blend for 30 minutes, or until the mixture reaches 149°F (65°C): the friction of the blender will heat the oil sufficiently. Test the temperature periodically using the instant-read thermometer. Strain through the coffee filter and let sit for 4 hours in the refrigerator.

PREPARING THE CUCUMBER GELÉE

Soak the gelatin in a bowl of cold water until softened. Wash the cucumber, cut it into 8 pieces, and blend for 5 minutes on high speed. Strain the cucumber mixture through the fine-mesh sieve into a large bowl, without pressing down, then measure out ¾ cup (180 ml) of the cucumber juice and combine it with the rice vinegar and salt in a bowl. Squeeze the gelatin to remove excess water, then melt it in a bowl set over a pan of barely simmering water. Whisk 3½ tbsp (50 ml) of the seasoned cucumber juice into the gelatin, then pour this mixture into the bowl with the remaining cucumber juice and whisk to combine. Pour into a tray, to a thickness of about ⅛ in. (4 mm), and let set for 2 hours in the refrigerator. Once the cucumber gelée has set, cut out 24 diamond shapes using the cookie cutter.

PREPARING THE RED ONION

Peel the red onion and slice it thinly crosswise. Let the slices soak in ice water for 15 minutes, then drain on paper towels.

PREPARING THE YELLOWTAIL

Cut the yellowtail fillet in half lengthwise. Remove any remaining pin bones using the tip of a knife. Remove the skin (see technique p. 41). Cut the fish into slices, ¼ in. (5 mm) thick, and let it marinate in the ponzu sauce with the fleur de sel for up to 15 minutes.

PREPARING THE PONZU-GINGER EMULSION

Peel the ginger and place it in a bowl with the egg white, lime juice, ponzu sauce, and salt. Using the immersion blender, process until smooth. Add the oil and blend until the mixture emulsifies. Adjust the consistency with a little water, if necessary, then transfer to the sauce bottle.

TO SERVE

Arrange the yellowtail slices on each serving plate, then add the danmuji and cucumber gelée diamonds. Fill in the empty spaces with ponzu-ginger emulsion and dots of chive oil. Garnish with the red onion rings, shiso microgreens, and marigold petals.

CAJUN-MARINATED SWORDFISH WITH CORN

Espadon mariné aux épices cajun et au maïs

Serves 4

Active time

1¼ hours

Cooking time

1½ hours

Marinating time

2 hours

Equipment

Instant-read thermometer

Food processor

Fine-mesh sieve

Kitchen torch

Mandoline

Microplane grater

Ingredients

Marinated swordfish

1 lb. (480 g) skinless, boneless swordfish fillet

3 tbsp (20 g) Cajun spice mix

1¼ tsp (6 g) salt

Scant ½ cup (100 ml) canola oil

Roasted vegetable jus

8¾ oz. (250 g) white onions

1 head garlic

8¾ oz. (250 g) cluster tomatoes

1¾ oz. (50 g) sweet red chili peppers (*piment long rouge*)

Vegetables

6 ears corn

7 tbsp (3½ oz./100 g) salted butter, at room temperature

2 pink radishes

1 scallion

To serve

½ tsp (2 g) fleur de sel

Juice and finely grated zest of 1 lime

PREPARING THE MARINATED SWORDFISH

Cut the swordfish into 4 cylindrical pieces weighing 4¼ oz. (120 g) each. Toast the Cajun spice mix for 1 minute in an ungreased skillet over medium heat, then transfer it to a bowl, add the salt and canola oil, and stir to combine. Pour over the swordfish and let marinate for 2 hours in the refrigerator. Sear the swordfish tataki-style in a hot, ungreased skillet for 1 minute on each side, or until the internal temperature reaches 100°F (38°C). Reserve at room temperature.

PREPARING THE JUS

Preheat the oven to 400°F (200°C/Gas Mark 6). Peel and quarter the onions. Cut the head of garlic in half crosswise. Wash the tomatoes and chili peppers and cut them in half as well. Place the vegetables in a baking dish and roast them in the oven until completely tender and deeply golden brown (about 30 minutes). Purée the vegetables in the food processor, then strain through the fine-mesh sieve into a saucepan and reduce until thickened.

PREPARING THE VEGETABLES

Shuck the corn and cook it in a pot of boiling salted water for 45 minutes. As soon as it is cool enough to handle, cut eight 1¼ × 2¾-in. (3 × 7-cm) strips of kernels off the cobs, then remove the remaining kernels. Char the strips using the kitchen torch. Place the loose kernels in the food processor with the butter and process until smooth, then strain through the fine-mesh sieve. Wash the radishes and cut them into paper-thin slices, about 1⁄16 in. (1 mm) thick, using the mandoline. Wash the scallion and cut it at an angle into ⅛-in. (2-mm) slices.

TO SERVE

Preheat the oven to 325°F (160°C/Gas Mark 3), then reheat the corn strips, processed corn, and swordfish in the oven for 2 minutes. For each serving, cut a swordfish cylinder into 3 pieces, place on a plate, and sprinkle with fleur de sel. Add a little roasted vegetable jus, drizzle a little lime juice over the fish, and scatter with lime zest. Serve the vegetables in individual bowls on the side.

*Classed as a flatfish yielding 2 fillets in France (see p. 16)

FLATFISH

SOLE MEUNIÈRE GRENOBLOISE WITH CREAMY POLENTA

Filet de sole meunière, garniture grenobloise

Serves 4

Active time
1½ hours

Cooking time
30 minutes

Equipment
Fine-mesh sieve
Whipping siphon + 1 N2O gas cartridge
8 skewers

Ingredients

Grenobloise garnish
- 4 slices sandwich bread
- 3 tbsp (1¾ oz./50 g) clarified butter
- 2 lemons
- 1½ oz. (40 g) capers
- ¼ bunch parsley

Fried capers
- Oil for deep-frying
- 1¾ oz. (50 g) capers

Brown butter emulsion
- 1 stick + 2 tsp (4½ oz./125 g) butter
- 2 tsp (10 ml) lemon juice
- ⅔ cup (150 ml) heavy cream, min. 35% fat
- 1 tsp (2 g) agar-agar powder
- Salt and ground white pepper

Sole meunière
- 4 whole soles
- ⅔ cup (2½ oz./75 g) all-purpose flour
- 4 tsp (20 ml) canola oil
- 1 stick (4 oz./120 g) butter, divided
- Lemon juice reserved from above, plus extra if needed
- Salt and freshly ground pepper

Creamy citrus polenta
- 2¾ cups (650 ml) whole milk
- Generous ¾ cup (4½ oz./130 g) fine polenta
- Finely grated zest and juice of ½ lime
- Scant ½ cup (100 ml) heavy cream, min. 35% fat
- ½ tsp (2 g) butter
- Salt

PREPARING THE GRENOBLOISE GARNISH
Cut the sandwich bread into approximately ⅛-in. (4-mm) dice and sauté in a hot skillet with the clarified butter until evenly golden brown. Peel the lemons, removing all the white pith. Holding the lemons over a bowl to catch any juice that runs out, remove the segments and cut them into small dice. Reserve the juice for the sole meunière. Drain the capers. Wash and dry the parsley and remove the stems.

PREPARING THE FRIED CAPERS
Heat the oil for deep-frying in a high-sided saucepan. Drain the capers and pat dry. Fry in the oil until lightly golden brown. Drain on paper towels.

PREPARING THE BROWN BUTTER EMULSION
Heat the butter in a large saucepan until it browns and has a nutty aroma. Add the lemon juice, followed by the cream and agar-agar powder. Season with salt and white pepper and let boil for a few seconds, then strain through the fine-mesh sieve. Transfer the emulsion to the whipping siphon, charge it with the cartridge, and shake the siphon to distribute the gas. Keep warm in a bain-marie until serving.

PREPARING THE SOLE MEUNIÈRE
Trim, gut, and fillet the soles (see techniques pp. 35, 50, and 90). Season the fillets with salt and pepper, then roll each one up, secure it with a skewer, and lightly coat with flour. Heat the oil and 3 tbsp (1½ oz./40 g) of the butter in a skillet until the butter begins to foam. Add the fish rolls and cook for 2–4 minutes on each flat side, depending on the thickness of the rolls, basting regularly with the oil and butter. Transfer the fish to a baking dish and keep warm, or finish cooking in the oven at 350°F (180°C/Gas Mark 4), if necessary. Add the remaining butter to the same skillet and heat it until it browns and has a nutty aroma. Add the reserved lemon juice, plus extra if needed, to the sauce, season with salt and pepper, and strain through the fine-mesh sieve.

PREPARING THE CREAMY CITRUS POLENTA
Bring the milk to a boil in a large saucepan. Stirring continuously with a spatula, add the polenta and cook over low heat until the polenta has absorbed the milk, has thickened, and leaves the sides of the pan (about 15 minutes). Season with salt, then stir in the lime zest and juice, followed by the cream. Stir in the butter and adjust the seasonings if necessary.

TO SERVE
Carefully remove the skewers from the rolled sole fillets and place two on each serving plate. Top each one with a fried caper. Dispense brown butter emulsion around the fish, then arrange the croutons, diced lemons, capers, and parsley leaves attractively around the emulsion. Serve the polenta and meunière sauce in separate bowls on the side.

SALT-CRUSTED SEA BREAM* WITH CHERMOULA

Daurade en croûte de sel, chermoula

Serves 4

Active time
2 hours

Chilling time
1 hour

Soaking time
20 minutes

Cooking time
20 minutes

Equipment
Stand mixer + dough hook
Mortar + pestle
Instant-read thermometer
Mandoline

Ingredients

Salt and seaweed crust
- 8 cups (2¼ lb./1 kg) all-purpose flour
- 14 oz. (400 g) coarse sea salt
- 1⅔ cups (400 ml) water
- Scant ½ cup (3½ oz./100 g) egg white (about 3 whites)
- ⅔ oz. (20 g) wakame seaweed flakes

Chermoula
- ½ bunch parsley
- ½ bunch cilantro
- 1 clove garlic
- ⅓ oz. (10 g) preserved lemon
- Generous ¾ cup (200 ml) olive oil
- 3½ tbsp (50 ml) lemon juice
- ¾ tsp (2 g) paprika
- ¾ tsp (2 g) ground cumin
- Salt

Salt-crusted sea bream
- 2 sea bream
- 1 lemon

Fennel and orange salad
- ⅓ cup (25 g) raisins, soaked in warm water for 30 minutes
- 2 bulbs fennel
- Finely grated zest and juice of 1 orange
- 2 tsp (10 ml) olive oil
- ¾ tsp (2 g) ground cumin
- Scant ½ tsp (2 g) salt

PREPARING THE SALT AND SEAWEED CRUST
Place all the salt and seaweed crust ingredients in the stand mixer bowl fitted with the dough hook and beat until the mixture comes together into a smooth dough. Let rest for 1 hour in the refrigerator.

PREPARING THE CHERMOULA
Wash, dry, and finely chop the parsley and cilantro. Peel and finely chop the garlic. Finely chop the preserved lemon. Place the herbs, garlic, and preserved lemon in the mortar and pound to a coarse purée using the pestle. Mix in the olive oil, lemon juice, and spices and season with salt.

PREPARING THE SALT-CRUSTED SEA BREAM
Preheat the oven to 350°F (180°C/Gas Mark 4). Trim and gut the sea bream (see techniques pp. 36 and 48), but do not scale them (this makes the salt crust easier to remove and prevents damaging the flesh). Dry them thoroughly with paper towels. Thinly slice the lemon and place in the belly cavities of the fish to flavor the flesh. Divide the salt and seaweed crust dough into 4 equal pieces and roll each piece to a thickness of 1⁄16–⅛ in. (2–3 mm), ensuring they are ¾–1¼ in. (2–3 cm) bigger than the sea bream. Place each sea bream on a piece of dough, brush a little water over the edges, and cover with a second piece of dough. Press the dough edges together to seal them and decorate if you wish. Immediately place in the oven and bake for 20 minutes, until the internal temperature reaches 122°F (50°C)—the temperature will continue to rise, to 131°F (55°C), when you remove the fish from the oven.

PREPARING THE FENNEL AND ORANGE SALAD
Meanwhile, drain the raisins. Wash the fennel, cut it into 1⁄16-in. (1-mm) slices using the mandoline, and place it in a large bowl with the raisins. In a small bowl, whisk together the orange zest and juice, olive oil, cumin, and salt. Pour over the fennel and toss to coat.

TO SERVE
Crack the salt crusts open at the table. Lift the sea bream out and serve with the chermoula and fennel and orange salad in bowls on the side.

*Classed as a flatfish yielding 2 fillets in France (see p. 16)

ROAST TURBOT WITH WHITE ASPARAGUS, MOREL MUSHROOMS, AND VIN JAUNE SAUCE

Côte de turbot rôti avec asperges blanches, morilles et sauce au vin jaune

Serves 4

Active time

1 hour

Cooking time

1 hour 50 minutes

Equipment

Fine-mesh sieve

Large oven-safe skillet

Ingredients

Turbot

1 turbot, weighing 4½ lb. (2 kg)

Vin jaune sauce

1 turbot head and tail (see above)

3½ oz. (100 g) shallots

2 cloves garlic

1¾ oz. (50 g) celery

1¾ oz. (50 g) carrot

5 tbsp (3 oz./80 g) butter, divided

Generous ¾ cup (200 ml) vin jaune, divided

1⅔ cups (400 ml) water

1 bouquet garni (thyme and bay leaf)

1½ tsp (3 g) coriander seeds

1½ tsp (3 g) fennel seeds

Scant ½ cup (3½ oz./100 g) crème fraîche

Mashed potatoes

⅓ oz. (10 g) parsley

14 oz. (400 g) floury potatoes, preferably Agria

Coarse sea salt

3½ tbsp (50 ml) olive oil

3 tbsp (1¾ oz./50 g) butter

Salt and freshly ground pepper

Garnishes

8 stalks white asparagus

1¾ oz. (50 g) shallots

4 tbsp (2 oz./60 g) butter, divided

¼ cup (60 ml) water

3½ oz. (100 g) fresh morel mushrooms

Salt and freshly ground pepper

To cook and serve

2 cloves garlic

3½ tbsp (50 ml) grape-seed oil

3 tbsp (1¾ oz./50 g) butter

4 sprigs thyme

Pea shoots

Salt and freshly ground pepper

PREPARING THE TURBOT

Trim and gut the turbot (see techniques pp. 35 and 50), then dry it thoroughly using paper towels. Cut off the head and tail and reserve them for the vin jaune sauce. Cut the turbot halfway between the head and tail ends to obtain 2 equal pieces. Carefully cut away the fillets from the top part of the tail end, on both sides of the fish, to expose the ribs (see technique p. 94), keeping the skin intact. Do the opposite on the head end: remove the fillets from the lower part of the fish, exposing the ribs of the top part. Reserve the removed fillets for another recipe. Fill a saucepan large enough to hold the turbot with water and bring to a boil. For each piece of turbot, dip the exposed ribs into the boiling water for 5–10 seconds (see technique p. 94). Thoroughly clean the bones with a dish towel, removing any remaining flesh. At this stage, the ribs should be exposed on one-half of each turbot piece, and the flesh with the skin on should be intact on the other half.

PREPARING THE VIN JAUNE SAUCE

Cut the turbot head in half, remove the gills and eyes, and thoroughly rinse the head and tail under running water. Peel and finely chop the shallots, garlic, celery, and carrot. Melt 3 tbsp (1¾ oz./50 g) of the butter in a medium saucepan over medium-low heat, add the chopped vegetables, and sweat them gently, still over medium-low heat with the pan covered, for about 10–15 minutes. Add the turbot head and tail, replace the lid, and cook over medium heat for 5–10 minutes. Deglaze with ⅔ cup (150 ml) of the vin jaune and let it reduce by two-thirds. Add the water, bouquet garni, and coriander and fennel seeds. Simmer gently for 25 minutes, skimming any foam from the surface. Strain the sauce through the fine-mesh sieve into a clean saucepan and reduce until it coats the back of a spoon. Remove from the heat and stir in the crème fraîche and remaining butter, followed by the remaining vin jaune.

PREPARING THE MASHED POTATOES

Wash and dry the parsley, remove the stems, and finely chop the leaves. Wash and peel the potatoes and cut them into approximately ¾-in. (2-cm) pieces. Place in a large saucepan, cover with cold water, and season generously with coarse sea salt. Gently simmer over low heat for 35 minutes, or until the potatoes are completely tender. Drain the potatoes and return them to the still-hot saucepan, add more salt if necessary, and season with pepper. Mash the potatoes with a fork, incorporating the olive oil and butter as you mash. Stir in the parsley.

PREPARING THE GARNISHES

Thoroughly wash the white asparagus stalks, then peel them and gently snap off the tough ends where they break naturally. Cut the stalks in half. Peel and finely chop the shallots. Melt 2 tbsp (1 oz./30 g) of the butter in a saucepan, add the shallots and a pinch of salt, and sweat until softened but not browned. Add the asparagus and water, cover, and cook over medium heat for 7–10 minutes, adding a little more water, if necessary, until the asparagus is tender and glazed. Place the morel mushrooms in a colander and shake them firmly, but not too violently, to remove as much dirt as possible, then rinse several times in a large bowl of cold water. Pat dry with paper towels and trim the stems using a paring knife. Melt the remaining butter in a large saucepan, add the morels, and season with salt and pepper. Cover the pan and cook over low heat for 5–10 minutes, or until the morels are tender.

COOKING THE TURBOT

Preheat the oven to 300°F (150°C/Gas Mark 2). Peel and roughly crush the garlic cloves and generously season the prepared turbot on all sides with salt and pepper. Warm the grape-seed oil in the large oven-safe skillet over medium-high heat, then place the fish in the pan with the dark side facing down. Sear until deeply golden brown underneath, then turn the fish over and add the butter, garlic, and thyme sprigs. Transfer the skillet to the oven and finish cooking for 12–14 minutes, or until the tip of a paring knife enters the flesh with no resistance. Transfer the fish to a rack.

TO SERVE

Reheat the garnishes if necessary. Reheat the vin jaune sauce, if necessary, and drizzle it down one side of each serving plate, then arrange the asparagus and morels over it. Scatter with pea shoots to add fresh notes and vibrant color. Place a scoop of mashed potatoes on each plate. Lean a piece of turbot, with the exposed ribs facing upward, against the potatoes on 2 of the plates, to serve. At the table, remove the fillets from the ribs and place a fillet on each plate.

JOHN DORY* WITH BROCCOLI PURÉE AND PASSION FRUIT SAUCE

Saint-Pierre et purée de brocoli

Serves 4

Active time
45 minutes

Cooking time
40 minutes

Equipment
Food processor

Ingredients

Passion fruit sauce
- 7 oz. (200 g) shallots
- 2 cups (500 ml) dry white wine
- Scant ½ cup (100 ml) white balsamic vinegar
- 1 stick + 2 tsp (4½ oz./125 g) salted butter, diced
- 1 passion fruit

John Dory
- 4 John Dory fillets
- Scant ½ tsp (2 g) salt
- 3½ tbsp (50 ml) olive oil

Garnishes
- 2 heads broccoli
- Scant ½ cup (100 ml) olive oil
- 10 Brussels sprouts
- 2 tbsp (25 g) butter
- ½ passion fruit
- Salt

PREPARING THE PASSION FRUIT SAUCE

Peel the shallots, cut them crosswise into 1⁄16-in. (2-mm) slices, and place them in a large saucepan with the white wine. Reduce until nearly all the liquid has evaporated, then remove from the heat and add the vinegar. Remove the shallots from the pan, warm the reduced white wine and vinegar mixture, and whisk in the butter piece by piece. Cut the passion fruit in half, scoop out the pulp and seeds, and add them to the sauce.

PREPARING THE JOHN DORY

Preheat the oven to 126°F (52°C/Gas on the lowest setting). Skin the John Dory fillets (see techniques pp. 41–44), season them with the salt, and brush them with the olive oil. Bake the fish for at least 30 minutes. Do not remove from the oven until right before serving.

PREPARING THE GARNISHES

Wash the broccoli and separate the florets from the stalks, then peel and finely chop the stalks. Set aside 12 small, attractive florets for garnishing and cook the rest along with the stalks in boiling, generously salted water until tender. While the broccoli is still hot, purée it in the food processor with the olive oil. Wash the Brussels sprouts, cut them in half, and blanch them in a saucepan of boiling water together with the 12 reserved broccoli florets for 1 minute. Drain, refresh them in ice water, then drain again. Melt the butter in a skillet, add the Brussels sprouts cut sides down, and brown them. Scoop out the pulp and seeds from the passion fruit and set aside.

TO SERVE

For each serving, cut a John Dory fillet in half, place it on one side of a serving plate, and coat it with passion fruit sauce. Spread a little broccoli purée alongside the fish and top with shallot slices, Brussels sprouts, and 3 blanched broccoli florets. Spoon over the passion fruit seeds and serve with the remaining sauce on the side.

* Classed as a flatfish yielding 2 fillets in France (see p. 16)

SEA BREAM* TARTARE WITH ZUCCHINI AND CITRUS

Tartare de daurade aux courgettes colorées et agrumes

Serves 4

Active time
30 minutes

Chilling time
Overnight

Equipment
Fish bone tweezers
Mandoline
3½-in. (9-cm) round cookie cutter
1¼-in. (3-cm) round cookie cutter

Ingredients

Pickled red onion
½ red onion
¼ cup (60 ml) water
2½ tbsp (40 ml) red wine vinegar
5 tsp (20 g) sugar
1 tsp (5 g) salt

Sea bream tartare
1 lb. 2 oz. (500 g) gilthead bream fillets (*daurade royale*)
½ bunch chives
⅔ oz. (20 g) shallot
1 red bell pepper
1 green zucchini
1 yellow zucchini
Piment d'Espelette
Fleur de sel

Chive mayonnaise
½ bunch chives
1 egg yolk
4 tsp (20 ml) lime juice
Piment d'Espelette
Scant ½ cup (100 ml) grape-seed oil
Salt

Garnishes
2 mini cucumbers
1 grapefruit
4 caper berries, stems trimmed

To serve
Purple basil flowers
Red-veined sorrel
4 tsp (20 ml) olive oil
1 pinch fleur de sel

PREPARING THE PICKLED RED ONIONS (1 DAY AHEAD)
Peel and thinly slice the red onion. Place it in a bowl with a lid. Heat the water, vinegar, sugar, and salt in a saucepan until the sugar and salt have dissolved to make a brine and it begins to boil. Pour the brine over the onions, cover, and let sit overnight in the refrigerator.

PREPARING THE SEA BREAM TARTARE
Remove the skin and any pin bones from the bream fillets (see techniques pp. 41–44 and 52). Cut the fish into ¼-in. (5-mm) dice (see technique p. 100) and set it aside in a bowl over ice. Wash and finely chop the chives, then peel and finely chop the shallot. Wash and quarter the bell pepper, remove the white ribs and seeds, then finely dice it. Wash the green and yellow zucchini. Using the mandoline, cut thin strips, 1⁄16 in. (2 mm) thick, off the outside. Finely dice the strips. Place the fish, shallot, chives, bell pepper, and zucchini in a bowl and stir to combine. Season to taste with *piment d'Espelette* and fleur de sel.

PREPARING THE CHIVE MAYONNAISE
Wash, dry, and finely chop the chives. Whisk together the egg yolk and lime juice in a bowl with a pinch of salt and *piment d'Espelette*. Whisking continuously, gradually drizzle in the grape-seed oil in a thin, steady stream until the mixture is pale, thick, and emulsified. Stir in the chives and adjust the seasonings, if necessary.

PREPARING THE GARNISHES
Wash the mini cucumbers and cut them lengthwise into thin strips using the mandoline. Cut the strips in half lengthwise, then roll them up to make small spirals. Peel the grapefruit, removing all the bitter white pith, then remove the segments and cut them into triangles with ¼-in. (6-mm) sides. Quarter the caper berries.

TO SERVE
Mix the sea bream tartare with the chive mayonnaise, reserving some mayonnaise for garnishing. For each serving, place the 3½-in. (9-cm) cookie cutter in the center of the plate and position the 1¼-in. (3-cm) cookie cutter inside the larger one. Spoon the tartare between the two cutters to make a ring. Arrange the pickled red onions and other garnishes attractively over the tartare, then add dashes of chive mayonnaise all around the ring, creating a symmetrical pattern. Remove the cookie cutters. Garnish the tartare with basil flowers and red-veined sorrel, drizzle with a little olive oil, and sprinkle with fleur de sel.

*Classed as a flatfish yielding 2 fillets in France (see p. 16)

DAB *EN PAPILLOTE* WITH POMELO SAUCE VIERGE

Limande en papillote, sauce vierge

Serves 4

Active time

30 minutes

Cooking time

20 minutes

Equipment

Fine-mesh sieve

8 sheets of parchment paper (see technique p. 134) or 4 roasting bags

Kitchen twine (if using roasting bags)

Ingredients

Toasted pine nuts

Scant ¾ cup (3½ oz./100 g) pine nuts

Sauce vierge

¾ lb. (350 g) pomelo

5¼ oz. (150 g) vine tomatoes

2 tsp (10 ml) red wine vinegar

3½ tbsp (50 ml) olive oil

Scant ½ tsp (1 g) freshly ground pepper

Salt

Vegetables

7 oz. (200 g) red onions

5¼ oz. (150 g) carrots, preferably sand carrots (*carrotes des sables*)

5¼ oz. (150 g) zucchini

10 shiitake mushrooms

Scant ½ cup (100 ml) olive oil

½ tsp (2 g) salt

Dab *en papillote*

1¼ lb. (600 g) dab fillets, skinned

Generous ½ tsp (3 g) salt

2 tsp (10 ml) olive oil

To serve

½ bunch scallions

Toasted pine nuts (see above)

PREPARING THE TOASTED PINE NUTS

Preheat the oven to 325°F (160°C/Gas Mark 3). Spread the pine nuts over a rimmed baking sheet and toast in the oven for 8 minutes, or until golden brown. Remove from the baking sheet and set aside.

PREPARING THE SAUCE VIERGE

Working over a small saucepan to catch the juice, peel the pomelo, removing all the bitter white pith. Remove the segments and cut each one into quarters. Squeeze the remaining juice into the saucepan. Wash the tomatoes, quarter them lengthwise, and scoop out the seeds. Place the seeds in a fine-mesh sieve set over the saucepan and press to release the juice. Cut the deseeded tomato quarters into ¾-in. (1.5-cm) pieces and place in the saucepan with the pomelo and tomato juices, and reduce until syrupy. Whisk together the vinegar, olive oil, ground pepper, salt, and pomelo-tomato reduction to make a vinaigrette.

PREPARING THE VEGETABLES

Peel the onions and carrots and wash the zucchini. Cut all three into julienne strips, 2¾ in. (7 cm) long. Clean the shiitake mushrooms with a slightly damp towel, then cut them into ¼-in. (5-mm) slices. Sauté the vegetables in a skillet with the olive oil and salt for 3–4 minutes, until softened but not browned.

PREPARING THE DAB EN PAPILLOTE

Preheat the oven to 325°F (160°C/Gas Mark 3). Cut the dab into 1¾-oz. (50-g) pieces—you should have three per person. Season with the salt and coat with the olive oil. Divide the vegetables between 4 sheets of parchment paper and top with 3 pieces of dab per serving. Cover with the remaining 4 sheets and fold over the edges of the parchment to seal the parcels tightly (see technique p. 134). Alternatively you can use roasting bags tied with twine. Cook in the oven for 8 minutes.

TO SERVE

Wash the scallions and cut each one at an angle into ¹⁄₁₆-in. (2-mm) slices. Carefully open the dab parcels, sprinkle with the toasted pine nuts and scallions, and pour the sauce vierge over the top.

ROAST BRILL WITH PAN-SEARED RADICCHIO AND DATE AND PINE NUT QUENELLES

Barbue rôtie, trévise snackée et condiment dattes et pignons de pin

Serves 4

Active time

1¼ hours

Cooking time

1¾ hours

Resting time

10 minutes

Equipment

Fine-mesh sieve

Ingredients

Brill and chicken jus

- ¾ lb. (350 g) chicken wings
- 7 oz. (200 g) brill or other fish bones (ask your fishmonger)
- 3½ oz. (100 g) white onions
- ½ head garlic
- Scant ½ cup (100 ml) olive oil
- ¼ bunch thyme
- 7 tbsp (3½ oz./100 g) butter
- 4 cups (1 liter) vegetable stock, divided

Pine nut and date paste

- Generous ¼ cup (1½ oz./40 g) pine nuts
- 8 Medjool dates
- ⅔ cup (150 ml) hazelnut oil
- Fleur de sel

Pan-roasted brill

- 4 brill cross cut steaks (tronçons), weighing 5¾ oz. (160 g) each
- ½ tsp (2 g) salt
- 2 tsp (10 ml) olive oil
- 3 tbsp (1¾ oz./50 g) butter

Pan-seared radicchio

- 2 cloves garlic
- 1 head radicchio
- 7 tbsp (3½ oz./100 g) butter
- ¼ bunch thyme
- ¼ tsp (1 g) salt

To serve

- 4 cloves garlic confit

PREPARING THE BRILL AND CHICKEN JUS

Cut the chicken wings and brill bones into 1½-in. (4-cm) pieces. Peel the onions and cut them into 8 wedges. Separate the garlic cloves and, leaving the skin on, roughly crush them. Heat the olive oil in a large saucepan and brown the chicken wings and brill bones. Add the onions, garlic, thyme, and butter and cook until browned. Pour off the excess fat, then deglaze with 3½ tbsp (50 ml) of the vegetable stock to release the browned bits from the bottom of the pan. Add the remaining stock and let simmer for 1½ hours. Strain the jus through the fine-mesh sieve into a clean saucepan and reduce until thick.

PREPARING THE PINE NUT AND DATE PASTE

Preheat the oven to 325°F (160°C/Gas Mark 3). Spread the pine nuts over a rimmed baking sheet and toast them in the oven for 8 minutes, or until golden brown. Remove from the baking sheet. Pit the dates and chop them into a paste using a chef's knife. Place the dates, pine nuts, and hazelnut oil in a bowl, season with fleur de sel, and stir until well combined.

PREPARING THE PAN-ROASTED BRILL

Remove the skin from both sides of the brill steaks. Ten minutes before cooking the fish, season the steaks all over with the salt. Warm the olive oil and butter in a skillet over medium heat, then add the fish and cook the steaks for 5 minutes on each side. Remove them from the pan and let them rest for 10 minutes.

PREPARING THE PAN-SEARED RADICCHIO

Peel and roughly crush the garlic cloves. Wash and quarter the radicchio and trim the base of each head level. Melt the butter in a skillet over low heat, then add the radicchio, garlic, thyme sprigs, and salt. Sear the radicchio wedges for 5 minutes on each side, or until lightly golden, basting them with the melted butter.

TO SERVE

Preheat the oven to 350°F (180°C/Gas Mark 4), then reheat the fish in the oven for 2 minutes right before serving. Cut the garlic confit lengthwise into ⅟16-in. (2-mm) slices. Place a brill steak on each serving plate and spoon the reheated brill and chicken jus over it. Place a radicchio quarter next to each fish steak and top with garlic confit slivers. Add a quenelle of the pine nut and date paste. Serve the remaining jus on the side.

MOROCCAN-STYLE SKATE WING WITH ZAALOUK

Raie douce à la marocaine avec zaalouk

Serves 4

Active time

4 hours

Marinating time

2 hours

Cooking time

1½ hours

Equipment

Fine-mesh sieve

Large oven-safe skillet

Ingredients

Moroccan-style skate wing

- 1 skate wing, weighing 2½ lb. (1.2 kg)
- 1½ tsp (7 g) salt
- 1½ tsp (4 g) sweet paprika
- Scant ½ tsp (1 g) powdered saffron
- 1 tsp (3 g) ground cumin
- 1½ tsp (4 g) ground turmeric
- ¾ tsp (2 g) ground black pepper
- 1 tsp (3 g) ground ginger
- Finely grated zest and juice of 1 lime

Zaalouk

- 1 lb. 2 oz. (500 g) eggplants
- Generous ⅓ cup (90 ml) olive oil, divided
- 10½ oz. (300 g) vine tomatoes
- 1½ oz. (40 g) shallots
- 1 clove garlic
- 1 bouquet garni (thyme and bay leaf)
- Salt and freshly ground pepper

Garnishes

- ¼ bunch cilantro
- 3½ oz. (100 g) samphire
- Olive oil

To cook and serve

- 1 clove garlic
- 1⅔ cups (7 oz./200 g) all-purpose flour
- 3½ tbsp (50 ml) olive oil
- 3 tbsp (1¾ oz./50 g) butter, at room temperature

PREPARING THE MOROCCAN-STYLE SKATE WING

Remove the skin from both sides of the skate wing using your hands (see technique p. 43), then place the wing in a dish. Combine all the spices in a bowl, then generously season both sides of the skate with the spice mixture. Add the lime zest and juice, rubbing them over the entire surface of the fish. Press plastic wrap over the skate wing and let it marinate for 2 hours in the refrigerator.

PREPARING THE ZAALOUK

Preheat the oven to 325°F (160°C/Gas Mark 3). Wash the eggplants and cut them in half lengthwise, then score the cut sides in a crosshatch pattern, cutting three-quarters of the way through the flesh. Place on a rimmed baking sheet with the cut side up, season with salt and pepper, and drizzle or brush with 2½ tbsp (40 ml) of the olive oil. Roast in the oven for 40 minutes–1 hour, or until the eggplants are completely tender. Meanwhile, hull and peel the tomatoes and cut them in half. Set the fine-mesh sieve over a bowl and scoop the tomato seeds into it to collect the juice. Dice the tomato flesh. Peel and finely chop the shallots and garlic. Heat the remaining olive oil in a saucepan and sweat the shallots and garlic for 5–10 minutes, until softened but not browned. Add the diced tomatoes, tomato juice, and bouquet garni, and season with salt and pepper. Cover with a piece of parchment paper cut to fit snugly inside the pan and cook over medium heat for about 20 minutes, or until all the liquid has evaporated. Scoop out the roasted eggplant flesh and roughly chop it. When the tomato sauce is reduced, stir in the chopped eggplant. Remove from the heat and adjust the seasonings, if necessary.

PREPARING THE GARNISHES

Wash, dry, and remove the stems from the cilantro. Wash the samphire, then briefly blanch it in a saucepan of boiling water, just until the water returns to a boil. Drain and immediately refresh it in ice water. Drain again and drizzle with a little olive oil.

COOKING THE SKATE WING

At the end of the marinating time, preheat the oven to 300°F (150°C/Gas Mark 2). Peel and finely chop the garlic. Dredge the skate wing in the flour, coating it thoroughly on both sides. Heat the olive oil in the large oven-safe skillet and brown the skate wing on both sides, then finish cooking it in the oven for 8 minutes. Remove the skillet from the oven and immediately add the butter and garlic. When the butter melts, spoon it all over the skate wing, coating it thoroughly. Transfer the skate wing to a rack.

TO SERVE

Spread the zaalouk, reheated if necessary, into an even layer in a large serving dish and arrange the samphire and cilantro over it. Place the skate wing on top.

LE CREUSET

STUFFED PLAICE WITH MUSHROOMS

Carrelet farci et champignons

Serves 6

Active time

1¼ hours

Cooking time

1½ hours

Equipment

Fine-mesh sieve

Food processor

Steam oven (or steamer)

Ingredients

Toasted hazelnuts

1¾ oz. (50 g) hazelnuts

Plaice

1 whole plaice, weighing 1¾ lb. (800 g), trimmed and gutted (see techniques pp. 35 and 50)

Salt

Sauce

1 lb. 2 oz. (500 g) plaice bones, or use other fish bones (see above, or ask your fishmonger, if necessary)

3½ oz. (100 g) shallots

1¾ oz. (50 g) button mushrooms

5 tbsp (2½ oz./75 g) butter, divided

1 cup (250 ml) dry white wine

1 bouquet garni (thyme and bay leaf tied up in a leek green)

4 cups (1 liter) water

Scant 4 cups (925 ml) heavy cream, min. 35% fat

Mushrooms

10½ oz. (300 g) girolle mushrooms

4 king trumpet (king oyster) mushrooms

3½ oz. (100 g) shallots

3 cloves garlic

1 stick + 2 tbsp (5¼ oz./150 g) butter

¼ bunch thyme

2 tsp (10 g) salt

Stuffing

5¼ oz. (150 g) raw boneless white fish, skinned if necessary

⅓ cup (75 ml) heavy cream, min. 35% fat

2 tsp (10 g) butter, softened

1½ tbsp (20 g) egg white (about 1 white)

1½ tsp (8 g) salt

¼ bunch tarragon

¼ bunch chervil

1¾ oz. (50 g) shallots

1¾ oz. (50 g) sweet red chili peppers (*piment long rouge*)

4 tsp (20 ml) olive oil

To serve

6 small sprigs chervil

Chopped toasted hazelnuts (see left)

Finely grated zest of 1 lemon

PREPARING THE TOASTED HAZELNUTS

Preheat the oven to 325°F (160°C/Gas Mark 3). Spread the hazelnuts over a lined, rimmed baking sheet and toast for 8 minutes. Chop roughly.

PREPARING THE PLAICE

Remove the dark top skin of the plaice, but leave the white underside skin intact (see technique p. 43). Fillet the plaice (see technique p. 90), keeping the fillets joined together—the underside fillets will have white skin, while the top fillets will be skinless. Season with salt and set the bones aside.

PREPARING THE SAUCE

Cut the fish bones into 2½-in. (6-cm) pieces. Peel and finely chop the shallots. Wipe the button mushrooms and slice thinly. Heat half the butter in a Dutch oven and sweat the shallots and mushrooms until softened. Add the bones and sweat them. Deglaze with the white wine and reduce to a thin glaze. Add the bouquet garni and water and let simmer for 25 minutes. Strain through the fine-mesh sieve into a large clean saucepan and reduce until thickened. In a separate saucepan, reduce the cream by three-quarters, then whisk into the sauce with the remaining butter to emulsify.

PREPARING THE MUSHROOMS

Scrape the bases of the girolles, then rinse and dry. Repeat twice more. Halve the king trumpets crosswise, then cut each piece in half lengthwise. Peel and finely chop the shallots. Roughly crush the garlic, leaving the skin on. Heat the butter in a large skillet until it browns and smells nutty, then add the shallots, garlic, and thyme. Season with salt and cook until the shallots are tender and lightly browned. Sauté each type of mushroom in the same pan until softened and lightly browned. Return them all to the pan.

PREPARING THE STUFFING AND COOKING THE PLAICE

Preheat the steam oven, if using, to 200°F (100°C/Gas on the lowest setting). Place the white fish in the food processor and process. Mix in the cream, butter, egg white, and salt until smooth. Wash, dry, and finely chop the herbs. Peel and finely chop the shallots. Wash the peppers, halve, remove the seeds, then finely chop. Heat the olive oil in a saucepan over low heat and sweat the shallots and peppers for 3 minutes, until softened. Let cool. Stir the herbs, shallots, and peppers into the fish mixture. Place the fillets from the underside of the plaice on a work surface, skin facing down, and spread with the stuffing. Cover with the top fillets, then fold the excess white skin over to hold the fillets together. Cook in the steam oven (or steam) for 20 minutes.

TO SERVE

Pour half the sauce into a serving dish, then add the mushrooms. Slice the fish lengthwise and fan the slices over the mushrooms. Scatter with the lemon zest, toasted hazelnuts, and chervil. Serve the remaining sauce on the side.

BREADED HALIBUT

Poisson pané

Serves 4

Active time
30 minutes

Resting time
10 minutes

Cooking time
10 minutes

Equipment
- Microplane grater
- Immersion blender
- Squeeze bottle
- Fish scaler
- Mandoline
- Deep fryer
- Instant-read thermometer

Ingredients

Ginger-soy mayonnaise
- 1 clove garlic
- ⅓ oz. (10 g) fresh ginger
- 2 tbsp (1 oz./30 g) egg white (1 white)
- 1 tbsp (15 g) Savora mustard
- 4 tsp (20 ml) soy sauce
- Generous ¾ cup (200 ml) grape-seed oil

Breaded halibut
- 1 lb. (480 g) halibut, preferably line-caught
- 7 oz. (200 g) coarse sea salt
- ¾ cup + 2 tbsp (3½ oz./100 g) all-purpose flour
- 2 eggs, beaten
- 3 cups (5¼ oz./150 g) panko breadcrumbs

Salad
- 1¾ oz. (50 g) frisée lettuce hearts
- 1 oz. (25 g) baby beet greens
- 1 red endive
- ¼ bunch scallions
- 1 bunch round red radishes

To serve
- 4 cups (1 liter) neutral oil for deep-frying
- Olive oil
- Fleur de sel
- Freshly ground pepper

PREPARING THE GINGER-SOY MAYONNAISE

Peel and roughly chop the garlic, then peel and finely grate the ginger. Place the egg white, mustard, ginger, garlic, and soy sauce in a small bowl and process with the immersion blender until smooth. Add the oil and blend again until the mixture emulsifies and all the oil is incorporated. Adjust the consistency and seasonings, if necessary, then transfer to the squeeze bottle and chill until serving.

PREPARING THE BREADED HALIBUT

Trim, scale, and gut the halibut (see techniques pp. 35, 39, and 50), then fillet it (see technique p. 90). Cut the fillets into 4 portions weighing 4¼ oz. (120 g) each (see technique p. 98). Pour half of the coarse salt onto a large plate, place the halibut on top, and cover with the remaining salt. Let the fish sit in the refrigerator for 10 minutes, then rinse it thoroughly under running water, taking care not to damage the flesh. Place the flour, eggs, and breadcrumbs in three separate wide shallow bowls. Dredge each piece of fish in the flour to coat, then dip it in the egg, followed by the breadcrumbs. Dip once more in the egg, then coat with a second layer of breadcrumbs.

PREPARING THE SALAD

Remove the stems from the frisée and beet greens, then wash and dry them. Cut the endive leaves into a feather shape. Wash the scallions and cut them at an angle into 1/16-in. (2-mm) slices. Wash the radishes and cut them into approximately 1/16-in (1-mm) slices using the mandoline. Toss the salad ingredients together in a bowl.

TO COOK AND SERVE

Preheat the oven to 350°F (180°C/Gas Mark 4) and heat the oil for deep-frying to 338°F (170°C). Deep-fry the breaded halibut fillets until they are golden brown, then finish cooking them in the oven for 5 minutes. Just before serving, toss the salad with a little olive oil to coat. Place a piece of breaded halibut on each serving plate and drizzle it generously with ginger-soy mayonnaise. Place the salad next to the fish and serve immediately.

CEPHALOPODS

SÈTE-STYLE TOMATO AND OCTOPUS PIE

Tielle sétoise

Serves 8

Active time
1 hour

Cooking time
3 hours

Rising time
3 hours–overnight

Storage
2 days

Equipment
Stand mixer + dough hook (optional)
Instant-read thermometer
Fine-mesh sieve
9½-in. (24-cm) fluted round tart pan, 1 in. (2.5 cm) deep

Ingredients

Pie dough
⅓ oz. (10 g) fresh yeast
1 cup (250 ml) water
2 tsp (10 g) salt
1 tbsp (15 ml) olive oil
4 cups (1 lb. 2 oz./500 g) all-purpose flour

Tomato and octopus filling
3 qt. (3 liters) fish fumet (see technique p. 118)
1 whole octopus, weighing 3½ lb. (1.5 kg), gutted and defrosted if previously frozen (see Chefs' Notes)
7 oz. (200 g) onions
1 oz. (30 g) garlic (about 7 medium-large cloves)
2¼ lb. (1 kg) tomatoes
2 tbsp (30 ml) olive oil
1 tsp (3 g) smoked paprika
20 saffron threads (about 1 tsp)
2 generous tbsp (1¼ oz./35 g) tomato paste
Sugar
1 cup (250 ml) octopus cooking liquid (see above)
Salt

To assemble
Olive oil

To serve
14 oz. (400 g) arugula
Olive oil
Fleur de sel

PREPARING THE PIE DOUGH

Place the yeast in a bowl with the water and stir until the yeast is dissolved. Whisk in the salt and olive oil until the salt is dissolved. Sift the flour into the stand mixer bowl or onto a work surface and make a well in the center. Add the wet ingredients and knead for 10 minutes on medium speed or by hand, until the dough is smooth and elastic and the temperature of it reaches 77°F (25°C). Press plastic wrap over the surface of the dough and let it rise for 1 hour at room temperature. Punch the dough down, cover it with plastic wrap, and let it rest for at least 2 hours, or overnight, in the refrigerator.

PREPARING THE TOMATO AND OCTOPUS FILLING

Bring the fish fumet to a boil in a large pan, then add the whole octopus. Let simmer for 2 hours 40 minutes, or until the tip of a knife pierces the octopus flesh with no resistance. Meanwhile, peel and finely chop the onions and garlic. Peel and quarter the tomatoes. Set the fine-mesh sieve over a bowl, scoop the tomato seeds into the sieve, and press down on them to collect the juice. Cut the tomato flesh into ¼-in. (5-mm) dice. In a large heavy-bottomed saucepan, warm the olive oil over low heat and sweat the onions and garlic for 10 minutes, until they are translucent. Add the paprika, saffron, and tomato paste, increase the heat to medium, and cook for 2 minutes. Add the diced tomatoes and tomato juice. Cover with a piece of parchment paper cut to fit snugly inside the pan and cook over low heat until all the liquid has evaporated. Add a little sugar, if necessary, to correct the acidity. Add 1 cup (250 ml) of the octopus cooking liquid and cook over low heat until thickened. Season with salt. Cut the octopus into ¼-in. (5-mm) dice and add it to the tomato sauce. Let cool.

ASSEMBLING AND BAKING THE PIE

Preheat the oven to 430°F (220°C/Gas Mark 7) and grease the tart pan with olive oil. Weigh out 1 lb. 2 oz. (500 g) of the dough. Roll it into a 12-in. (30-cm) disk, ⅛ in. (3 mm) thick, and line the tart pan with it. Add the tomato and octopus filling, spreading it in an even layer. Roll the remaining 10½ oz. (300 g) dough into another 12-in. (30-cm) disk, ⅛ in. (3 mm) thick. Lightly brush this second dough disk with water to moisten it, then place it over the filling with the moistened side down. Run a rolling pin over the edges of the pan once or twice to trim off the excess dough. Using a skewer, make a hole in the center to allow steam to escape, then crimp the edges for an attractive finish. Brush the dough with olive oil and bake for 25–30 minutes, until the crust is golden.

TO SERVE

Wash and dry the arugula and toss it with olive oil to coat lightly. Season with fleur de sel. Cut the pie into 8 equal pieces and serve with the salad on the side. The pie can be served hot, or left to cool on a wire rack and eaten warm or cold.

CHEFS' NOTES

To tenderize the octopus, you can freeze it in advance, then thaw it in the refrigerator the day before cooking. Freezing helps to break down the muscle fibers.

FRIED CALAMARI WITH SPICY BELL PEPPER MAYONNAISE

Calamars frits, mayonnaise piquante aux poivrons

Serves 4

Active time
1 hour

Marinating time
1 hour

Cooking time
30 minutes

Equipment
Juicer
Fine-mesh sieve
Electric hand whisk
Drum sieve
Deep fryer
Instant-read thermometer

Ingredients

Marinated calamari
- 1½ lb. (750 g) squid
- Scant ½ cup (100 ml) olive oil
- ½ tsp (2 g) chili paste
- 4 tsp (20 ml) lemon juice
- ¾ tsp (2 g) smoked paprika
- Salt

Red bell pepper glaze
- 1 lb. 2 oz. (500 g) red bell peppers

Bell pepper mayonnaise
- 2 egg yolks
- 2 tsp (10 g) Dijon mustard
- 4 tsp (20 ml) apple cider vinegar
- 1½ tbsp (25 ml) canola oil
- ¼ tsp (1 g) chili paste
- Red bell pepper glaze (see above)
- Salt

Breadcrumb coating and frying
- 1⅔ cups (7 oz./200 g) all-purpose flour
- ¾ cup + 2 tbsp (3½ oz./100 g) cornstarch
- ¾ tsp (2 g) sweet paprika
- Scant 1 cup (3½ oz./100 g) fine dried breadcrumbs
- Salt and freshly ground pepper
- Oil for deep-frying

PREPARING THE MARINATED CALAMARI

Clean the squid (see technique p. 72), then cut them into rings, ¼ in. (5 mm) wide (see technique p. 104). Dry thoroughly with paper towels. Whisk together the olive oil, chili paste, lemon juice, and smoked paprika, and season with salt. Coat the calamari rings with the mixture and let marinate for 1 hour in the refrigerator.

PREPARING THE BELL PEPPER GLAZE

Wash the bell peppers, halve them, and remove the stems and seeds. Pass the peppers through the juicer, then strain the juice through the fine-mesh sieve into a saucepan. Reduce the juice over low heat for 30 minutes, or until it coats the back of a spoon.

PREPARING THE BELL PEPPER MAYONNAISE

Whisk together the egg yolks, mustard, and vinegar in a large bowl and season with salt. Whisking continuously, gradually drizzle in the canola oil in a thin, steady stream until the mixture is pale, thick, and emulsified. Stir in the chili paste and all of the red pepper glaze.

PREPARING THE BREADCRUMB COATING

Whisk together all the ingredients in a large bowl. Drain the calamari rings and toss them in the breadcrumb mixture to coat, then shake them gently in the drum sieve to remove any excess.

TO COOK AND SERVE

Heat the oil for deep-frying to 355°F (180°C). Deep-fry the calamari rings for 2–3 minutes, until they are golden brown and crisp. Using a slotted spoon, remove the calamari rings, drain on a plate lined with paper towels, and season immediately with salt. Serve with the bell pepper mayonnaise on the side.

BASQUE-STYLE STUFFED SQUID

Calamars farcis, basquaise

Serves 4

Active time

45 minutes

Cooking time

2½ hours

Resting time

5 minutes

Equipment

Food processor

Whipping siphon + 2 N2O gas cartridges

Disposable pastry bag

Wooden toothpicks

Large oven-safe skillet

2-in. (5-cm) round cookie cutter

Ingredients

Garlic and parsley foam

1 bunch flat-leaf parsley

8 cloves garlic

⅓ cup (3½ oz./100 g) egg yolk (5 yolks)

1 stick + 2 tbsp (5¼ oz./150 g) butter, melted and cooled

Scant ½ cup (100 ml) olive oil

Juice of 1 lemon

Salt and white pepper

Piperade

1 red bell pepper

1 green bell pepper

1 red onion

4 tsp (20 ml) olive oil

6 slices Spanish chorizo

2¾ oz. (75 g) Taggiasca olives, pitted

2 tbsp finely chopped parsley

Salt, as needed

To assemble

14 oz. (400 g) small squid (*supions*)

Piperade (see above)

Garnishes

½ bunch parsley

2 cloves garlic

Scant ½ cup (100 ml) olive oil, divided

2 fresh Spanish chorizo sausages for grilling

4 eggs

To serve

12 Taggiasca olives, pitted

Daikon radish microgreens

PREPARING THE GARLIC AND PARSLEY FOAM

Wash the parsley and remove the stems. Peel and chop the garlic. Blanch the parsley leaves in boiling salted water for 5 minutes, then cool them over a bed of ice and drain on paper towels. Place the parsley, garlic, egg yolks, butter, and olive oil in the food processor and process until smooth. Incorporate the lemon juice and season with salt and white pepper. Transfer to the whipping siphon and cook in a bain-marie maintained at 145°F (63°C) for 1½ hours.

PREPARING THE PIPERADE

Peel the red and green bell peppers, remove the seeds, and thinly slice the peppers. Peel and thinly slice the onion. Warm the olive oil in a large saucepan over low heat, add the bell peppers and onion, and cook, covered, until very soft (15–20 minutes). Meanwhile, cut the chorizo and olives into ¼-in. (5-mm) dice. Finely chop the bell pepper and onion mixture, then stir in the chorizo, olives, and parsley. Adjust the seasonings if necessary, then transfer the piperade to the pastry bag.

ASSEMBLING THE STUFFED SQUID

Prepare the squid (see technique p. 72). Set the tentacles aside. Snip off the tip of the pastry bag and pipe some of the piperade into the squid bodies, then close the ends with toothpicks, ensuring they are not packed too tightly, to prevent them opening during cooking. Reserve the remaining piperade for serving.

PREPARING THE GARNISHES AND COOKING THE STUFFED SQUID

Preheat the oven to 350°F (180°C/Gas Mark 4). Wash and dry the parsley and finely chop the leaves. Peel and finely chop the garlic. Heat half of the olive oil in the large oven-safe skillet and brown the chorizo sausages all over, then finish cooking them in the oven for 5 minutes. Remove the sausages from the skillet and let them rest on a rack for 5 minutes. In the same skillet, quickly sauté the stuffed squid and tentacles in the fat from the sausages with the chopped garlic and parsley, until just cooked through and browned in places. Reserve on a clean dish towel. In a separate skillet, fry the eggs in the remaining olive oil. Using the 2-in. (5-cm) cookie cutter, cut around the yolks so the white is a narrow, even ring. Cut the chorizo sausages at an angle into thick slices.

TO SERVE

Charge the siphon with one of the cartridges and shake to distribute the gas, using the second cartridge, if necessary. Pipe a ring of piperade onto each serving plate and place a fried egg in the center. Arrange the stuffed squid, tentacles, and chorizo slices attractively around the plate, then scatter over Taggiasca olives and Daikon microgreens. Dispense mounds of garlic and parsley foam around the other elements of the dish. Serve the remaining foam on the side.

OCTOPUS WITH CHORIZO AND SPICED BEET PURÉE

Poulpe au chorizo et condiment de betterave

Serves 8

Active time
1½ hours

Freezing time
30 minutes

Thawing time
30 minutes

Cooking time
1½ hours

Equipment
Large cast-iron skillet
Food processor or immersion blender

Ingredients

Octopus
1 whole octopus, weighing 3½ lb. (1.5 kg)
⅔ cup (150 ml) olive oil
3 cloves garlic, unpeeled
¼ bunch thyme

Sweet potatoes
3½ lb. (1.5 kg) white sweet potatoes
1¾ sticks (7 oz./200 g) salted butter, divided
2 cloves garlic, unpeeled
¼ bunch thyme

Spiced beet purée
1 lb. 2 oz. (500 g) raw red beets
2 tsp (15 g) honey
1¾ tsp (5 g) smoked chili powder
¾ tsp (2 g) ground cumin
Scant ½ tsp (2 g) salt
Scant ½ cup (100 ml) aged red wine vinegar

Chorizo
2¾ oz. (80 g) fresh Spanish chorizo

To serve
Herb-infused oil (optional)
½ bunch scallions
Golden sesame seeds
Piment d'Espelette

PREPARING THE OCTOPUS

Separate the octopus tentacles from the head (see technique p. 72), reserving the latter for another recipe. Freeze the tentacles for about 30 minutes, or until they are firm to the touch, to break down the muscle fibers. Thaw the tentacles at room temperature for about 30 minutes. Warm the olive oil in a Dutch oven over high heat until shimmering, then add the garlic, thyme, and tentacles. Sear the tentacles for 2 minutes on each side, then cover the pan, reduce the heat to low, and cook the tentacles for an additional 25 minutes on each side. They will slowly release their juices, which will gently poach the flesh.

PREPARING THE SWEET POTATOES

Wash and peel the sweet potatoes, then cut them at an angle to obtain 40 slices about 1½ in. (4 cm) long and ½ in. (1 cm) thick. Reserve all the peeled trimmings for the purée. Melt half the butter in the large cast-iron skillet with the garlic and thyme. Add the sweet potato slices and cook them, covered, for 5–10 minutes, turning them over halfway through the cooking time. Cook until they are tender and golden brown. Meanwhile, dice the reserved sweet potato trimmings and cook them in a saucepan of boiling salted water until tender. Drain, then purée in the food processor or using an immersion blender with the remaining butter until completely smooth.

PREPARING THE SPICED BEET PURÉE

Wash the beets, then peel and finely dice them (mirepoix). Warm the honey, spices, and salt in a large saucepan, then add the beets and stir to coat. Deglaze with the vinegar and cook, covered, over low heat until the beets are completely tender (about 10 minutes), adding a little water if necessary to prevent burning. Purée in the food processor or using an immersion blender.

PREPARING THE CHORIZO

Cut the chorizo into 40 slices, 1⁄16 in. (2 mm) thick. Brown them on both sides in an ungreased skillet.

TO SERVE

Wash the scallions and cut them at an angle into 1⁄16-in. (1-mm) slices. Reheat the octopus tentacles and garnishes as necessary. Drizzle each serving plate with a little herb-infused oil, if desired, then add 2 scoops of sweet potato purée, a quenelle of spiced beet purée, and 5 slices each of browned chorizo and sweet potato. Add several pieces of octopus tentacle, scatter with scallion slices and golden sesame seeds, and dust with *piment d'Espelette*.

SÈTE-STYLE CUTTLEFISH

Seiche à la sétoise

Serves 4

Active time

1½ hours

Cooking time

2 hours

Soaking time

1 hour

Marinating time

15 minutes

Equipment

Food mill

Fine-mesh sieve

Mandoline or crinkle cutter

Mortar + pestle

Electric hand whisk or balloon whisk

3½-in. (9-cm) stainless-steel ring

Ingredients

Tomato stock

⅕ oz. (5 g) white onion

⅓ oz. (10 g) carrot

⅓ oz. (10 g) celery

1 small clove (about 1 g) garlic

1½ lb. (750 g) vine tomatoes

4 tsp (20 ml) olive oil

1 tsp (5 g) salt

¾ tsp (2 g) ground white pepper

Garnishes

5¾ oz. (160 g) black Camargue rice

1¾ oz. (50 g) white onion

Scant ½ cup (100 ml) olive oil, divided

Scant ½ tsp (2 g) salt

Tomato stock (see above)

1 lb. 2 oz. (500 g) floury potatoes, preferably Agria

Rouille

1¾ oz. (50 g) waxy potato, preferably Charlotte

⅔ cup (150 ml) tomato stock (see left)

Scant ½ tsp (2 g) salt

2 saffron threads

¾ tsp (2 g) *piment d'Espelette*

4 cloves garlic confit

4 confit tomatoes

1 egg yolk

1 cup (250 ml) olive oil

Cuttlefish

4 cuttlefish, weighing 7 oz. (200 g) each, cleaned, skinned, and tentacles removed (see technique p. 75)

4 tsp (20 ml) olive oil

3 saffron threads

Scant ½ tsp (2 g) salt

To serve

Sundried tomatoes

PREPARING THE TOMATO STOCK

Peel and finely chop the onion, carrot, celery, and garlic. Wash and quarter the tomatoes. Heat the olive oil in a large saucepan and sweat the onion, carrot, celery, and garlic. Season with the salt and pepper, add the quartered tomatoes, and simmer for 1 hour. Pass everything in the saucepan through the food mill, then strain the stock through the fine-mesh sieve into a clean saucepan.

PREPARING THE GARNISHES

Place the rice in a large saucepan, add enough water just to cover, and let soak for 1 hour. Drain the rice, return it to the saucepan, add enough water just to cover, and heat until the water begins to boil. Drain the rice again. Peel and finely chop the onion, and sweat it in 1½ tbsp (25 ml) olive oil in a large saucepan with the salt. Reheat the tomato stock. When the onion has softened, add the rice and sauté until the grains are translucent. Add the tomato stock a ladleful at a time, stirring until the rice absorbs the liquid before adding the next. Continue for 45 minutes, or until the rice is al dente. Reserve the remaining stock. Peel the potatoes, then cut them into 2¾-in. (7-cm) disks, ¾ in. (1.5 cm) thick. Cut ridges on one side of each potato disk using a mandoline or crinkle cutter, then trim the edges. Brown the potatoes on both sides in a large skillet with the remaining olive oil, then add enough stock to just cover and cook until softened.

PREPARING THE ROUILLE

Peel, wash, and quarter the potato. Cook the potato in a saucepan with the remaining tomato stock, salt, saffron, and *piment d'Espelette* until it is tender and the liquid has reduced (the potato will absorb some of the stock). Place the garlic confit in the mortar and pound it to a paste using the pestle. Cut the confit tomatoes into small pieces, add to the mortar, and pound to crush and blend. Add the potato with the reduced stock and pound until smooth. Incorporate the egg yolk and transfer to a bowl. Whisking continuously, gradually drizzle in the olive oil in a thin, steady stream until the mixture is pale, thick, and emulsified, like a mayonnaise. Reserve at room temperature.

PREPARING THE CUTTLEFISH

Using a small, sharp knife, score the inside of the cuttlefish in a crosshatch pattern. Cut 3 of the cuttlefish into 4 pieces and let them marinate in the olive oil with the saffron for 15 minutes. Sauté for 30 seconds in a skillet with a little salt. Cut the fourth cuttlefish into strips, ½ in. (1 cm) wide, and sauté them for 30 seconds in a separate skillet with a little olive oil and salt.

TO SERVE

Cut the sundried tomatoes into petal-like slices. Reheat the cuttlefish and garnishes. For each serving, place the ring in the center of a shallow bowl and fill it with black rice. Remove the ring and top with strips of marinated and plain cuttlefish, a potato slice, and tomato petals. Serve the rouille on the side.

BABY SQUID WITH PIQUILLO PEPPERS AND SQUID INK TUILES

Chipirons, piquillos et tuiles à l'encre de seiche

Serves 4

Active time

2 hours

Cooking time

1½ hours

Marinating time

30 minutes

Equipment

Food processor

Drum sieve

Juicer

Fine-mesh sieve

Ingredients

Cured ham powder

5¼ oz. (150 g) cured ham, preferably jambon de Bayonne, thinly sliced

Gnocchi

1¾ lb. (800 g) potatoes, preferably Bintje, unpeeled

Coarse sea salt

Scant ¼ cup (2 oz./60 g) egg yolk (3 yolks)

3½ oz. (100 g) Ossau-Iraty cheese, grated

1 cup (4½ oz./125 g) all-purpose flour, plus extra for dusting

2 tbsp + 2 tsp (25 g) potato starch

Piment d'Espelette

Salt

Baby squid

1¾ lb. (800 g) baby squid

4 tsp (20 ml) olive oil

¾ tsp (2 g) *piment d'Espelette*

2 tsp (10 ml) lemon juice

1 clove garlic

5¼ oz. (150 g) sweet Basque chili peppers (*piparras*), preferably *piments doux d'Anglet*, cut in half lengthwise

Salt

Yellow bell pepper glaze

14 oz. (400 g) yellow bell peppers

Piquillo pepper coulis

7 oz. (200 g) piquillo peppers

1¾ oz. (50 g) *sobrasada* (soft cured pork sausage)

¾ tsp (2 g) *piment d'Espelette*

Salt

Squid ink tuiles

⅔ cup (150 ml) water

Scant 2 tbsp (18 g) all-purpose flour

2½ tbsp (40 ml) canola oil

¼ tsp (2 g) squid ink

Salt

To serve

4 tsp (20 ml) canola oil

1 tbsp (20 g) butter

Marigold petals

Red-veined sorrel leaves

PREPARING THE CURED HAM POWDER

Preheat the oven to 350°F (180°C/Gas Mark 4). Spread out the cured ham on a baking sheet lined with parchment paper and dry in the oven for 10 minutes, until dried out. Let cool completely, then grind to a fine powder in the food processor.

PREPARING THE GNOCCHI

Preheat the oven to 350°F (180°C/Gas Mark 4). Wash and dry the potatoes, then place them on a rimmed baking sheet on a bed of coarse sea salt and roast until a knife inserted into the center meets no resistance (30–45 minutes). Peel the potatoes and pass the flesh through the drum sieve. Weigh out 1 lb. 3 oz. (550 g) of the flesh and place it in a large bowl with the egg yolks, grated Ossau-Iraty cheese, flour, and potato starch. Season with *piment d'Espelette* and salt. Using a spatula or your hands, mix the ingredients together to make a soft dough. Shape into long logs, ½ in. (1 cm) in diameter, then cut into ½-in. (1-cm) cubes. Reserve on a lightly floured surface.

PREPARING THE BABY SQUID

Clean the baby squid (see technique p. 72). Cut the bodies in half lengthwise, then rinse them and score the flesh with a crosshatch pattern (see technique p. 104). Place the bodies and tentacles in a baking dish and add the remaining ingredients. Toss to coat the squid well and let it marinate for 30 minutes in the refrigerator.

PREPARING THE YELLOW BELL PEPPER GLAZE AND PIQUILLO PEPPER COULIS

Wash the bell peppers and remove the stems and seeds. Pass the peppers through the juicer, then strain the juice through the fine-mesh sieve into a saucepan. Reduce over low heat for 30 minutes, or until it coats the back of a spoon. Place the piquillo peppers and sobrasada in the food processor and process until smooth. Add the *piment d'Espelette* and season with salt to taste. Strain through the fine-mesh sieve into a saucepan.

PREPARING THE SQUID INK TUILES

Whisk together all the ingredients. Season with salt. Warm a large nonstick skillet over high heat, then ladle in the batter to make 4 tuiles. Cook for 1–2 minutes on each side and remove. Break each tuile into 3.

TO SERVE

Warm the piquillo pepper coulis. Poach the gnocchi in a saucepan of boiling salted water until they float. Drain. Warm the butter and canola oil in a skillet and brown the gnocchi. Warm a separate large skillet over high heat and sauté the baby squid and marinade for 2 minutes. For each serving, brush a line of yellow glaze across the plate, then ladle piquillo pepper coulis into the center. Add the squid and gnocchi, and dust with cured ham powder. Top each one with 3 tuile pieces, marigold petals, and sorrel.

SHELLFISH

MUSSEL VELOUTÉ WITH MUSHROOMS, KOHLRABI, AND BOTTARGA

Velouté de moules de la baie du Mont-Saint-Michel et poutargue

Serves 4

Active time
1½ hours

Cooking time
45 minutes

Equipment
Kitchen twine
Fine-mesh sieve
¾-in. (1.5-cm) melon baller
Immersion blender

Ingredients

Mussels marinière
- 3½ lb. (1.5 kg) mussels, preferably from the Bay of Mont Saint-Michel
- 3½ oz. (100 g) shallots
- 2 cloves garlic
- 5 sprigs parsley
- 5 sprigs thyme
- 1 bay leaf
- 2 tbsp (1 oz./30 g) butter
- 2 cups (500 ml) dry white wine

Garnishes
- 2 kohlrabi
- Scant ½ cup (100 ml) fish fumet (see technique p. 118)
- 1 tsp (2.5 g) ground turmeric
- 5¼ oz. (150 g) button mushrooms
- 1¼ cups (300 ml) water
- 1 tbsp (20 g) butter
- Juice of 1 lemon
- Salt

Velouté
- 2 cups (500 ml) fish fumet (see technique p. 118)
- Generous ¾ cup (200 ml) mussel pan juices (see above)
- 1¼ cups (300 ml) crème fraîche
- 2 tbsp (1¼ oz./35 g) butter
- ¼ cup (1¼ oz./35 g) all-purpose flour
- 3½ tbsp (50 ml) mushroom cooking liquid (see above)
- Salt and freshly ground pepper

To serve
- ¼ bunch chervil
- 12 thin slices bottarga

PREPARING THE MUSSELS MARINIÈRE

Clean the mussels (see technique p. 60) and let them drain. Peel and finely chop the shallots and garlic. Wash and dry the parsley and remove the stems, reserving them for the bouquet garni. Finely chop the leaves. Using the kitchen twine, tie the parsley stems, thyme sprigs, and bay leaf together to make the bouquet garni. Melt the butter in a Dutch oven over low heat and sweat the shallots and garlic for 5 minutes. Add the bouquet garni and mussels. Pour in the white wine, cover, and cook over high heat for 4 minutes, shaking the pan often, or until the mussels have opened. Discard any that do not open. Stir in the parsley, then remove the mussels from the pot. Strain the pan juices through the fine-mesh sieve into a bowl and measure out a generous ¾ cup (200 ml) for the velouté. Remove the mussel shells and reserve the mussels in the remaining pan juices.

PREPARING THE GARNISHES

Wash and peel the kohlrabi and scoop out twelve ¾-in. (1.5-cm) spheres using the melon baller. Place them in a saucepan with the fish fumet and turmeric and cook over medium heat for 15 minutes, or until completely tender. Reserve in the saucepan. Peel the mushrooms and cut off the stems, then scallop them: cut the caps in half at an angle, then cut each half into 2 or 3 equal pieces an angle. Place the water, butter, and lemon juice in a large saucepan and add a pinch of salt. Bring to a boil, then add the mushrooms and cover with a piece of parchment paper cut to fit snugly inside the pan. Cook over high heat for 3 minutes. Strain the cooking liquid through the fine-mesh sieve and reserve for the velouté.

PREPARING THE VELOUTÉ

Warm the fish fumet, measured mussel pan juices, and crème fraîche in a large saucepan until they begin to simmer. In a separate large saucepan, prepare a roux: melt the butter until foaming, then whisk in the flour until smooth. Whisking continuously, cook for a couple of minutes until slightly thickened but not browned. Remove from the heat and let cool for 5 minutes. Pour half of the hot fumet mixture into the roux, whisking continuously, and bring to a boil quickly. Whisk in the rest of the fumet mixture, then whisk in enough of the mushroom cooking liquid to obtain a pourable consistency. Adjust the seasonings if necessary.

TO SERVE

Wash and dry the chervil and remove the stems. Gently reheat the kohlrabi, mussels, and mushrooms. Reheat the velouté and process with the immersion blender until smooth. Transfer to a pitcher. Arrange the kohlrabi, mushrooms, and mussels in shallow bowls and garnish with bottarga slices and chervil leaves. At the table, right before serving, pour the hot velouté into the bowls.

CHAMPAGNE OYSTERS

Huîtres gratinées au champagne

Serves 4

Active time
30 minutes

Chilling time
30 minutes

Cooking time
20 minutes

Equipment
Oyster knife
Kitchen torch

Ingredients

Oysters
12 meaty oysters (*huîtres spéciales*)

Champagne sabayon
3 egg yolks
2 tbsp (30 ml) champagne
1 pinch *piment d'Espelette*
1 tbsp (20 g) clarified butter, melted and cooled slightly
Salt

Champagne-braised leeks
3½ oz. (100 g) leeks (white parts only)
1 tbsp (20 g) butter
Oyster liquor (see above)
3½ tbsp (50 ml) champagne
2 tbsp (1 oz./30 g) crème fraîche
1 pinch *piment d'Espelette*
Salt

To serve
Coarse gray sea salt

PREPARING THE OYSTERS

Preheat the oven to 250°F (120°C/Gas Mark ½) and place the oysters on a rimmed baking sheet with the rounded side facing down. Bake for 5–8 minutes, keeping a close eye on them: remove them as soon as the shells begin to open, even slightly. Cool the oysters in the refrigerator for at least 30 minutes, keeping them flat so that the liquor stays in the shells. When the oysters have cooled completely, carefully pour their liquor into a bowl and reserve for the leeks. Open the oysters completely by sliding the blade of the oyster knife between the shells and twisting it to pry them apart (see technique p. 65). Remove the oysters from the shells and reserve them in the refrigerator. Keep the shells for serving.

PREPARING THE CHAMPAGNE SABAYON

Whisk together the egg yolks and champagne in a medium bowl and place the bowl over a saucepan of barely simmering water. Cook, whisking in a figure-eight motion, until the mixture thickens slightly. Remove from the heat and season with a pinch of *piment d'Espelette* and salt. Whisking continuously, gradually drizzle in the clarified butter in a thin, steady stream until the mixture is thick, smooth, and creamy. Cover with plastic wrap and set aside at room temperature.

PREPARING THE CHAMPAGNE-BRAISED LEEKS

Wash and thinly slice the leek whites. Melt the butter in a medium saucepan over low heat and sweat the leeks with a pinch of salt until softened but not browned. Add the oyster liquor and champagne and reduce until nearly all the liquid has evaporated. Stir in the crème fraîche and season with salt and a small pinch of *piment d'Espelette*. Simmer gently for 5 minutes, or until the leeks are completely tender.

TO SERVE

Reheat the leeks and sabayon, if necessary. Spoon a small amount of the leeks into each reserved half-shell and top with an oyster. Cover with champagne sabayon and quickly pass the kitchen torch over them to brown the tops. Serve immediately, setting each one on a bed of coarse gray sea salt.

LOBSTER BISQUE

Bisque de homard

Serves 4

Active time

1 hour

Cooking time

1 hour

Equipment

2 metal skewers

Tea infuser

Pestle

Immersion blender

Fine-mesh sieve

Ingredients

Lobster

1¾ lb. (800 g) whole lobster (2 lobsters)

1 orange

1 lemon

6½ cups (1.5 liters) water

3 tsp (15 g) salt

1 stalk celery

1¾ oz. (50 g) fennel

1¾ tsp (5 g) peppercorns

Lobster bisque

1¾ tsp (5 g) assorted star anise pods, fennel and coriander seeds, and peppercorns

1¾ oz. (50 g) shallots

1¾ oz. (50 g) carrots

1 oz. (25 g) fennel

1 oz. (25 g) celery

5¼ oz. (150 g) tomatoes

3½ tbsp (50 ml) canola oil

Lobster pieces (see above)

4 tsp (20 ml) cognac

Scant ½ cup (100 ml) Crémant d'Alsace

6½ cups (1.5 liters) fish fumet (see technique p. 118), cold

Scant 2 tbsp (25 g) tomato paste

1 bouquet garni (parsley and bay leaf tied up in a leek green)

Bisque liaison

⅓ cup (2½ oz./70 g) short-grain rice

1⅔ cups (400 ml) fish fumet (see technique p. 118)

Scant ½ cup (3½ oz./100 g) crème fraîche

3 tbsp (1¾ oz./50 g) butter, at room temperature

Salt

Fried rice noodles

1¾ oz. (50 g) rice vermicelli

Oil for deep-frying

Salt

Crémant d'Alsace foam

1⅔ cups (400 ml) Crémant d'Alsace

Scant ½ cup (100 ml) heavy cream, min. 35% fat

1 tsp (2 g) soy lecithin powder

Salt

To serve

4 pea shoots

¾ tsp (2 g) *piment d'Espelette*

PREPARING THE LOBSTER

Prepare the lobsters for cooking (see technique p. 109); twist the tails and claws off the lobster bodies and devein the lobster tails. Insert a metal skewer through each tail lengthwise to keep it straight during cooking, or use a fork. Using scissors, cut the lobster bodies into approximately 2-in. (5-cm) pieces and reserve for the bisque. Cut the orange and lemon crosswise into slices. Place the water in a large pot with the orange, lemon, salt, celery, fennel, and peppercorns, and bring to a boil. Add the lobster claws and let simmer for 6 minutes, then immediately plunge them into ice water to cool them quickly. Remove the meat from the claws, reserving the claws for serving; use the meat in another recipe. Return the water to a boil, add the lobster tails, and let simmer for 4 minutes. Plunge into the ice water, then remove the shells and cut the tail meat into ¼-in. (5-mm) pieces. Reserve the shells for the bisque.

PREPARING THE LOBSTER BISQUE

Place the assorted spices in the tea infuser. Peel and finely chop the shallots, carrots, fennel, and celery. Wash and quarter the tomatoes. Warm the canola oil in a rondeau pan over high heat and deeply brown the reserved lobster body pieces and shells, then reduce the heat. Add the shallots, carrots, fennel, and celery and sweat them for a few minutes with the reserved lobster pieces. Flambé with the cognac, then deglaze with the Crémant d'Alsace and reduce by half. Roughly crush the lobster body pieces using the pestle or a rolling pin, then add the fish fumet, tomato paste, quartered tomatoes, and bouquet garni. Place the tea infuser in the pan and bring the mixture to a boil. Reduce the heat and let simmer for 30–40 minutes, regularly skimming any foam from the surface. Remove the tea infuser, then process to a coarse purée using the immersion blender. Strain through the fine-mesh sieve into a clean pot, pressing down on the solids to extract as much liquid as possible.

PREPARING THE BISQUE LIAISON

While the bisque simmers, cook the rice in the fish fumet until it is completely tender. Drain. Add the rice to the pot with the strained bisque and bring to a boil. Let boil for a few minutes, then process until smooth with the immersion blender and strain through the fine-mesh sieve into a separate large clean saucepan. Whisk in the crème fraîche and butter to emulsify, then adjust the seasonings if necessary.

PREPARING THE FRIED RICE NOODLES

Heat the oil for deep-frying in a high-sided saucepan. Add the rice vermicelli and deep-fry for 30–40 seconds, or until crisp. Drain on paper towels and season with salt.

PREPARING THE CRÉMANT D'ALSACE FOAM

Reduce the Crémant d'Alsace by three-quarters, then stir in the cream. Add the soy lecithin and season with salt to taste. Using the immersion blender, process until emulsified and foamy.

TO SERVE

Reheat the lobster bisque, if necessary: it should be very hot. Reheat the pieces of lobster tail meat. Divide the pieces of lobster tail between four shallow bowls and pour the hot bisque over them. Place a lobster claw in each bowl, then ladle a little Crémant d'Alsace emulsion over the bisque. Garnish with the fried rice noodles and pea shoots and dust with *piment d'Espelette*.

LOBSTER WITH ASPIC

Homard bellevue

Serves 4

Active time

1½ hours

Cooking time

1½ hours

Chilling time

30 minutes

Equipment

Fine-mesh sieve

1½ -in. (4-cm) round cookie cutter

Mandoline

Instant-read thermometer

1¼-in. (3-cm) round cookie cutter

2-in. (5-cm) round cookie cutter

Ingredients

Lobster

4 lobsters

1 lemon

3 qt. (3 liters) water

⅔ cup (150 ml) white wine

⅕ oz. (5 g) dried fennel

3½ oz. (100 g) coarse sea salt

Lobster fumet

1 lb. 2 oz. (500 g) lobster carcasses (see above)

1¾ oz. (50 g) onion

1¾ oz. (50 g) fennel

3½ oz. (100 g) tomatoes

3½ tbsp (50 ml) olive oil

3 tbsp (1¾ oz./50 g) butter

Scant ½ cup (100 ml) dry white wine

Aspic

⅛ tsp (0.5 g) gelatin powder

½ tsp (2.5 ml) cold water

1 cup (250 ml) lobster consommé

Tomato and lobster butter

Lobster carcasses and vegetables from the fumet (see left)

2⅔ sticks (10½ oz./300 g) butter

Generous 3 tbsp (1¾ oz./50 g) tomato paste

Garnishes

5¼ oz. (150 g) long white turnips

2¾ oz. (80 g) carrots

3½ oz. (100 g) waxy potatoes, preferably Charlotte

2¾ oz. (80 g) shelled peas

6 confit tomatoes

¼ cup (2 oz./60 g) mayonnaise

3½ tbsp (50 ml) olive oil

4 quail eggs

To serve

1 tbsp (20 g) tomato and lobster butter (see above)

3½ oz. (100 g) cooked black truffle

PREPARING THE LOBSTER

Prepare the lobsters for cooking (see technique p. 109); twist the tails and claws off each lobster body, reserving the bodies for the lobster fumet, and devein the lobster tails. Cut the lemon crosswise into slices. Place the water in a large pot with the wine, dried fennel, lemon, and coarse salt and bring to a boil. Simmer the larger lobster claws for 8 minutes, the smaller ones for 6 minutes, and the tails for 4 minutes. As soon as the tails are done, plunge them into ice water to cool them quickly, then remove the shells, reserving them for the lobster fumet, and set aside the tail meat to serve. Remove the meat from the claws, reserving the claws for serving in a little of the cooking liquid; use the meat in another recipe.

PREPARING THE LOBSTER FUMET

Roughly chop the lobster carcasses (the bodies and shells). Peel and finely chop the onion and fennel, then wash and quarter the tomatoes. Heat the olive oil and butter in a large pot and brown the lobster carcasses. Add the onions and fennel, followed by the tomatoes. Cook for 5 minutes, then deglaze with the white wine. Add enough water to just cover the ingredients and let simmer for 25 minutes over low heat. Strain the fumet through the fine-mesh sieve into a clean saucepan, reserving the lobster carcasses and vegetables for the tomato and lobster butter. Reduce the fumet until it coats the back of a spoon.

PREPARING THE ASPIC

Sprinkle the gelatin over the water in a small bowl and let soak for 10 minutes. Heat the lobster consommé, then stir in the gelatin until dissolved. Pour the gelatin mixture into a rimmed baking sheet to a thickness of ¾ in. (2 cm) and chill for about 30 minutes, or until set. Cut out four aspic disks using the 1½-in. (4-cm) cookie cutter.

PREPARING THE TOMATO AND LOBSTER BUTTER

Preheat the oven to 325°F (160°C/Gas Mark 3). Place the lobster carcasses and vegetables reserved from the fumet in a small Dutch oven and dry them over medium heat. Add the butter and tomato paste and cook in the oven for 30 minutes. Strain through the fine-mesh sieve and reserve at room temperature.

PREPARING THE GARNISHES

Peel the turnip and cut off four thin 5 × 1½-in. (12 × 4-cm) strips using the mandoline, then cut the rest into fine dice. Peel and finely dice the carrots and potatoes. Cook the turnip, carrots, potatoes, and peas together in a large saucepan of boiling salted water until just tender. Drain and let cool in a large bowl. Cut the confit tomatoes into ¼-in. (5-mm) dice and add to the bowl with the vegetables. Add the mayonnaise and gently stir to coat. Warm the olive oil in a skillet, add the quail eggs, and cook them for 3–4 minutes. Carefully remove them from the pan, then cut around the yolks using the 1½-in. (4-cm) cookie cutter to give the eggs a perfectly round shape.

TO SERVE

Warm 1 tbsp (20 g) of the tomato and lobster butter to 122°F (50°C) in a small saucepan. Add the lobster tails and gently reheat them in the butter. Cut sixteen ⅛-in. (2-mm) slices from the truffle using the mandoline, then trim the slices into disks using the 1¼-in. (3-cm) cookie cutter. Make 4 crosswise slits in each lobster tail and place the black truffle disks in the slits. For each serving, place the 2-in. (5-cm) round cookie cutter on one side of the plate and line the inside edge with a turnip strip, slightly overlapping the edges of the strip so it holds together. Fill with the finely diced vegetables and peas until level with the top edge of the turnip. Carefully set a quail egg on top. Remove the cutter. Place a truffle-stuffed lobster tail and 1 or 2 claws on each plate, then add an aspic medallion. Serve with the fumet and remaining tomato and lobster butter on the side.

LOBSTER ROLLS

Serves 2

Active time
1½ hours

Chilling time
1½ hours

Cooking time
50 minutes

Resting time
15 minutes

Equipment
Stand mixer + dough hook (optional)
1¾ × 7-in. (4.5 × 18-cm) loaf pan, 1¾ in. (4.5 cm) deep
Instant-read thermometer

Ingredients

Puff pastry bun
1 tbsp (18 g) unsalted butter
Scant 6 cups (1 lb. 6 oz./625 g) pastry flour (T45)
Scant 6 cups (1 lb. 6 oz./625 g) rye flour
1 tsp (5 g) salt
Scant ⅓ cup (70 ml) water
7 tbsp (3½ oz./105 g) butter, preferably 84% butterfat, well chilled

Lobster
2 lobsters
2 tsp (10 g) lobster butter (*beurre de homard*, store-bought or homemade)
⅔ oz. (20 g) dried fennel

Garnishes
3½ oz. (100 g) white cabbage
¼ bunch scallions
Generous ½ tsp (3 g) salt
Juice of ½ lemon

Mayonnaise
Scant ½ tsp (2 g) salt
3½ tbsp (50 ml) apple cider vinegar
2 tsp (10 g) Dijon mustard
1 egg yolk
⅔ cup (150 ml) grape-seed oil

PREPARING THE PUFF PASTRY BUN

Place the 1 tbsp (18 g) unsalted butter in the bowl of the stand mixer with the pastry and rye flours, salt, and water and mix until smooth. Alternatively, mix by hand. Shape the dough into a ball, cover with plastic wrap, and chill for 30 minutes. Using a rolling pin, flatten the 84% butter into a square. Make sure it stays cold. Roll the dough into a rectangle twice as long as the butter. Place the butter on one side of the dough and fold the other side over, enclosing the butter completely. Roll the dough into a rectangle three times as long as it is wide, keeping it roughly the same width as the square of butter. With one short side facing you, fold the dough into three, like a letter, then rotate it 90° clockwise to give it a single turn. Roll it into a rectangle and fold it into three again, giving it a second single turn. Cover with plastic wrap and chill for 30 minutes. Give the dough two more single turns as above, rotating it 90° between turns. Cover with plastic wrap and chill for an additional 30 minutes. Preheat the oven to 400°F (200°C/Gas Mark 6). Roll the dough into a 3 × 8-in. (8 × 20-cm) rectangle, ¼ in. (5 mm) thick, and line the loaf pan with it. Place a weight in the center to form a hot-dog bun shape and bake for 40 minutes, until crisp and golden. Remove from the pan and let cool completely.

PREPARING THE LOBSTER

Prepare and clean the lobsters (see technique p. 109). Cut the lobster meat into pieces weighing 1 oz. (30 g) each. Heat the lobster butter to 122°F (50°C) in a large saucepan, add the lobster meat and dried fennel, and cook at this temperature for 10 minutes.

PREPARING THE GARNISHES

Wash and thinly slice the cabbage and scallions, place them in a bowl with the salt, and let sit for 15 minutes to release excess water. Rinse and drain well, then toss with the lemon juice.

PREPARING THE MAYONNAISE

Place the salt in a large bowl with the vinegar and stir to dissolve. Whisk in the mustard and egg yolk. Whisking continuously, gradually drizzle in the grape-seed oil in a thin, steady stream until the mixture is pale, thick, and emulsified.

TO SERVE

Gently reheat the lobster meat if needed. Cut the puff pastry bun in two at an angle, then spread mayonnaise inside each half and add some of the cabbage and scallion mixture to each one. Top with warm lobster pieces and serve with the remaining mayonnaise on the side.

SPAGHETTI WITH CLAMS

Spaghettis à la vongole

Serves 4

Active time
45 minutes

Cooking time
20 minutes

Resting time
1 hour

Equipment
Fine-mesh sieve

Ingredients

Clams
- 1¾ oz. (50 g) celery
- 1 clove garlic
- 3½ oz. (100 g) shallots
- 3½ tbsp (50 ml) olive oil
- 2¼ lb. (1 kg) small clams, soaked for 4 hours in 2–3 changes of salted water (see p. 21)
- Scant ½ cup (100 ml) white wine

Spaghetti
- 14 oz. (400 g) spaghetti
- Salt

To serve
- ¼ bunch parsley
- ½ cup (100 ml) pasta cooking liquid (see above)
- Clam pan juices (see above)
- 3½ tbsp (50 ml) olive oil
- Juice and finely grated zest of 1 lime
- 1¾ oz. (50 g) bottarga
- Scant ½ tsp (1 g) *piment d'Espelette*

PREPARING THE CLAMS
Wash and peel the celery and cut it into ¼-in. (5-mm) dice. Peel and finely chop the garlic and shallots. Heat the olive oil in a large skillet and sauté the clams with the garlic, shallots, and celery for 2 minutes. Deglaze with the white wine and reduce by half. Remove the clams from the skillet and remove three-quarters of them from their shells; discard any that do not open. Strain the pan juices through the fine-mesh sieve into a bowl and reserve.

COOKING THE SPAGHETTI
Cook the spaghetti in a large pan of boiling salted water for 7 minutes, or until slightly underdone. Reserve a scant ½ cup (100 ml) of the pasta cooking liquid.

TO SERVE
Wash, dry, and finely chop the parsley. Finish cooking the spaghetti in a sauté pan, gradually adding the pasta cooking liquid and the clam pan juices. When the spaghetti is al dente, or cooked to your liking, toss in the olive oil, parsley, clams, and lime juice and zest. Remove from the heat and adjust the seasonings if necessary. Divide the pasta and clams between four shallow bowls and grate over the bottarga. Dust with the *piment d'Espelette* and serve immediately.

SURIMI WITH LOBSTER ROE

Surimi au corail

Serves 4

Active time

25 minutes

Cooking time

1 hour

Storage

3 days

Equipment

Steam oven

Fish bone tweezers

Food processor

Fine-mesh drum sieve

Silicone mold with half-cylinder cavities, approximately 6 in. (15 cm) long and 2 in. (5 cm) wide

Ingredients

Whiting surimi

8¾ oz. (250 g) skinless, boneless whiting fillets

2 egg whites

Scant ½ cup (100 ml) heavy cream, min. 35% fat

1 cup (250 ml) neutral oil

1¼ tsp (6 g) salt

10 g lobster roe (coral)

Vinaigrette

Scant ½ cup (100 ml) aged wine vinegar

1 tsp (5 g) black sesame paste (tahini)

2 tsp (10 g) Dijon mustard

Scant ½ cup (100 ml) neutral oil

Salad

8 shiso leaves

5¼ oz. (150 g) cucumber

1 sheet nori

Vinaigrette (see above)

To serve

1½ tsp (5 g) white sesame seeds

1½ tsp (5 g) black sesame seeds

PREPARING THE WHITING SURIMI

Preheat the steam oven to 195°F (90°C/Gas on the lowest setting). Remove any remaining pin bones from the whiting fillets (see technique p. 52), then cut the fillets into pieces weighing ½ oz. (15 g) each. Process the fish until smooth in the food processor, then mix in the egg whites, cream, oil, and salt. Press the mixture through the drum sieve. Stir the lobster roe into one-third of the fish mixture and spread it evenly over the base of the mold cavities. Cover with the remaining fish mixture, filling the cavities completely. Cook in the steam oven for 1 hour, then remove from the molds and let cool completely.

PREPARING THE VINAIGRETTE

Whisk together the vinegar, sesame paste, and mustard in a bowl. Whisking continuously, gradually drizzle in the oil in a thin, steady stream until emulsified. Set aside at room temperature.

PREPARING THE SALAD

Wash and dry the shiso leaves. Wash the cucumber, then cut it in half lengthwise, leaving the skin on, and scrape out the seeds. Cut at an angle into ¾-in. (2-cm) slices. Julienne the nori. Place the shiso leaves, cucumber, and nori in a bowl, add the vinaigrette, and toss to coat.

TO SERVE

Slice the surimi. Divide the salad between four serving plates, arrange the surimi over the top, and sprinkle with white and black sesame seeds.

SCALLOP CARPACCIO WITH BLACK RADISHES, BEET PURÉE, AND CHARCOAL FRITTERS

Coquille Saint-Jacques, radis noir et bouillon de barbes

Serves 4

Active time
1½ hours

Marinating time
4 hours

Cooking time
30 minutes

Rising time
2 hours

Equipment
Mandoline
Stand mixer + dough hook
Deep fryer
Instant-read thermometer
Fine-mesh sieve

Ingredients

Soy-cured egg yolks
⅔ cup (150 ml) soy sauce
3½ tbsp (50 ml) beet juice
4 egg yolks, left whole

Pickled black radishes
7 oz. (200 g) black radishes
Generous ¾ cup (200 ml) water
1¼ cups (300 ml) spirit vinegar
½ cup (3½ oz./100 g) sugar
Scant ½ tsp (2 g) salt
1 tbsp (10 g) mustard seeds

Charcoal fritters
1¼ tsp (4 g) active dry yeast
Scant ½ cup (100 ml) lukewarm water
1⅔ cups (7 oz./200 g) all-purpose flour
2½ tsp (10 g) sugar
2½ tsp (5 g) activated charcoal powder
Generous ½ tsp (3 g) salt + more for sprinkling
¼ tsp (1 g) baking soda
Neutral oil for greasing and deep-frying

Beet purée
8¾ oz. (250 g) peeled, cooked red beet, warm
4 tsp (20 ml) beet juice
Scant ½ tsp (1 g) ground ginger
2 tsp (10 g) butter
Salt

Scallop carpaccio
10 scallops in their shells

Scallop broth
8¾ oz. (250 g) scallop mantles reserved from above (or ask your fishmonger)
1 tbsp (20 g) butter
1¾ oz. (50 g) shallots, peeled and finely chopped
3½ tbsp (50 ml) white wine
2 cups (500 ml) water

To serve
Olive oil
Purple and green oxalis leaves

PREPARING THE SOY-CURED EGG YOLKS
Combine the soy sauce and beet juice in a medium bowl, then carefully place the egg yolks in the bowl. Let cure in the refrigerator for 2 hours.

PREPARING THE PICKLED BLACK RADISHES
Wash the black radishes and cut them, unpeeled, into 1⁄16-in. (1-mm) slices using the mandoline. Place in a heatproof bowl. Place the water, vinegar, sugar, salt, and mustard seeds in a saucepan and heat until the sugar and salt have dissolved, then bring to a boil. Immediately pour the hot brine over the radishes, cover with plastic wrap, and let marinate for 2 hours at room temperature.

PREPARING THE CHARCOAL FRITTERS
Dissolve the active dry yeast in a bowl of lukewarm water and let sit until foaming (about 10 minutes). Place all the remaining charcoal fritter ingredients, except the oil, in the stand mixer, then add the yeast mixture and knead until the dough is elastic and pulls away from the sides of the bowl. Lightly grease the surface of the dough with oil, cover with a dish towel, and let rise for 1–2 hours at room temperature until doubled in volume. Preheat the oil for deep-frying to 374°F (190°C). Shape the dough into logs, 4 in. (10 cm) in length and ¾ in. (2 cm) in diameter. Deep-fry for 3 minutes, then remove from the oil, carefully split each fritter open lengthwise, separate the two halves, and return to the oil for an additional 30 seconds. Drain on paper towels and sprinkle with salt.

PREPARING THE BEET PURÉE
Place the beet in the food processor with the beet juice, ground ginger, and butter. Purée until smooth. Season with salt, pass through the fine-mesh sieve, and chill until serving.

PREPARING THE SCALLOP CARPACCIO
Shuck the scallops and remove them from their shells (see technique p. 62), reserving the mantles (frills) for the scallop broth. Clean the scallops and slice them thinly crosswise.

PREPARING THE SCALLOP BROTH
Thoroughly rinse the scallop mantles to remove any sand. Heat the butter in a large saucepan and sweat the shallots until softened. Add the mantles and cook for 1 minute, or until firm. Deglaze with the white wine and reduce by half, then add the water and let simmer for 20 minutes. Strain through the fine-mesh sieve and adjust the seasonings if necessary. Transfer to a pitcher.

TO SERVE
For each serving, place beet purée in the base of a shallow bowl. Arrange the scallop and radish slices in a ring. Drizzle with olive oil, place an egg yolk in the center, and garnish with oxalis leaves. Serve the broth and fritters on the side.

STUFFED RAZOR CLAMS WITH A CITRUS CRUST

Couteaux farcis, croûte d'agrumes

Serves 4

Active time
45 minutes

Soaking time
2 hours

Cooking time
10 minutes

Chilling time
30 minutes

Ingredients

Razor clams

24 razor clams

Citrus crust

3 tbsp + 2 tsp (2 oz./55 g) butter, softened

1½ tbsp (10 g) finely grated lemon, orange, and grapefruit zest

⅓ cup (1¼ oz./35 g) dried breadcrumbs

1 scant tbsp (10 g) grated Parmesan

Scant ½ tsp (2 g) salt

¾ tsp (2 g) ground sumac

Stuffed razor clams

24 razor clams (see above)

Scant ½ cup (100 ml) olive oil

1¾ oz. (50 g) scallions

1 clove garlic

⅕ oz. (5 g) chervil

Scant ¼ cup (1¾ oz./50 g) mascarpone

Juice of ½ lemon

¾ tsp (2 g) sweet paprika

SOAKING THE RAZOR CLAMS

To remove the sand from the razor clams, soak them in cold salted water for 2 hours.

PREPARING THE CITRUS CRUST

Combine the butter and citrus zest in a large bowl, then add the breadcrumbs, Parmesan, salt, and ground sumac. Stir until well combined. Between two sheets of parchment paper, roll the mixture to a thickness of 1⁄16 in. (1–2 mm). Place in the refrigerator until firm, then cut out 12 rectangles measuring about 4 × 1½ in. (10 × 4 cm), or the size of the razor clam shells when open. Reserve in the refrigerator.

PREPARING THE STUFFED RAZOR CLAMS

Preheat the oven to 400°F (200°C/Gas Mark 6) with the broiler on. Rinse the soaked razor clams, then dry them well with paper towels. Warm the olive oil in a skillet over high heat, add the clams, and cook them for 2–3 minutes, or just until they open. Remove the clams from their shells, reserving the shells for serving. Wash and finely chop the scallions, then peel the garlic and crush it with a garlic press. Wash, dry, and finely chop the chervil. Cut the shelled razor clams into ½-in. (1-cm) pieces and place them in a large bowl with the scallions, garlic, mascarpone, lemon juice, chervil, and sweet paprika. Stir to combine. Open 12 of the reserved razor clam shells like a book and cover them with the filling. Top each one with a citrus crust rectangle and place under the broiler for 3–4 minutes, or until golden brown. Serve immediately.

CARAMELIZED ABALONE WITH FOIE GRAS AND POTATO FOAM

Ormeaux rôtis au beurre, foie gras et espuma de pommes de terre

Serves 4

Active time

1½ hours

Cooking time

40 minutes

Equipment

Immersion blender

Fine-mesh sieve

Whipping siphon + 1 N2O gas cartridge

Scallop knife

Meat tenderizer

Oval cookie cutter, 4 in. (10 cm) long

Ingredients

Potato foam

1 lb. 2 oz. (500 g) waxy potatoes, preferably Bintje

1 cup (250 ml) heavy cream, min. 35% fat

Scant ⅓ cup (70 ml) olive oil

Salt

Abalones

4 large abalones, weighing 2 oz. (60 g) each

1 clove garlic

3 tbsp (1¾ oz./50 g) butter

4 sprigs thyme

Salt and freshly ground pepper

Spinach and foie gras

7 oz. (200 g) spinach

1 clove garlic

2 tbsp (1 oz./30 g) butter

4 raw foie gras escalopes, weighing 1½ oz. (40 g) each

Salt and freshly ground pepper

To serve

12 Mertensia (oyster plant) leaves

PREPARING THE POTATO FOAM

Peel and rinse the potatoes and cut them into large pieces. Place in a large pot, cover with cold water, and add salt. Let simmer for 30 minutes, or until the potatoes are completely tender. Transfer the potatoes to a bowl with a generous ¾ cup (200 ml) of the cooking water. Add the cream and olive oil and process until smooth using the immersion blender. Season with salt and pepper, then strain through the fine-mesh sieve. Transfer the potato mixture to the whipping siphon, charge it with the cartridge, and shake the siphon to distribute the gas. Keep warm in a bain-marie.

PREPARING THE ABALONES

Remove the abalones from their shells using the scallop knife, then remove the guts. Rinse the abalones under running water, rubbing them to remove any residual dirt or debris. Wash the shells and reserve them for serving. Wrap the abalones in a clean dish towel. Using the meat tenderizer, pound them with a swift, clean blow to break down the muscle fibers and make the meat more tender when cooked. Season both sides with salt and pepper. Peel and roughly crush the garlic. Warm the butter in a sauté pan over high heat until foaming, then add the abalones and quickly caramelize them on both sides, basting them with the butter. Add the garlic and thyme after turning them over. Reserve on paper towels.

PREPARING THE SPINACH AND FOIE GRAS

Wash the spinach and remove the stems. Peel and roughly crush the garlic. Heat the butter in a large saucepan with the garlic until the butter browns and has a nutty aroma. Add the spinach and cook for 3 minutes, until wilted. Transfer the spinach to a colander, season it with salt and pepper, and set aside. Season the foie gras on both sides with salt and pepper, then sear in an ungreased skillet over high heat until browned on both sides and a knife inserted into the center meets with no resistance. Reserve on paper towels.

TO SERVE

For each serving, place the oval cookie cutter on one side of the plate and line the base with spinach. Remove the cookie cutter and place a foie gras escalope over the spinach. Cut each abalone into thick slices and place the slices on top of each foie gras escalope. Garnish with Mertensia leaves. Place an abalone half-shell on each plate next to the abalone and fill with potato foam. Serve immediately.

SHELLFISH MARINIÈRE WITH LEEKS AND CAULIFLOWER FOAM

Coquillages en marinière, poireaux et purée de chou-fleur

Serves 4

Active time

2 hours

Soaking time

4 hours

Cooking time

2 hours 40 minutes

Resting time

30 minutes

Equipment

Food processor

Fine-mesh sieve

Whipping siphon + 1 N2O gas cartridge

Coffee filter

Kitchen torch

Ingredients

Shellfish

1 lb. 2 oz. (500 g) cockles (*coques*)

1 lb. 2 oz. (500 g) periwinkles (*bigorneaux*)

¾ lb. (350 g) warty Venus clams (*praires*)

Seawater or salted water, 2 generous tbsp salt (1¼ oz./35 g) per 4 cups (1 liter) water

Candied leek greens

1¼ lb. (600 g) leeks

Generous ¾ cup (200 ml) water

½ cup (3½ oz./100 g) sugar

Cauliflower foam

½ head cauliflower

2 cups (500 ml) whole milk

Generous ¾ cup (200 ml) heavy cream, min. 35% fat

2 tbsp (25 g) butter

Salt and white pepper

Roasted leek whites

Leek whites (see left)

3½ tbsp (50 ml) olive oil

Salt

Shellfish marinière

Shellfish (see left)

3½ oz. (100 g) shallots, divided

1 bunch (1¾ oz./50 g) parsley, divided

3 tbsp (1¾ oz./50 g) butter, divided

⅔ cup (150 ml) white wine, divided

Marinière sauce

1¼ cups (300 ml) marinière pan juices (see above)

3 tbsp (1½ oz./40 g) butter

Fried leek roots

Leek roots (see left)

White vinegar

1¼ cups (300 ml) oil for deep-frying

Salt

To serve

Borage flowers and leaves

SOAKING THE SHELLFISH

To remove the sand from the cockles, periwinkles, and clams, place them in a large bowl and cover them halfway with seawater or generously salted water. Let soak for at least 4 hours, changing the water once or twice if necessary.

PREPARING THE CANDIED LEEK GREENS

Preheat the oven to 175°F (80°C/Gas on the lowest setting) and line a rimmed baking sheet with parchment paper. Cut the roots and green parts off the leeks. Set the whites aside for roasting and the roots for frying. Thoroughly wash the leek greens, then cut them into 4-in. (10-cm) pieces. Blanch in boiling water for 10 seconds, then immediately plunge into ice water to cool quickly. Drain the leek greens and lay them flat on a cutting board. Using a knife held parallel to the work surface, cut each green in half lengthwise. Place on the prepared baking sheet. Heat the generous ¾ cup (200 ml) water and sugar in a saucepan until the sugar dissolves, then bring to a boil. Let the syrup cool for a few minutes, then brush it over the leek greens and dry them in the oven for 2 hours.

PREPARING THE CAULIFLOWER FOAM

Cut the cauliflower into florets, wash them, and cook in a large saucepan with the milk and cream until tender. Place the florets in the food processor with a scant ½–⅔ cup (100–150 ml) of the milk and cream mixture and process until very smooth. Incorporate the butter, season with salt and pepper. The purée should have a fairly liquid consistency, so add more of the milk and cream mixture if necessary. Strain through the fine-mesh sieve, transfer to the whipping siphon, and charge it with the cartridge. Shake the siphon to distribute the gas and keep warm in a bain-marie.

PREPARING THE ROASTED LEEK WHITES

Preheat the oven to 350°F (180°C/Gas Mark 4). Thoroughly wash the reserved leek whites, wrap them in an aluminum foil parcel with the olive oil and salt, and roast for 30 minutes. Let the leeks cool, then cut them at an angle into 2½-in. (6-cm) pieces.

PREPARING THE SHELLFISH MARINIÈRE

Rinse the soaked cockles, periwinkles, and clams separately under running water. Peel and finely chop the shallots. Wash and dry the parsley. Divide the butter between 3 large saucepans with lids and melt over low heat. Add one-third of the shallots to each and sweat for 5 minutes, then add one-third of the parsley and wine to each saucepan. It is necessary to cook the shellfish separately, as they have different cooking times. Place the cockles and periwinkles separately in two of the saucepans, cover, and cook over high heat for 3 minutes, shaking the pan often, or until the shells have opened. Place the clams in the third saucepan, cover, and cook for 5 minutes. Once all the shells have opened, remove the shellfish from the pans and let them cool. Discard any that do not open. Strain the pan juices through the fine-mesh sieve into a single bowl and let sit for 30 minutes to allow any remaining sand or impurities to sink to the bottom. Remove the cockles, periwinkles, and clams from their shells.

PREPARING THE MARINIÈRE SAUCE

Carefully pour the marinière pan juices through the coffee filter into a clean bowl, taking care to avoid pouring in the impurities that have settled at the bottom of the bowl. Measure 1¼ cups (300 ml) of the juices into a saucepan and reduce over low heat to a glaze that coats the back of a spoon. Whisk in the butter until smooth and reserve in the saucepan.

PREPARING THE FRIED LEEK ROOTS

Thoroughly wash the leek roots in water with vinegar, then dry them well with a clean dish towel. Heat the oil for deep-frying in a high-sided saucepan and deep-fry the leek roots until crisp. Remove them with a slotted spoon, place on paper towels, and season with salt.

TO SERVE

Using the kitchen torch, char some of the roasted leek whites and reheat the rest. Reheat the shellfish in the marinière sauce. Dispense cauliflower foam onto the center of each serving plate and top with an assortment of the shellfish. Arrange leek whites alongside, then top with candied leek greens and fried leek roots. Garnish with borage flowers and leaves.

CRAB WITH SEAWEED SALAD AND CRAB GELÉE

Tourteau, salade d'algues et gelée

Serves 4

Active time
1 hour

Cooking time
6 hours 40 minutes

Chilling time
Overnight + 1 hour

Soaking time
20 minutes

Equipment
Fine-mesh sieve

Ingredients

Crab

- 2 edible or brown crabs (*tourteaux*)
- 3 qt. (3 liters) vegetable stock
- 1 clove garlic, unpeeled
- 2 bay leaves
- 1/5 oz. (5 g) dried fennel
- 2/3 cup (150 ml) white wine
- 1/3 oz. (10 g) coarse sea salt

Crab gelée

- 1 lb. 2 oz. (500 g) crab carcasses (see above)
- 3½ oz. (100 g) celery
- 3½ oz. (100 g) onions
- 3½ oz. (100 g) carrots
- 5¼ oz. (150 g) tomatoes
- 3½ tbsp (50 ml) neutral oil
- 4 qt. (4 liters) water
- Generous ¼ tsp (1.5 g) fish gelatin powder
- Scant 2 tsp (9.5 g) cold water

Seaweed salad

- 1/3 oz. (10 g) kombu
- 1/3 oz. (10 g) wakamé
- 3½ oz. (100 g) cucumber
- 1 kiwi
- 1 Granny Smith apple
- Juice of 1 lime

To serve

- Chervil leaves
- Finely grated zest of ½ lime

PREPARING THE CRABMEAT (1 DAY AHEAD)

If using live crabs, kill them according to the chefs' note p. 126. Place the vegetable stock, garlic, bay leaves, dried fennel, white wine, and coarse sea salt in a large pot and bring to a boil. Lower the crabs into the water and let boil for 20 minutes, then remove the crabs and let them cool for 20 minutes. Shell the crabs (see technique p. 106), reserving the carcasses for the crab gelée. Shred the crabmeat, excluding the claw and knuckle meat (reserve these for serving), then stir in the roe (coral). Place the meat in airtight containers and set aside in the refrigerator.

PREPARING THE CRAB GELÉE (1 DAY AHEAD)

Preheat the oven to 175°F (80°C/Gas on the lowest setting). Cut the crab carcasses into pieces using scissors. Peel and thinly slice the celery, onions, and carrots. Wash and chop the tomatoes. Heat the neutral oil in a Dutch oven and lightly brown the crab carcasses, then add the celery, onions, carrots, and tomatoes and cook until softened and browned. Add the 4 qt. (4 liters) water, cover with a paper towel, and place the lid on the pot. Cook in the oven for 6 hours. Remove from the oven and let sit at room temperature to allow the solids to settle at the bottom. Using a ladle, carefully strain through the fine-mesh sieve into a clean container, avoiding stirring the solids, to obtain a clear broth. Let sit overnight in the refrigerator. The following day, sprinkle the gelatin over the scant 2 tsp (9.5 ml) cold water in a small bowl and let soak for 10 minutes. Skim any fat off the broth, if necessary, then measure out 4 cups (1 liter), warm it in a saucepan, and stir in the gelatin mixture until dissolved. Chill for about 1 hour, or until set.

PREPARING THE SEAWEED SALAD

Soak the kombu and wakame in a bowl of water for 10 minutes to remove excess salt. Peel and finely dice the cucumber, kiwi, and apple, and place them in a bowl. Drain the kombu and wakame, then cut them into fine dice, ensuring they are the same size as the other elements. Add the seaweed to the bowl, then add the lime juice and toss to coat.

TO SERVE

Divide the seaweed salad between the serving plates and shape it into a circle, ¾ in. (2 cm) high, in the center. Cover with a ¾-in. (2-cm) layer of shredded crabmeat, then top with claw and knuckle meat. Spoon crab gelée around the salad and crab, and garnish with chervil leaves and lime zest.

PARISIAN-STYLE GNOCCHI WITH WHELKS *EN PERSILLADE*

Gnocchis à la parisienne et bulots en persillade

Serves 4

Active time

40 minutes

Cooking time

2 hours

Equipment

Fine-mesh sieve

Mandoline

1¼-in. (3-cm) round cookie cutter

Ingredients

Chicken jus

2¼ lb. (1 kg) chicken carcasses

⅔ oz. (20 g) peeled white onion

½ head garlic

2 tsp (10 ml) olive oil

¼ bunch thyme

1 tbsp (20 g) butter

8 cups (2 liters) vegetable stock, divided

Parisian-style gnocchi

Generous ¾ cup (200 ml) whole milk

4 tbsp (2 oz./60 g) butter

Generous ½ tsp (3 g) salt

¾ cup + 2 tbsp (3½ oz./100 g) all-purpose flour

3 eggs

2 cups (500 ml) heavy cream, min. 35% fat

Sautéed mushrooms, whelks, and garlic and parsley butter

6 brown button mushrooms

5 tbsp (3 oz./80 g) butter, at room temperature, divided

½ tsp (2 g) salt

¼ bunch thyme

28 cooked whelks

1 clove garlic

½ bunch parsley

Juice of ½ lemon

Garnishes

4 brown button mushrooms

1¾ oz. (50 g) Comté cheese

PREPARING THE CHICKEN JUS

Cut the chicken carcasses into 1½-in. (4-cm) pieces. Cut the onion into 8 pieces. Separate the garlic cloves and roughly crush them, unpeeled, using the flat side of a chef's knife blade. Heat the olive oil in a large saucepan and sear the carcasses until pale golden brown. Add the onions, garlic, thyme, and butter and continue to cook until the meat is deeply browned. Skim off excess fat using a skimmer, then deglaze with 3½ tbsp (50 ml) of the vegetable stock to release the browned bits from the bottom of the pan. Add the remaining stock and simmer, uncovered, for 1½ hours. Strain the jus through the fine-mesh sieve into a clean saucepan and reduce over low heat until it has a syrupy consistency that coats the back of a spoon.

PREPARING THE PARISIAN-STYLE GNOCCHI

Bring the milk, butter, and salt to a boil in a large saucepan, then add the flour all at once. Whisking vigorously, cook over low heat until the mixture dries and pulls away from the sides of the pan. Remove from the heat. As soon as the mixture has cooled, stir in the eggs one at a time using a spatula. Shape the mixture into quenelles weighing 1½ oz. (40 g) each, then poach in a large pot of simmering water. Once the gnocchi rise to the surface, leave them for 5 minutes, turning them regularly to cook all sides. Using a slotted spoon, transfer the gnocchi to a lightly oiled baking sheet. In a large saucepan, reduce the cream by three-quarters.

PREPARING THE MUSHROOMS, WHELKS, AND GARLIC AND PARSLEY BUTTER

Clean the mushrooms and cut each one into 6 pieces. Heat 1 tbsp (20 g) of the butter in a large saucepan with the salt and thyme and sauté the mushrooms until browned. Set aside. Remove the whelks from their shells, then remove the hard end of the foot (operculum) and intestinal tract. To prepare the garlic and parsley butter, peel and finely chop the garlic, and wash and dry the parsley, remove the stems, and finely chop the leaves. Place the garlic and parsley in a bowl, add the lemon juice and remaining butter, and stir to combine.

PREPARING THE GARNISHES

Clean the mushrooms and cut them into 1⁄16-in. (1-mm) slices using the mandoline. Cut the Comté into ⅛-in. (2-mm) slices, then cut out 20 Comté disks using the 1¼-in. (3-cm) cookie cutter.

TO SERVE

Melt the garlic and parsley butter in a saucepan, add the whelks, and stir to coat them well. Reheat for 2–3 minutes. Cut the gnocchi in half at a slight angle to give them a pyramid shape, then reheat them in the reduced cream. Reheat the sautéed mushrooms and chicken jus, if necessary. Arrange the gnocchi, whelks, and sautéed mushrooms in serving bowls, then pour chicken jus over them. Garnish with the Comté disks and mushroom slices.

AVOCADO *FÉROCE* WITH PRAWNS AND EGGS MIMOSA

Féroce d'avocat, crevettes impériales charentaises et mimosa

Serves 4

Active time
45 minutes

Soaking time
Overnight

Chilling time
2 hours

Cooking time
30 minutes

Equipment
Food processor
Pastry bag + plain round tip
Fine-mesh drum sieve
Bowl scraper
1¼-in. (3-cm) round cookie cutter

Ingredients

Salt cod
2¾ oz. (80 g) salt cod fillet

Poached prawns
12 prawns, preferably Kuruma (*crevettes impériales charentaises*)
1 onion
1 carrot
1 stalk celery
2 cloves garlic, unpeeled
4 cups (1 liter) water
1 lemon
1 bouquet garni (bay leaf and thyme)
2 tbsp (30 ml) champagne vinegar
2 tsp (10 g) salt
2 tsp (5 g) *piment d'Espelette*
1 tsp (3 g) black peppercorns
2¼ lb. (1 kg) ice cubes

Avocado *féroce*
½ oz. (15 g) cilantro
⅕ oz. (5 g) fresh red chili pepper, preferably *piment du Maroc* (optional)
2 ripe avocados (15¾ oz./450 g)
⅓ oz. (10 g) sandwich bread
Juice and finely grated zest of 2 limes
2 tbsp (30 ml) olive oil
Prepared salt cod (see above), broken into pieces
Salt and freshly ground pepper

Garnishes
4 eggs
1 pomegranate
1 red chili pepper, preferably *piment du Maroc*
1¾ oz. (50 g) small-leafed basil

PREPARING THE SALT COD (1 DAY AHEAD)

Soak the cod in cold water overnight, changing the water at least three times. The following day, drain and rinse the cod, then place it in a saucepan, cover with cold water, and bring to a simmer. Remove the cod and chill it for at least 1 hour, or until it has completely cooled. Break the cod into small pieces, removing any remaining bones.

PREPARING THE POACHED PRAWNS

Shell and devein the prawns (see technique p. 58). Peel and finely chop the onion, carrot, and celery. Crush the garlic with the flat side of a knife blade. Place the onion, carrot, celery, and garlic in a large pot, bring to a boil, and let simmer for 10 minutes. Cut the lemon crosswise into slices and add to the pot with the bouquet garni, vinegar, salt, *piment d'Espelette*, and peppercorns. Let simmer for 5 minutes, then add the prawns and cook for 3–4 minutes, or until just pink. Immediately add the ice cubes to the pot to cool the prawns quickly, then place in the refrigerator and chill for 1 hour. Drain the prawns, dry them carefully, and reserve them in the refrigerator.

PREPARING THE AVOCADO FÉROCE

Wash the cilantro and remove the stems. Wash the chili pepper, if using, and remove the seeds. Peel the avocados, remove the pits, and place the flesh in the food processor with the cilantro leaves, chili pepper, sandwich bread, and lime juice and zest. Process until smooth. With the motor running, drizzle in the olive oil. Season with salt and pepper, then gently fold in the salt cod. Transfer the *féroce* to the pastry bag.

PREPARING THE GARNISHES

Hard-boil the eggs for 9 minutes, then cool them in ice water and remove the shells. Pass the yolks and whites separately through the drum sieve, pushing down on them with the bowl scraper. Cut the pomegranate open and remove the arils. Wash and thinly slice the chili pepper and remove the seeds. Wash and dry the basil.

TO SERVE

Scatter the egg whites and yolks across the base of a serving dish in a thin layer, taking care not to crush them. With the aid of the 1¼-in. (3-cm) cookie cutter, pipe disks of avocado *féroce* over the eggs. Place a prawn on each disk with the tail facing upward. Garnish with the pomegranate arils, chili pepper slices, and sprigs of basil.

SHRIMP FRIED RICE

Riz sauté aux crevettes bouquet

Serves 4

Active time
20 minutes

Cooking time
1¼ hours

Equipment
Fine-mesh sieve
Wok

Ingredients

Shrimp and shrimp butter

- 7 oz. (200 g) shrimp, preferably common prawns (*crevettes bouquet*)
- 1¾ oz. (50 g) onion
- 2 tomatoes
- 1¾ sticks (7 oz./200 g) butter, divided
- 1½ tsp (10 g) tomato paste
- Scant ½ cup (100 ml) cognac

Fried rice

- 1 bunch scallions
- 6 eggs
- 1 tsp Vietnamese fish sauce
- Scant ½ cup (100 ml) neutral oil
- 7 oz. (200 g) day-old cooked rice
- 1 tbsp soy sauce

PREPARING THE SHRIMP AND SHRIMP BUTTER

Preheat the oven to 325°F (160°C/Gas Mark 3). Shell and devein the shrimp (see technique p. 58), leaving 4 attractive ones unshelled for serving. Reserve the shells for the shrimp butter. Peel and finely chop the onion. Wash and quarter the tomatoes. Heat 2 tsp (10 g) of the butter in a small Dutch oven and sweat the onions until softened but not browned. Add the tomato paste and tomatoes, then deglaze with the cognac. Add the shrimp shells and remaining butter, cover the pot, and cook in the oven for 1 hour. Strain the shrimp butter through the fine-mesh sieve and set aside.

PREPARING THE FRIED RICE

Wash the scallions and cut them at an angle into thin slices; keep the white parts and green parts separate, reserving the latter for garnishing. Whisk together the eggs and fish sauce until light and airy. Heat the wok over high heat, then add the oil and stir to coat. Add the eggs and cook, stirring vigorously with a spatula. When the eggs are set, add the scallion whites and rice and cook, stirring energetically. Add the soy sauce at the end and stir-fry until the rice and eggs are evenly coated. Meanwhile, cook the peeled shrimp in the shrimp butter until just pink; they are delicate, so it is best to cook them separately. Add the shrimp to the rice and toss gently to distribute them evenly. Cook the 4 reserved shrimp in a skillet with a little shrimp butter for 30 seconds per side.

TO SERVE

Using a large ladle as a mold, scoop a quarter of the fried rice into each of four serving bowls. Top each serving with an unshelled shrimp and garnish with sliced scallion greens.

POACHED LANGOUSTINES WITH THAI BROTH

Langoustines pochées et bouillon thaï

Serves 4

Active time

2 hours

Chilling time

1 hour

Cooking time

45 minutes

Soaking time

15 minutes

Equipment

Food processor

Fine-mesh sieve

Muslin or a coffee filter

Wooden skewers

Mandoline

Deep fryer (or skillet)

Instant-read thermometer

Teapot or heatproof pitcher

Ingredients

Thai basil oil and chili oil

1 bunch Thai basil

1¼ cups (300 ml) canola oil, divided

2 bird's eye chili peppers

Salt

Thai broth

8¾ oz. (250 g) red bell peppers

⅔ oz. (20 g) fresh red chili peppers

1¾ oz. (50 g) fresh ginger

1¾ oz. (50 g) garlic

1 stalk lemongrass

Generous ¾ cup (200 ml) rice vinegar

¼ cup (1¾ oz./50 g) sugar

2 tsp (10 g) salt

4 cups (1 liter) water

Langoustines

1 lb. 2 oz. (500 g) langoustines

Lemongrass-infused langoustine gelée

2½ sheets (5 g) gelatin, 200 Bloom

2 cups (500 ml) Thai broth (see left)

1¾ oz. (50 g) shallots

3½ oz. (100 g) carrots

3½ tbsp (50 ml) canola oil

Langoustine shells (see above)

1 stalk lemongrass

4 tsp (20 ml) white wine

4 cups (1 liter) water

Salt

Bok choy

1 head bok choy

Salt

Lotus chips

4 cups (1 liter) water

3½ tbsp (50 ml) white vinegar

1 fresh lotus root

Oil for deep-frying

Salt

To serve

Enoki mushrooms

Marigold petals

Nasturtium leaves

PREPARING THE THAI BASIL OIL AND THE CHILI OIL

Wash and dry the Thai basil and remove the stems, reserving them for the Thai broth, if desired. Place the leaves in the food processor with half the canola oil and process until smooth. Strain through the fine-mesh sieve and let rest for at least 1 hour in the refrigerator, allowing the clear green oil to rise to the surface. Wash and dry the food processor bowl, then wash the chili peppers, remove the seeds, and cut the peppers into pieces. Process with the remaining oil until smooth, then strain through the fine-mesh sieve and let rest for at least 1 hour in the refrigerator.

PREPARING THE THAI BROTH

Wash the bell and chili peppers, then cut the chili peppers in half. Peel the ginger and garlic. Cut the bell peppers, ginger, and lemongrass into ½-in. (1-cm) dice and place them in a large saucepan with the garlic, chili peppers, rice vinegar, sugar, and salt. Add the Thai basil stems, if desired. Add the water and bring to a boil, then lower the heat and let simmer for 30–45 minutes. Strain through the fine-mesh sieve and adjust the seasonings if necessary.

PREPARING THE LANGOUSTINES

Peel the langoustines, reserving the shells for the gelée. Remove the veins by pulling on the central part of the tail (see technique p. 56). Spear the langoustines with wooden skewers to keep them straight.

PREPARING THE LEMONGRASS-INFUSED LANGOUSTINE GELÉE

Soak the gelatin in a bowl of cold water until softened. Measure out 2 cups (500 ml) of Thai broth, reserving the rest for serving. Warm the broth, then squeeze the gelatin to remove excess water and stir it into the hot broth until dissolved. Peel and dice the shallots and carrots and sweat them in a large saucepan with the canola oil until softened but not browned. Add the langoustine shells. Break the lemongrass stalk in half and add it to the pan. Deglaze with the white wine, then add the water and bring to a boil, skimming any foam from the surface. Let simmer for 30–45 minutes. Strain through the muslin or coffee filter into a large clean saucepan, add the Thai broth and gelatin mixture, and bring to a boil. Season with salt, then pour into four serving bowls and let set in the refrigerator until serving.

PREPARING THE BOK CHOY

Separate and wash the bok choy leaves. Cut any large leaves in half midway between the top and bottom. Cook in boiling salted water for 3–4 minutes, then immediately refresh in cold water.

PREPARING THE LOTUS CHIPS

Combine the water and vinegar in a large bowl. Wash and peel the lotus root, then cut it into 1⁄16-in. (1-mm) slices using the mandoline. Soak the slices in the water and vinegar mixture for 15 minutes to reduce their bitterness. Meanwhile, heat the oil for deep-frying to 338°F (170°C). Drain the lotus root slices and dry well on paper towels, then deep-fry until crisp. Remove, drain on paper towels, and season with salt.

TO SERVE

Heat the remaining Thai broth until simmering, then transfer it to the teapot. Place bok choy over the gelée in each serving bowl, then add the langoustines. Drizzle with a little Thai basil oil and chili oil and garnish with enoki mushrooms, marigold petals, and nasturtium leaves. Top with the lotus chips. At the table, just before serving, pour the hot Thai broth over the langoustines to poach them and liquefy the gelée.

CRAYFISH RAGOUT WITH SAUSAGE AND WHITE BEANS

Ragoût d'écrevisse à la saucisse et haricots blancs

Serves 4

Active time

45 minutes

Cooking time

3½ hours

Equipment

Fine-mesh sieve

Ingredients

White bean and tomato ragout

3½ oz. (100 g) shallots

¼ bunch marjoram

1 lb. 2 oz. (500 g) cluster tomatoes

⅔ cup (160 ml) olive oil, divided

Scant ½ tsp (2 g) fine sea salt

1 bunch scallions

1 tsp (2 g) fennel seeds

7 oz. (200 g) white beans, soaked for at least 6 hours

3 bay leaves

8 cloves garlic, unpeeled

½ tsp (2 g) baking soda (optional)

1 tsp (5 g) coarse sea salt

Crayfish and sausage

28 small crayfish

2 tbsp (30 ml) olive oil, divided

2 dried sweet red chili peppers (*piments longs*)

2 tsp (10 ml) cognac

4 Italian sausages with fennel

Pork belly and crayfish jus

1 lb. 2 oz. (500 g) pork belly

10½ oz. (300 g) crayfish heads, claws, and shells (see above)

7 oz. (200 g) white onions

½ head garlic

2 tsp (10 ml) olive oil

½ bunch thyme

1¾ sticks (7 oz./200 g) butter

8 cups (2 liters) vegetable stock, divided

To serve

2 generous tbsp (20 g) black peppercorns

PREPARING THE WHITE BEAN AND TOMATO RAGOUT

Peel and finely chop the shallots. Wash and dry the marjoram and set aside 5 whole sprigs for cooking the beans. Remove the stems from the rest and chop the leaves. Peel, seed, and roughly chop the tomatoes. Heat ⅓ cup (80 ml) of the olive oil in a sauté pan and sweat the shallots for 5 minutes. Add the chopped marjoram, tomato, and fine sea salt and cook over low heat for about 30 minutes, or until all the excess liquid has evaporated and the compote is thick and jammy. Meanwhile, wash the scallions and cut them at an angle into 1/16-in. (2-mm) slices; keep the white parts and green parts separate, reserving the latter for garnishing. Heat the remaining olive oil in a large pot and sweat the scallion whites until softened but not browned. Add the fennel seeds, soaked white beans, and enough water to cover, then add the bay leaves, garlic, and reserved marjoram sprigs. Add the baking soda, if desired (this can make the beans softer and reduce the cooking time). Let simmer for 1–1½ hours, or until the beans are completely tender but not falling apart, adding the coarse salt three-quarters of the way through the cooking time, when the beans have begun to soften. Drain the beans and remove the bay leaves, marjoram sprigs, and garlic. Peel the garlic, cut it into slivers, ¾ in. (1.5 cm) long and 1/16 in. (2 mm) wide, and set aside for garnishing. Combine the white beans and tomato compote in a single pot.

PREPARING THE CRAYFISH AND SAUSAGE

Remove the heads and veins from the crayfish (see technique p. 56), reserving the heads and claws for the jus. Heat 4 tsp (20 ml) of the olive oil with the dried chili peppers in a Dutch oven, then add the crayfish tails and cook, stirring, for 30 seconds. Add the cognac and flambé. Cover the pot and cook over low heat for 2–3 minutes, swirling the pot continuously. Remove the shells from the crayfish tails, reserving the shells for the jus. Return the tails to the olive oil to prevent discoloration, and reserve at room temperature. Remove the chili peppers from the oil, cut them at an angle into ¾-in. (1.5-cm) slices, and add them to the pot with the tomato compote and white beans. Remove the skin from the Italian sausages, then pinch off pieces weighing ½–⅔ oz. (15–20 g) each. Cook in a skillet with the remaining olive oil for 5 minutes, or until browned.

PREPARING THE PORK BELLY AND CRAYFISH JUS

Cut the pork belly into 1½-in. (4-cm) cubes and roughly chop the crayfish heads, claws, and shells. Peel the onions and cut each one into 8 pieces. Separate the garlic cloves and roughly crush them, leaving them unpeeled. Heat the olive oil in a sauté pan and sear the pork belly and crayfish carcasses until pale golden brown. Add the onions, garlic, thyme, and butter, and continue to cook until the meat and carcasses are deeply browned. Pour off the excess fat and deglaze with 2 cups (500 ml) of the stock to release the browned bits from the bottom of the pan. Add the remaining stock and let simmer, uncovered, for 1½ hours. Strain the jus through the fine-mesh sieve into a clean saucepan and reduce until it coats the back of a spoon.

TO SERVE

Crush the peppercorns using the flat side of a chef's knife blade. Reheat the crayfish tails and sausage pieces in the jus and reheat the white bean and tomato ragout. Ladle ragout into serving bowls, add the crayfish tails and sausage, and garnish with the reserved garlic slivers and scallion greens.

GRILLED LANGOUSTES WITH TIMUT PEPPER AND CARAMELIZED FENNEL

Langouste grillée aux baies de Timur, fenouil caramélisé et jus corsé

Serves 4

Active time

30 minutes

Cooking time

1½ hours

Equipment

Mortar + pestle

Grill

Fine-mesh sieve

Ingredients

Grilled langoustes with Timut pepper

2 langoustes, weighing 1¼ lb. (600 g) each

½ lemon

1 clove garlic

2 tbsp (30 ml) olive oil

10 sprigs thyme

Timut peppercorns

Salt and freshly ground black pepper

Langouste jus

1 leek

1 onion

1 carrot

2 cloves garlic

3½ oz. (100 g) Roma tomatoes

2 langouste heads (see above)

2 tbsp (30 ml) grape-seed oil

2 tbsp (1 oz./30 g) butter

2 tbsp (1 oz./30 g) tomato paste

2½ tbsp (40 ml) cognac

Scant ½ cup (100 ml) dry white wine

2 cups (500 ml) fish fumet (see technique p. 118)

1 bouquet garni (thyme, bay leaf, and parsley stems)

1 pinch *piment d'Espelette*

Caramelized fennel

1¼ lb. (600 g) fennel

1¼ cups (300 ml) water

2 tbsp (1 oz./30 g) butter

2 bay leaves

⅓ oz. (10 g) parsley

Salt and freshly ground pepper

To serve

Fleur de sel

Marigold petals

Oxalis leaves

PREPARING THE GRILLED LANGOUSTES WITH TIMUT PEPPER

Prepare the langoustes for cooking (see technique p. 109); twist the tails off each langouste body, then cut the tails in half lengthwise. Reserve the head sections for the jus. Cut the lemon crosswise into slices and roughly crush the garlic cloves, leaving them unpeeled. Heat the olive oil in a small saucepan over low heat with the lemon, garlic, and thyme, just long enough to delicately flavor the oil, without letting it simmer. Remove from the heat. Place several Timut peppercorns in the mortar and pound them to a powder using the pestle. Preheat the grill to a high temperature. Season the tail meat with salt and freshly ground black pepper, then lightly brush it with the flavored olive oil, reserving the rest for serving. Place the langouste tails on the grill with the open sides facing down, then grill for 2–3 minutes on each side. A few seconds before finishing, lightly sprinkle ground Timut pepper over the meat to draw out the spice's flavor without burning it. Carefully remove the meat from the shells and set aside.

PREPARING THE LANGOUSTE JUS

Peel and finely chop the leek, onion, and carrot. Peel and roughly crush the garlic cloves. Wash and roughly chop the tomatoes. Cut the langouste heads into pieces using scissors and cook them in a large pot with the grape-seed oil over high heat until deeply browned. Add the butter along with the leek, onion, carrot, and garlic, and sweat for 8 minutes, then add the tomatoes and tomato paste and stir gently to coat. Deglaze with the cognac, then add the white wine and reduce by two-thirds. Add the fish fumet and bouquet garni, season with a pinch of *piment d'Espelette*, and let simmer for 40 minutes. Strain through the fine-mesh sieve into a clean saucepan, pressing down on the solids to extract as much flavor as possible. Reduce over low heat until the jus is intensely flavorful and has a lightly syrupy consistency that coats the back of a spoon.

PREPARING THE CARAMELIZED FENNEL

Peel and wash the fennel, cut it into ¼-in. (5-mm) dice, and place it in a sauté pan with the water, butter, and bay leaves. Season with salt and pepper. Cover the pan with a piece of parchment paper cut to fit snugly inside, to ensure even cooking. Gently simmer over low heat until the fennel is completely tender, adding water as needed to prevent it from browning too quickly. When the liquid has evaporated completely, continue cooking, stirring continuously, until the fennel is lightly caramelized. Meanwhile, wash and finely chop the parsley, then stir it in when the fennel is done. Adjust the seasonings if necessary.

TO SERVE

Place half a langouste tail on each serving plate and cut it at an angle into two pieces. Season each piece with a pinch of fleur de sel and a few drops of the garlic and lemon-flavored oil used for grilling. Shape the caramelized fennel into small quenelles using two spoons and arrange several on each plate alongside the langouste tail. Spoon several drops of jus onto each plate and garnish with marigold petals and oxalis leaves.

GOOSENECK BARNACLE MARINIÈRE

Pouces-pieds en marinière

Serves 4

Active time
30 minutes

Cooking time
10 minutes

Equipment
Fine-mesh sieve

Ingredients

Vegetables

- 1 bunch multicolored radishes
- 3 cloves garlic, divided
- 3½ tbsp (50 ml) neutral oil, divided
- 5 sprigs thyme, divided
- 2 tsp (10 ml) aged wine vinegar, divided
- Vegetable stock, as needed
- 3 tbsp (1¾ oz./50 g) butter
- 5¾ oz. (160 g) shelled peas
- ½ tsp (2 g) salt

Gooseneck barnacle marinière

- 7 oz. (200 g) gooseneck barnacles
- 3½ oz. (100 g) onions
- 3½ oz. (100 g) carrots
- 3½ oz. (100 g) celery
- ½ head garlic
- 3½ tbsp (50 ml) olive oil
- 3 bay leaves
- ¼ bunch thyme
- 1 cup (250 ml) red wine

Gooseneck barnacle vinaigrette

- 5 drops red Tabasco sauce
- 8 drops Worcestershire sauce
- Scant ½ cup (100 ml) gooseneck barnacle pan juices (see above)
- Scant ½ cup (100 ml) olive oil

To serve

- ½ bunch scallions

PREPARING THE VEGETABLES

Cut the radishes in half, leaving ¼ in. (5 mm) of the green tops attached. Peel the garlic cloves. Place the radishes in separate saucepans by color, and divide the olive oil, thyme, vinegar, and garlic between the saucepans, reserving 1 garlic clove and 2 thyme sprigs for cooking the peas. Add enough vegetable stock to each pan to just cover the radishes, cover the pans, and cook over low heat until the tip of a knife slides in easily and the pan juices have reduced to a glaze. Melt the butter in a separate saucepan with the reserved garlic clove and thyme sprigs, then add the peas and salt and cook for 2–3 minutes, until the peas are cooked but still slightly firm.

PREPARING THE GOOSENECK BARNACLE MARINIÈRE

Trim the gooseneck barnacle bases to ensure they are level. Rinse the barnacles three times under cold, running water. Peel and thinly slice the onions, carrots, and celery. Separate the garlic cloves, leaving them unpeeled. Heat the olive oil in a large saucepan and sweat the carrots, onions, and celery along with the garlic, bay leaves, and thyme until softened but not browned. Add the gooseneck barnacles and deglaze with the red wine. Cover and let simmer for 3 minutes, or until the skin separates from the meat. Remove the gooseneck barnacles, then strain the pan juices through the fine-mesh sieve into a bowl. Using scissors, cut the tough, leathery skin off each barnacle, up to the hard, plated head, exposing the meat but leaving it attached. Measure out a scant ½ cup (100 ml) of the gooseneck barnacle pan juices into a small bowl and set aside. Reserve the barnacles in the remaining strained pan juices.

PREPARING THE GOOSENECK BARNACLE VINAIGRETTE

Add the Tabasco and Worcestershire sauce to the reserved warm gooseneck barnacle pan juices. Whisking continuously, drizzle in the olive oil in a thin, steady stream until emulsified. Keep warm.

TO SERVE

Wash the scallions and slice them thinly at an angle. Reheat the peas and radishes, divide them between four shallow bowls, and add the gooseneck barnacles. Drizzle with the warm vinaigrette and garnish with the sliced scallions.

SEA URCHIN AND SCALLOP TARTARE WITH PEATED WHISKY FOAM

Langues d'oursin sur un lit de tartare de Saint-Jacques, espuma de whisky tourbé

Serves 4

Active time
40 minutes

Cooking time
30 minutes

Equipment
Immersion blender

Ingredients

Peated whisky foam
- 2 tsp (4 g) soy lecithin powder
- Generous 3/4 cup (200 ml) whole milk
- Generous 3/4 cup (200 ml) fish fumet (see technique p. 118)
- 3 1/2 tbsp (50 ml) peated whisky, such as Lagavulin

Sea urchin and scallop tartare
- 8 sea urchins
- 8 shelled sea scallops
- 2/3 oz. (20 g) shallot
- 1 bunch chives
- 2 tbsp (30 ml) olive oil
- Juice of 1/2 lemon

To serve
- Fleur de sel
- Freshly ground pepper

PREPARING THE PEATED WHISKY FOAM
Combine the soy lecithin powder, milk, and fish fumet in a large saucepan. Bring to a simmer, stirring often to dissolve the soy lecithin. Process the mixture with the immersion blender until well combined. Let cool, then incorporate the whisky.

PREPARING THE SEA URCHIN AND SCALLOP TARTARE
Clean and prepare the sea urchins, carefully removing the lobes of orange uni (see technique p. 70). Set 4 shells aside for serving, then tightly cover the uni with plastic wrap and keep refrigerated. Cut the scallops into approximately 1/4-in. (5-mm) dice and reserve in a bowl set over a bed of ice. Peel and finely chop the shallot. Wash and finely chop the chives. Add the olive oil, lemon juice, shallot, and chives to the bowl with the scallops. Gently stir to combine, taking care not to damage the scallops. To prepare the reserved sea urchin shells for serving, boil them for about 15 minutes, then drain and rinse with cold water. Using the back of a knife blade, scrape off any remaining spines to achieve a clean, smooth surface. Dry the shells.

TO SERVE
Divide the scallop tartare between the 4 cleaned urchin shells and season with fleur de sel and freshly ground pepper. Gently arrange the sea urchin uni over the tartare. Just before serving, blend the peated whisky mixture with the immersion blender to obtain an airy, stable foam. Spoon the foam over the sea urchin and scallop tartare.

SNAIL RAVIOLI WITH RAMSON GARLIC SPONGE CAKE

Raviole d'escargots et sponge cake à l'ail des ours

Serves 4

Active time

2 hours

Cooking time

1 hour 10 minutes

Chilling time

1 hour

Equipment

Food processor

Instant-read thermometer

Muslin

Stand mixer + paddle beater and dough hook

Small oven-safe saucepan

Mortar + pestle (optional)

Pasta maker

Fine-mesh sieve

Whipping siphon + 1 N2O gas cartridge

2 (1-cup/250-ml) paper cups

Ingredients

Parsley chlorophyll

7 oz. (200 g) parsley

Ravioli dough

2¼ cups (10 oz./280 g) all-purpose flour

¾ cup (4 oz./120 g) semolina flour

4 eggs

1¾ oz. (50 g) parsley chlorophyll (see above)

Puréed garlic confit

2 heads garlic

⅔ cup (150 ml) olive oil

Garlic and parsley butter

⅓ oz. (10 g) flat-leaf parsley

3 cloves garlic

7 tbsp (3½ oz./100 g) butter, softened

Salt and freshly ground pepper

Sautéed snails

20 large canned snails, preferably from Burgundy

1 tbsp (20 g) butter

Salt

Snail ravioli

Ravioli dough (see left)

Sautéed snails (see above)

Garlic and parsley butter (see above), well chilled

Ramson garlic coulis and dried ramson garlic leaves

10½ oz. (300 g) ramson garlic leaves

4 tsp (20 ml) neutral oil

Ramson garlic siphon sponge

⅓ oz. (10 g) shelled peas

1 oz. (30 g) ramson garlic leaves

2 eggs

4 tsp (20 ml) canola oil

2 tbsp water

Scant ½ tsp (2 g) salt

2 tbsp (20 g) all-purpose flour

To serve

12 ramson garlic flowers (optional)

Salt

PREPARING THE PARSLEY CHLOROPHYLL

Wash and dry the parsley, then blend it with a little water in the food processor to obtain a liquid purée. Transfer the purée to a small saucepan and warm it to 160°F (70°C). Maintain this temperature until the chlorophyll rises to the surface, then skim this thick layer off and strain it through the muslin, letting it drain for several minutes.

PREPARING THE RAVIOLI DOUGH

Fit the stand mixer with the paddle beater. Place the all-purpose and semolina flours and the eggs in the bowl, and knead until the dough comes together into a ball. Add the chlorophyll and continue kneading for a few minutes, until the color is evenly distributed. Cover with plastic wrap and let rest for 1 hour in the refrigerator.

PREPARING THE PURÉED GARLIC CONFIT

Preheat the oven to 175°F (80°C/Gas on the lowest setting). Separate the garlic cloves and place them unpeeled in the small oven-safe saucepan with the olive oil, which should cover the garlic completely. Cook in the oven for 1 hour. When the garlic is cool enough to handle, drain and peel it, then grind or pound it until smooth and creamy using the food processor or mortar and pestle.

PREPARING THE GARLIC AND PARSLEY BUTTER

Wash and dry the parsley, remove the stems, and finely chop the leaves. Peel the garlic and chop it very finely. Place the butter, garlic, and parsley in a bowl and stir until well blended. Season with salt and pepper.

PREPARING THE SAUTÉED SNAILS

Drain the snails and rinse them thoroughly. Melt the butter in a skillet over medium heat and sauté the snails for 4–5 minutes. Remove from the skillet, season with salt, and let cool.

ASSEMBLING THE SNAIL RAVIOLI

Roll the ravioli dough through the pasta maker to a thickness of approximately 1⁄16 in. (1 mm). Cut the dough into twenty 1½-in. (4-cm) squares. Place a sautéed snail and about ½ tsp of garlic and parsley butter on each dough square, then brush a little water around the edges to moisten them. Fold each square in half to form a triangle, then press the edges to seal them. Pinch the two bottom corners together.

PREPARING THE RAMSON GARLIC COULIS AND DRIED RAMSON GARLIC LEAVES

Wash the ramson garlic and set aside 4 attractive leaves for garnishing. Blanch the remaining leaves in a pot of boiling water for a few seconds, then immediately plunge them into ice water to preserve the vibrant green color. Drain the leaves, then purée them in the food processor, strain through the fine-mesh sieve into a bowl, and season with salt. To prepare the dried ramson garlic leaves, line a plate with microwave-safe plastic wrap and brush with the neutral oil. Place the 4 reserved leaves on the plastic wrap, then cover them with another piece of plastic wrap. Make a few holes in the plastic and microwave on high for three 1½ -minute bursts.

PREPARING THE RAMSON GARLIC SIPHON SPONGE

Blanch the peas in boiling water, then plunge them into ice water to stop the cooking process. Wash and dry the ramson garlic leaves and place them in the food processor with the eggs, peas, and oil. Process until smooth, then add the water and salt and process until well combined. Strain through the fine-mesh sieve into a bowl. Add the flour and mix until smooth. Transfer to the whipping siphon, charge it with the cartridge, and shake the siphon to distribute the gas. Dispense the mixture into the two paper cups, filling them halfway. Using the tip of a knife, pierce a few holes in the bottom of each paper cup and microwave on high for 1 minute.

TO SERVE

Just before serving, cook the ravioli in a large pot of boiling salted water until they float to the surface. Ladle ramson garlic coulis into the base of each serving bowl and arrange 5 ravioli over it, making a tight ring in the center. Arrange pieces of siphon sponge around the ravioli, add a few spoonfuls of puréed garlic confit, and top each serving with a dried ramson garlic leaf. Garnish with ramson garlic flowers, if desired.

FROG LEGS WITH GARLIC FLAN AND SNAIL CROQUETTES

Cuisses de grenouille, flan d'ail de Lautrec et cromesquis d'escargots

Serves 4

Active time

1½ hours

Cooking time

1 hour

Chilling time

5 minutes

Freezing time

30 minutes

Equipment

Pastry bag + plain ½-in. (1-cm) tip

Immersion blender

Fine-mesh sieve

4 silicone timbale molds, 1½ in. (4 cm) in diameter

Instant-read thermometer

Ingredients

Croquettes

1 oz. (30 g) shallots

4 cloves garlic

¼ oz. (8 g) parsley

⅔ oz. (20 g) Spanish chorizo

1 stick + 2 tbsp (5¼ oz./150 g) butter, softened

Scant ½ cup (1¾ oz./50 g) dried breadcrumbs

12 shelled snails

Salt and freshly ground pepper

Garlic flan

6 cloves garlic, preferably pink

Scant ½ cup (100 ml) heavy cream, min. 35% fat

Scant ½ cup (100 ml) whole milk

1 egg

1 egg yolk

Salt and freshly ground pepper

Parsley coulis

1 bunch parsley

4 cups (1 liter) water

4 tsp (20 g) salt

2 tbsp (1 oz./30 g) butter

Frog legs and snails

¼ bunch flat-leaf parsley

20 snails in their shells

10 pairs of frog legs

Scant ½ cup (1¾ oz./50 g) all-purpose flour

3 tbsp (1½ oz./40 g) clarified butter

Salt and freshly ground pepper

Croquette breading

¾ cup + 2 tbsp (3½ oz./100 g) all-purpose flour

Scant ½ cup (3½ oz./100 g) egg white (about 3½ whites)

1¾ cups (7 oz./200 g) dried breadcrumbs

Oil for deep-frying

CHEFS' NOTES

To retain their vibrant color, blanch green vegetables in boiling salted water (up to 4 tsp/20 g salt per 4 cups/1 liter water), then shock by quickly plunging in ice water.

PREPARING THE SNAIL CROQUETTES

Peel and finely chop the shallots and garlic. Wash, dry, and finely chop the parsley. Finely dice the chorizo. Sweat the shallots and garlic in a small saucepan with the chorizo until softened but not browned, then season with salt and pepper and let cool. Place the softened butter in a bowl with the chorizo mixture, parsley, and breadcrumbs and stir until well combined. Transfer the croquette mixture to the pastry bag and pipe out 12 mounds with the same diameter as the snails. Place a snail in the center of each, then pipe more mounds of the same size to cover them. Place the croquettes in the refrigerator for at least 5 minutes to firm them up slightly, then roll them in your hands to form balls. Freeze for 30 minutes.

PREPARING THE GARLIC FLAN

Preheat the oven to 200°F (100°C/Gas Mark ¼). Peel the garlic and remove the germs, then place the cloves in a small saucepan, cover with cold water, and bring to a boil. Drain and repeat this process once more. Place the blanched garlic in a saucepan with the cream and milk and let simmer for 10 minutes, until the garlic is tender. Using the immersion blender, process the mixture until smooth, then season with salt and pepper and strain through the fine-mesh sieve into a bowl. In a separate large bowl, whisk together the egg and egg yolk, then add the garlic and cream mixture and whisk until well combined, without incorporating too much air. Fill the silicone timbale molds with the flan mixture and cook in a bain marie in the oven for 20–25 minutes, or just until set.

PREPARING THE PARSLEY COULIS

Remove the stems from the parsley and wash the leaves. Bring the water to a boil, add the salt, and blanch the leaves for 3–5 minutes, then drain and place in ice water to cool quickly. Drain the cooled leaves and blend with the 4 cups (1 liter) water using the immersion blender. Heat the butter in a small saucepan until it browns and has a nutty aroma, then stir it into the parsley coulis.

PREPARING THE FROG LEGS AND SNAILS

Wash, dry, and very finely chop the parsley. Rinse the snails under cold running water. Separate the frog legs by cutting between the tops of the two legs and through the hip bone. Cut off the feet and remove the meat from the lower parts of the legs, leaving only the thigh meat. Scrape the exposed bones using the back of a paring knife. Season the drumsticks with salt and pepper, then dredge them in the flour to coat and shake them in a colander to remove any excess. Warm the clarified butter in a sauté pan, add the frog drumsticks, and brown them all over. Add the snails and cook until heated through, then season with salt and pepper and stir in the parsley. Reserve the frog legs and snails on paper towels.

BREADING AND FRYING THE CROQUETTES

Preheat the oil for deep-frying to 338°F (170°C). Place the flour, egg whites, and breadcrumbs in three separate bowls. Roll each croquette in the flour to coat, then dip in the egg white, followed by the breadcrumbs. Repeat this process a second time for a second layer of coating. Deep-fry for 2 minutes.

TO SERVE

For each serving, place a garlic flan in the center of a bowl, top it with a croquette, and pour parsley coulis around it. Arrange the frog legs and snails in their shells around the flan, alternating the two. Serve the remaining croquettes on the side.

INDEX